Poverty Amid Plenty

World and Irish Development Reconsidered

D1369754

Do m'iníon is óige, Caoimhe.

Rugadh í tar éis dom an chéad chaibidil den leabhar seo a scríobh agus críochníodh an leabhar cúpla lá tar éis a dara breithlá. Go bhfeice sí le linn a saoil domhan níos cothroime agus níos cirte.

Poverty Amid Plenty

World and Irish Development Reconsidered

Peadar Kirby

 TRÓCAIRE
and
GILL and MACMILLAN

Published in Ireland by

TRÓCAIRE

Catholic Agency for World Development
169 Booterstown Ave.,
Blackrock, Co. Dublin
and
Gill and Macmillan Ltd,
Goldenbridge, Dublin 8
with associated companies throughout the world.

First reprint March 1997
Second reprint October 1997

© Trócaire 1997
ISBN 0 7171 2607 2

Design: Public Communications Centre
Index: Fergus Mulligan
Print origination by Typeform Ltd
Printed in Ireland by Genprint (Ireland) Ltd

A catalogue record is available for this book from the British Library.

Published as part of Trócaire's Programme of Research and Development Education. The views expressed are the author's and do not necessarily coincide with those of Trócaire.

Contents

Foreword

This was a book I never planned to write. After the publication of my last book *Ireland and Latin America: Links and Lessons* (Trócaire and Gill & Macmillan) in April 1992 I turned my attention to academic study and registered as a part-time doctoral research student at the London School of Economics. I therefore expected it would be many years before I would publish another book. The idea for this book came from Andy Storey who was then Trócaire research officer. He expressed an interest in reading the initial outline of my doctoral research; his response was to suggest drafting a book proposal for Trócaire's research advisory committee drawing on some of the ideas in my doctoral outline. My initial scepticism turned to more positive interest as we discussed the idea and so I was set on the road that led to this book. I am therefore very grateful to him for sowing that initial seed as I am to the Trócaire research advisory committee for their interest in it and their helpful comments at the initial stage of firming up an outline of what it would cover.

Then came the hard part of the work which has covered two and a half years. I owe a great debt of gratitude to my PhD supervisor, Professor Fred Halliday, for his constant encouragement both for the initial idea and for the work as it has proceeded. It is certainly true to say that without his support, the book would never have been written. I know he doesn't agree with all that is in it but his sharp and highly perceptive comments on draft chapters have always given me pause to ponder and have helped me deepen my own thinking on many issues.

I have also been helped considerably in developing my ideas and been on many occasions challenged to reconsider assumptions by many friends. In particular I want to acknowledge the support and interest of Larry Bond, Ann-Louise Gilligan and Katherine Zappone. They are always stimulating and challenging company. I can say the same about many colleagues in Dublin City University who have shown a critical interest in and a support for this work as it has progressed. Furthermore, DCU is a university which values interdisciplinary work and, through its own links with the area partnerships on Dublin's northside and its outreach programme in Ballymun, is showing a practical commitment to fostering links between academia and marginalised communities. It is therefore an excellent setting in which to develop the perspectives contained in this book.

I have received generous financial support from a number of sources towards the writing of this book and towards my PhD, without which this work could never have been completed. Trócaire was extremely generous in its grant towards the book as was the National Development Education Committee which on two occasions gave me grants towards my PhD. I have more recently received a grant from the Research and Postgraduate Studies Committee of Dublin City University. I am delighted to be able to take this opportunity to put my gratitude on public record.

I have used a number of libraries during my research in all of which I found staff unfailingly helpful even with the most insignificant query. These are Dublin City University library, University College Dublin library and in particular its Centre for Development Studies, the Trócaire library, the British Library of Political and Economic Science, Trinity College Dublin library and the National Library, Dublin. I would like to express my special gratitude to three librarians for the help they have given me in identifying sources and getting copies of works I sought – Ann Kinsella of Trócaire library and Edel O'Brien and Seán Mac Philibín of DCU library.

Numerous people were kind enough to read a draft of the book or of parts of it; to them all I am very grateful for their comments from which I have learnt a lot. These include Tony Fahey, Frank Barry, Packie Commins and Eoin O'Malley of the Trócaire research advisory committee, Cristóbal Kay of the Institute for Social Studies in The Hague, and Larry Bond, Fred Halliday, Denis O'Hearn of Queen's University Belfast, Susan O'Donnell and Roddy Flynn, both PhD students at DCU, Luke Gibbons of DCU, and Niall Crowley of the Community Workers' Co-operative. My gratitude in a special way goes to Maura Leen, Trócaire's Research Officer. She inherited this project but, in her efficient way of dealing with the many practical tasks it entails, has shown a commitment to seeing it through which I greatly appreciate.

Last but certainly not least, my deepest thanks go to the little community of three women with whom I live. Caoimhe has not known a daidí who was not preoccupied by some intellectual problem associated with this book while Bríd has got used to Daidí using the excuse "Caithfidh mé leabhar Chaoimhe a scríobh" to extricate myself from her requests to play. And Toni has grown used to my being distracted by the many mental and even emotional preoccupations which writing a book of this kind entails. I hope none of them feel I take them for granted and I also hope that Toni realises not just how much I depend on the practical and the emotional support she gives me but also how much I learn from her own restless spirit and the exciting paths it is exploring.

Finally, I don't need to say that I alone take responsibility for what is contained in these pages. I have taken into account the many comments I received from those who read earlier drafts but I would be surprised if they were all entirely satisfied with what I made of those comments. I offer this work as a contribution to ways of considering development. I have changed many ideas a lot in writing it and I am sure I will continue to change my ideas. I do not therefore see it as a final definitive word on anything but as part of an ongoing debate. What matters most to me is fostering approaches to understanding and resolving social problems which are broad and humanistic enough to attempt to capture something of the richness and unpredictability of the human condition. I hope this book imposes an intellectual straitjacket on nobody; I wish it to open new perspectives and avenues of exploration for building a more just and inclusive world.

Peadar Kirby,
School of Communications,
Dublin City University,
January 1997

Preface

The first question to some people reading this book may well be: "Why is Trócaire publishing a book which focuses equally on Ireland as on the developing world as a whole?". There are several reasons.

The first is that simply stated it is only through understanding the Irish development experience, in which we are rooted, that we can hope to understand the complex range of development paths chosen or in some cases largely thrust upon, developing countries. Second the study looks at inequality and poverty, issues which are at the core of Trócaire's mission statement which reads: *"Trócaire envisages a just world where people's dignity is ensured, where basic needs are met, where there is equity in the distribution of resources and where people are free to be instruments of their own development"*.

Thirdly, at the United Nations World Summit on Social Development last year the focus was on three core themes: "poverty eradication, productive employment and social integration". Trócaire participated actively in this Summit and Peadar Kirby's text takes up these themes by focusing on the challenges. in these areas for developing countries and Ireland. NGOs and civil society groups from Ireland and the developing world were to the fore at the Summit in pushing a shared approach to this agenda. Their vigour and vision is part of the inspiration behind this book. Fourthly, the author's investigation of the thorny question "is Ireland a developing country?" has a broader European interest as Ireland experiences steady progress in raising its levels of income per head so as to approach the EU average. As the highest per capita recipient of EU aid with current transfers averaging one billion pounds a year the development path chosen by Ireland is of particular significance in the context of declining aid flows to some of the world's poorest nations. At the same time these countries are expected to integate themselves smoothly and quickly into the global economy.

Fifth and finally, there is at present no single textbook which addresses the issue of Irish and world development using development theory and comparative analysis. Yet over the past five years in particular there has been a rapid growth in the number of courses on development studies and numbers of students taking up these courses here in Ireland. The enthusiasm for such studies is a sign of hope that various models of development pursued and their outcomes will be examined and questioned by a wide range of people from different perspectives.

The publication of this book as we approach the end of UN year for the eradication of poverty is fitting. Its title *Poverty Amid Plenty* is apt. While tremendous progress has been made overall in raising life expectancy, adult literacy and other social indicators, the income gap between the haves and have nots widens daily. As the 1996 United Nations Development Programme (UNDP) *Human Development Report* shows while the world economy has become more globalised so too has it become even more polarised. The richest 20% of the world's population has seen its ratio of global wealth rise from 30 to 61 times that of the poorest 20% since 1960. Even more startling, the riches of the world's record number of billionaires – 358 in total - now exceeds the combined incomes of countries with nearly half of the world's population. When one looks at absolute poverty levels the picture is equally alarming. According to UN sources more than one billion people subsist on the equivalent of less than US$370 a year.

To some observers Northern governments prefer the poverty spotlight to be on the problems in developing countries. This is ironic as in Europe 55 million people live below the poverty line and in the USA one child in five lives in poverty. There are many dangers of compartmentalising poverty into developed versus developing country poverty. A major one is that it limits the scope for building solidarity between sectoral interest groups world-wide, e.g. trade unions, women's groups and student movements, as well as between domestic and development NGOs. Kirby's analysis reinforces the need for such links.

This book which applies development theory to Ireland and the wider world brings to the fore the need for more debate on the global nature of poverty. By highlighting the issues raised in this book the reader is challenged to examine what is meant by development as against success in purely economic terms.

Justin Kilcullen
Director
Trócaire
January 1997

Introduction

"*I am keenly aware that there are, at the moment, powerful revisions and perspectives flowing around that concept [of sustainable development], pressing against it, refusing to allow it to set into a Western platitude, vehemently demanding that the life-and-death resonances be looked at in the most unswerving way, even if that leads us to a far less comfortable view of the subject.*

"...*We need to be vigilant about using the term 'sustainable development' because the very words themselves are deceptive. For some of the poorest developing countries – another term I think we need to investigate – a great deal of their reality and their future is not literally sustainable development: quite the contrary. Instead of sustenance and development, they are actually being subjected to an ordeal of survival through a depletion of their assets. I suppose the historical parallel would be Irish tenant farmers in the 1840s, who, in order to make their way through a terrible famine, had to pay their rent with the very crops which might have kept them alive. Rain forests, topsoil, animal habitats, plant diversity – these are the priceless and irreplaceable fuel for the fires of so-called development. Many millions are not beneficiaries of development – let us be honest – they are victims of it. But what do we do about it?*

"*We can start by re-defining the terms.... One of the tasks we need to undertake is a rigorous examination of the words we use, and the way we lock realities into those words, and influence approaches to the problem through relatively poor definitions of it. Until our definitions are made in a collaborative way by those who have a day-to-day knowledge of the reality and suffering, those definitions will be wanting. Until we make a coherent picture which includes crippling debt as well as international assistance, cultural dignity as well as political need, and embark on a genuine process of structural change in the ordering of our world, we will not have respected the profound moral implications of the concept of sustainable development.*

"...*The consumer societies in which we live are rapidly becoming ethics-resistant. They are more prosperous and more wasteful than any in human history. They have put considerable amounts of their resources behind glittering opportunities such as modern technology, which could arguably also be – to use another old ethical word – deeply selfish ones.*

"...*We need to acknowledge that Western industrialised societies do not offer a blueprint for development but rather have much to*

*learn in addressing the historic capacity of Africa and other regions
to sustain their peoples, and much to offer in assessing the most
effective and environmentally sustainable technology to serve the
common needs of the planet.*

*"...We cannot afford to be silent. We cannot afford to break the
silence with careless words and unexamined concepts. If there is to be
a future meeting, of an emblematic kind, between a child of the
North and a child of the South, grown into adults, if they are to be
able to meet without bitterness and shame and as true partners, we
need to prepare that meeting now – by our words, our actions and
our commitments."*

– President Mary Robinson,
Catholic Fund for Overseas Development
Pope Paul VI Memorial Lecture,
Manchester, April 1994.

Interest in and knowledge about the developing world has
perhaps never been greater in Ireland. Irish people contribute
generously to many relief and development agencies, so much so
that Irish voluntary contributions to Third World causes per head
of population are among the highest in the world. Thousands of
Irish people serve in developing countries, many of them living
and working among the poorest of the poor. Since 1993 the
Irish state has responded to this concern by increasing its
development assistance at a time when many developed countries
are reducing their aid budgets. Solidarity groups work to raise
awareness about the plight of the oppressed in various Third
World countries and some of these have had a major influence on
Irish government policy – most notably the East Timor Ireland
Solidarity Campaign in the 1990s and the Irish Nicaragua
Support Group in the mid 1980s. Irish non-governmental
organisations (NGOs) have taken an active part in preparations
for the series of major UN world summits in the early 1990s and
representatives of a wide range of Irish NGOs have attended
these summits – from Rio on the environment in 1992, through
Vienna on human rights in 1993, Cairo on population in 1994,
to Copenhagen on poverty and Beijing on women in 1995. Irish
people have made films, written plays and composed songs on
these and other issues relating to development. And few Irish
people are not aware of the plight of various Third World
countries from blanket coverage by the Irish media at various
periods since the early 1980s.

But a focus on Irish interest and commitment should not

allow us forget that in some places things are getting worse. We have witnessed ever more horrifying scenes of human suffering and social breakdown from various parts of Africa since the early 1980s – first Ethiopia, then Mozambique, Somalia, Angola, Sudan and Liberia, to Rwanda and Burundi in the mid 1990s. People must wonder where will be next and whether the horrors can become any worse. Alongside crises in many parts of Africa, however, have been successes in other parts of the developing world. Countries like South Korea and Taiwan have virtually graduated to First World status while close behind them are following Thailand, Indonesia and Malaysia. Latin America, for long associated with regular military coups and guerrilla warfare, has become a region of relatively stable elective democracies with some countries, most notably Chile, regarded as showcases of successful economic development.

It is not surprising therefore that the dualistic picture of a world divided into developed and developing countries, a picture that has since the 1950s dominated the way we conceive of the world, has begun to break down. It is being replaced by a more multi-dimensional picture of a world in which the simple division between developed and developing becomes harder and harder to sustain. On the one hand, it is clear that much of sub-Saharan Africa is being left further and further behind with some countries collapsing in chaos and ceasing to exist as functioning states. On the other hand, some of the East Asian and Latin American countries are so dynamic economically as to put the developed countries of western Europe and north America on the defensive. And, with the persistence of serious problems of unemployment and poverty at the heart of the developed world, we hear talk of a Third World within some of the most prosperous societies history has ever known. Furthermore, as new divisions emerge around the world, so too do new issues of common concern such as environmental damage that threatens all our futures or the huge numbers of refugees from wars, famines and economic breakdown that pose dilemmas for developed and underdeveloped alike.

Examining deeper questions

It is then an opportune time for a book on development, particularly one that offers an overview (as well as an underview) of some of the key trends that are shaping our world today. This it does by stepping back from the day-to-day practice of development to examine, as President Robinson asked us in the quote with which this introduction opens, the words we use and the realities these words express or fail to express. This book therefore looks at some of the deeper questions raised by development practice, questions such as:

- What do we mean by development?

- Why are many countries underdeveloped?

- How does development happen?

- What are the results of half a century of development efforts?

This is a book about development theory as distinct from development practice and it offers something akin to a map of the main approaches to understanding development over the past half century. There are many such books available but two features distinguish this one. The first is that it takes into account the huge changes that are convulsing the world of development since the 1980s. It thus devotes attention to the effect on development of such issues as the collapse of eastern European communism, the rise of Islamic fundamentalism, the growing awareness of environmental concerns and the burgeoning of grassroots movements of the poor and marginalised throughout the South. Part I, where these issues are examined, is about development theory worldwide. It interrogates what we mean by development (Chapter 1) and goes on to outline the two major ways development was understood from the 1950s to the 1980s, modernisation theory and dependency theory (Chapter 2). Chapter 3 looks at the emergence of the neo-classical counter-revolution in the 1980s and the crisis in development theory while Chapter 4 looks at the new questions raised by environmental and feminist critiques, by Islamic fundamentalism and by grassroots movements. The second distinguishing feature of this book is that, for the first time, it applies this theory in a systematic way to the case of Ireland. This is done in Part II which asks whether Ireland is developed or underdeveloped (Chapter 5) and outlines the main ways in which Irish development has been understood (Chapter 6). It goes on to re-examine Irish nationalism (Chapter 7) and the links between the state and civil society (Chapter 8), arguing that the potential of these as resources for development has been neglected. The hope is that this treatment of development theory worldwide and its application to Ireland will contribute to a dialogue between such theory and the Irish development experience.

Readership

The book is written for two types of readers. The first is those many people whose interest has been awakened by practical involvement either in issues of world development or in issues like unemployment, poverty and social exclusion at home, in whatever form this involvement may take, from awareness-raising campaigns to practical service on the ground. Such people often fail to find accessible texts which link what can often be the very dry and abstract world of theory with the very real and immediate world of development efforts. I hope such readers may find this book accessible in that it shows how the questions which theory deals with derive from practice and influence that practice. For those for whom the practice of development, whether at home or abroad, is their primary interest, I believe that a knowledge of development theory can greatly deepen and enrich their practice since it deals with the wider questions raised by such practice.

This book is also written for a second set of readers. There is now a wide range of courses in Irish third-level colleges which deal with development – development studies, community development, sociology of development, development economics, the history and geography of developing areas. This book is intended as an introductory text for students of such courses, the first textbook of development theory written from an Irish perspective. Thus the copious footnotes, which the general reader may find irksome, serve to direct students to books and articles where they can explore their particular interests in greater depth.

Optimism, scepticism

This book is written at a time of optimism in mainstream development circles, both worldwide and in Ireland. World Bank and International Monetary Fund (IMF) reports paint a generally optimistic picture of the prospects for most developing countries with the exception of sub-Saharan Africa and parts of the former Soviet Union. In Ireland, healthy growth rates in the mid 1990s have led to the label "Celtic Tiger" being applied carrying the implication that Ireland is now in the same league as the East Asian Tigers of South Korea, Taiwan, Singapore and Hong Kong. This book, as its title indicates, is written from a more sceptical point of view. It gives priority to questions concerning the impact of economic growth on the marginalised, on women, on the environment. In the case of Ireland, it focuses on the disjuncture between economic growth and social development.

The reason for this scepticism is not begrudgery or defeatism as Professor Joseph Lee has alleged motivates criticism of Ireland's so-called economic miracle.[1] Rather is it motivated by a concern that uncritical acceptance of a form of development that benefits many but marginalises in a semi-permanent way a significant minority of our population is only shoring up the most serious problems for the future. Ireland is no exception in this regard as social exclusion has become perhaps the most worrying feature of social change throughout today's world; its link to the growth of terrorism, religious fundamentalism, racism and various forms of social breakdown warrants far closer scrutiny than it has so far received. Yet, leading multilateral agencies such as the World Bank and the IMF continue to promote a model of development which, in the opinion of some who work with the poor throughout the South, is generating ever greater inequality, poverty and marginalisation.[2] In this context, a period of economic growth demands that some hard questions be asked about the impact of this growth on society.

This is one of the reasons why, in both Parts I and II, the book looks beyond the strategies of governments and multilateral agencies to the burgeoning community sector and the large number of social movements that are allowing the poor and excluded become actors for social change, voice their needs and promote a model of development that includes rather than excludes. Paying due attention to this striking new political phenomenon serves to lessen the dominance of elites and technocrats in the drive for development. This emergence of civil society, as it is sometimes called, was clearly seen in the colourful presence of sectors of civil society at the NGO fora which were held alongside each of the major UN summits of the 1990s. Thus while this book offers an analysis of development that may be far from optimistic, it eschews the determinism of some development theorists and believes our future is more than ever in the hands of civil society. This is not to minimise the huge structural imbalances in power, wealth and resources which characterise today's world more than ever before in human history. But the emergence of the poor as the subjects of social change and development as much as its objects is a remarkable new phenomenon and one of the great hopes that we may win the race against time to create a sustainable and sane society on this planet.

Poverty Amid Plenty

Conclusion

It must be admitted in conclusion that the half-century of development efforts since the second World War has, more often than not, defied expectations. Well has it been said that each decade since the 1950s has confounded the predictions of the so-called experts and showed that human history is far more unexpected than we often allow for. The dominant view of the 1950s was that the countries of the Third World would gradually come to take on the economic, political, social and cultural attributes of the developed world through Western aid, know-how and technology. Yet, the 1960s were born under the shadow of the Cuban revolution and witnessed a determined swing against the West in the radicalisation of Arab nationalism and the emergence of African socialism. A new orthodoxy emerged that held development was only possible through breaking links with the world capitalist economy and following a path of self-reliance. The challenge to the West in the 1970s, however, came not from such an undermining of the capitalist economy but from the petroleum-producing states which quadrupled the price of oil in 1973 sending the economy of the West into crisis. This stimulated a determined attempt on the part of the South, through the Group of 77, to reform the international financial and trading system through its espousal of a New International Economic Order. Thus the 1980s opened with high hopes of development but these were quickly dashed as the international debt crisis and the way the West handled it plunged so many developing countries into deep crisis and led to a "lost development decade". Similarly the expectations raised by the collapse of eastern European communism and the hopes of a "peace dividend" at the very end of the 1980s were far from realised in the 1990s.

Prediction would thus be foolhardy indeed. If this book shows anything it is that there are no easy paths to development, that human resources count every bit as much as natural ones and that, while high hopes have usually been disappointed, neither have the prophets of doom been validated. If 50 years of development have left one legacy it is that popular aspirations for a decent and secure livelihood have spread widely throughout the world's population. Yet, not only have these aspirations not been fulfilled for countless millions but these people have in many cases seen the scales of progress tip against them. My hope is that this book may help readers understand why this is so and motivate them with a sense of urgency to contribute towards tipping the scales in the other direction, both in Ireland and wider afield.

Footnotes

1 See Joseph Lee: "Ireland's magnificent 7 per cent growth rate stuns the begrudgers" in *The Irish Times*, 4 January 1996 and "Economic defeatism does us no favours" in *The Sunday Tribune*, 28 January 1996.

2 See, for example, reports by Oxfam, *Economic Reform and Inequality in Latin America* and *Embracing the Future ... Avoiding the Challenge of World Poverty: Oxfam's response to the World Bank's 'vision' for the Bretton Woods System*, Oxfam Ireland, 1994. See also a Christian Aid report published to mark the 50th anniversary of the Bretton Woods institutions entitled *Who Runs the World?*, Christian Aid, 1994.

Part I

World Development

Chapter 1

A Developing World?

"The age we are now in is going to be the century of naked conflict. It will be between the quarter of the world that consumes three-quarters of the resources and the three-quarters that is left with a quarter of the resources."

– Ruben Zamora, Salvadorean politician[1]

Introduction

"Township squalor shocks Kitt" ran the headline on the front page of *The Irish Times* over a report of a visit by the then Minister of State for Overseas Development, Mr Tom Kitt, to a shanty town on the outskirts of Johannesburg, South Africa. The conditions encountered "caused a deep intake of breath from the official party", it was reported, and a brief description was given of what caused the shock: "... in Africa's most developed country, the open sewers ran and the people crowded into horrible shanties just a short drive from extravagant north Johannesburg suburbs". The Minister was reported to have used words like "deplorable, intolerable and unacceptable" to describe what he saw (and, presumably, smelt)[2].

The culture shock described in this piece has been the experience of many people from developed countries over recent decades when they see for the first time the dreadful conditions in which so many Third World people live. For many, the shock is so great as to motivate them to want to do something practical about it, a motivation tapped and given free rein through the many development programmes of governments and non-governmental organisations (NGOs) in the developed world. Among these, for example, is the Irish government's Overseas Development Assistance programme under the aegis of which Irish people with specialist skills spend periods in some of the programme's priority countries (all of them in Africa) transferring skills to local people. The Irish government also funds the Agency for Personal Service Overseas (APSO) and has set for it a target of funding 2,000 volunteer placements in Third World countries by 1997 (APSO expected to be funding 1,350 placements by the end of 1996)[3]. Among Irish NGOs which sponsor relief and development programmes in the Third World on which Irish personnel work are Concern and Goal. Other agencies such as Trócaire and Christian Aid prefer to spend their funds on supporting projects in developing countries organised and run by local people.

What motivates these programmes and those who work on them is the challenge of development. Yet, while there is a widespread desire to see a substantial and permanent improvement in the living conditions of the poorest throughout the world, there is less agreement on the means to achieve this. In the past, for example, it was often thought that providing schools or hospitals in developing countries would automatically serve the cause of development. Now, even the World Bank is critical of the fact that health spending in most Third World countries is skewed towards high-cost hospital services that disproportionately benefit better off urban groups while most of the poor have access to minimal services.[4]

An issue that often divides development workers – even ones working on the same programme – concerns how best to work with the poor. Westerners with skills in specific areas such as building, health care, engineering or agricultural development can seek to pass these skills on through involving local people in projects largely designed and run by the Westerners. Other development workers, however, believe that this approach may succeed in passing on skills that are not the most appropriate or may serve simply to help the social and economic advancement of some individuals while doing little to develop the community. This latter group may take the slower and more painstaking approach of working with local groups, supporting them in designing responses to their needs, and in this way mobilise community action for change.

Even without budging outside one's own country, fundamental differences in understanding development are encountered. To so many who contribute generously to appeals for Third World aid, it may seem self-evident that increasing the amounts of money or food aid sent to Third World countries will help alleviate poverty and underdevelopment provided the aid is honestly administered and gets to the poorest. Others, however, protest. Cheap food sent to aid starving people may undercut the price fetched by local foodstuffs and so undermine local production. Aid may largely be spent on buying goods from the donor country and so the motives for giving it may be less than altruistic. And, even in the case of aid that is wholly spent on improving the lives of the poorest in the Third World, some will

Poverty Amid Plenty

argue that this simply increases dependence. In this view, the main causes of underdevelopment lie in the developed world and its exploitation of the raw materials of the Third World at low prices while, at the same time, interfering with the attempts of Third World countries to build up manufacturing industry through restricting the imports of their goods into the rich consumer markets of the developed world.

These examples serve to show that there are no straightforward answers to the problems of development which face so many countries and peoples. Furthermore, different approaches to development – from the policies of agencies like the International Monetary Fund and the World Bank to the programmes and projects of NGOs at grassroots level – can involve different understandings of the goals to be achieved and the means to achieve them, understandings that can often contradict each other. Thus the World Bank can finance the building of a dam in a Third World country claiming this will irrigate arid land and boost agricultural production while NGOs working with local people can be to the forefront of protests to get the project stopped since it will flood the territory inhabited by these people and destroy their livelihood for good. In such a case, both the World Bank and the NGOs claim to be motivated by a desire for development, yet their understanding of what this entails is so different that each ends up seeing the other as obstacles to development.

Different understandings therefore motivate different practices of development. Recognising this draws attention to the importance of theory as different development practices can only be fully understood when the theories motivating them are understood. The first half of this book is devoted to explaining the main theories of development which have emerged over the past half century and the context in which they have been developed. As an introduction to these theories, this first chapter explores the meaning of the term "development" itself. Having introduced some of the complexities associated with the term, the chapter examines the nature of the global divisions which have caused categories like "developed" and "underdeveloped" to be coined. It then gives a brief history of how problems of global underdevelopment have been analysed and how the categories we use today emerged. The chapter goes on to assess the impact of almost 50 years of "development" and ends by offering a working definition of development and discussing whether the term should be rescued or discarded entirely.

A divided world

The terms "developed/underdeveloped", "First World/Third World" are fundamental contemporary categories for understanding the world. We take it for granted that we live in a divided world and it is rarely that we sit in front of our televisions or open our newspapers and do not find these divisions re-inforced through images of Third World poverty and destitution.[5] Yet what is the nature of this division and are the divisions as clear-cut as they are presented?

The most widely accepted classification of world economies in terms of development is that of the World Bank. The main criterion used is GNP per capita, defined by the Bank as "the value of the final output of goods and services produced by an economy ... divided by the midyear population"[6]. It is thus a measure of economic performance rather than of human wellbeing, something acknowledged by the Bank. However, it does provide a relatively straightforward basis for categorising levels of development, provided we limit the term to the relatively narrow and conventional meaning of economic growth rates. Based on 1994 figures, the Bank divides the 209 countries and regions of the world into four development categories:

- low, with average per capita GNP of $725 or less,

- lower-middle, with per capita GNP between $726 and $2,895,

- upper-middle, with per capita GNP between $2,896 and $8,955 and

- high, with per capita GNP of $8,956 or more

Table 1.1 – World GNP per capita

GNP per capita 1994	Number of economies	GNP (US$000,000) 1994	Population (000,000) 1994	GNP per capita (US$) 1994
Low	64	1,251,000	3,178	390
Lower-middle	66	1,818,000	1,100	1,650
Upper-middle	35	2,207,000	476	4,640
High	44	20,517,000	849	24,170
World	209	25,793,000	5,603	4,600

Source: The World Bank Atlas 1996, p.20. The table gives average per capita incomes for each group of countries whereas the accompanying text gives figures for the per capita income groups to which each country belongs.

The number of countries in each category is as follows: 64 in the low category, 66 in the lower-middle, 35 in the upper-middle and 44 in the high category. Yet, of the 5.6 billion people in the world in 1994, 3.1 billion were in the low category, 1.1 billion in the lower-middle category, 476 million in the upper-middle category and 849 million in the high category.

Looking at the countries which fall into each of the categories, one finds geographical clusters. Thus sub-Saharan African countries tend to predominate in the low-income category together with China, India, Pakistan and Bangladesh all of which have populations of over 100 million. The lower middle-income grouping is more geographically diverse with Azerbaijan, Indonesia, Senegal, Bolivia and Cameroon at the bottom (in that order from the bottom) and Iran, Turkey, Botswana, the Czech Republic and Panama in that order from the top. The upper middle-income group is rather more homogeneous being made up mostly of Latin American and eastern European countries with Venezuela, Belarus, Brazil, South Africa and Mauritius in that order at the bottom and Turkmenistan, Saudi Arabia, Portugal, South Korea and Greece in that order at the top. The high-income group is made up almost exclusively of the countries of western Europe, the United States, Canada, Australia, New Zealand and Japan, although it does include Singapore, Hong Kong, Kuwait, the United Arab Emirates and Israel. Switzerland is at the top and New Zealand is at the bottom of this group with Ireland second from the bottom.[7]

This therefore gives us a certain crude snapshot of the state of the world, at least in terms of the distribution of wealth globally. It shows it to be far more heterogeneous than crude categories of "developed" and "underdeveloped" would indicate, approximating much more to a long spectrum with the great bulk of the world's people crowded together at the poorer end – 4.2 billion with average per capita income of less than $1,650 annually in 1994 – while 1.3 billion people are strung along the spectrum on national average per capita incomes ranging from $2,840 to $35,760. It is a picture of enormous and gross inequality. Furthermore, it is getting substantially worse. As the UN Development Programme's *Human Development Report 1992* reported, between 1960 and 1989 the countries with the richest 20 per cent of world population saw their share of global GNP rise from 70.2 per cent to 82.7 per cent. Over the same period, the countries with the poorest 20 per cent of the world's population saw their share of global GNP fall from 2.3 per cent to 1.4 per cent. As the UNDP concluded: "In 1960, the top 20 per cent received 30 times more than the bottom 20 per cent, but by 1989 they were receiving 60 times more."[8]

This picture furthermore overlooks the inequality in income distribution within each country. For it is a misnomer to regard the countries of the Third World as poor, since many of them contain natural resources of great wealth and many have developed sophisticated high-tech industries which can successfully compete with the products of the developed world. India has its own space programme, for example, and has built an armaments industry largely through its own efforts. Brazil sells warplanes of its own design and manufacture to the British airforce and has developed a fuel from alcohol now used in half the country's cars. So it is a complete misunderstanding to regard the countries of the Third World as sunk in poverty and backwardness. Yet it is true to say that their social structure tends to concentrate wealth more inequitably than is the case in the developed world leaving large sectors of the population (the majority in many countries) living precariously.

At the lower end of the world class structure therefore is a concentration of people living in great poverty (at least when defined in terms of monetary income) whose situation in global historical terms the World Bank describes as follows: "Despite the vast opportunities created by the technological revolutions of the twentieth century, more than one billion people, one-fifth of the world's population, live on less than one dollar a day – a standard of living that Western Europe and the United States attained two hundred years ago".[9] At the other end of the class structure in most Third World countries is a small wealthy elite controlling a huge share of the national wealth. In Brazil, a notorious example, the richest 10 per cent of the population controls 51.3 per cent of the wealth and the richest 20 per cent controls 67.5 per cent. The poorest 20 per cent, on the other hand, controls only 2.1 per cent of the national wealth.[10]

For Latin America as a whole, Alejandro Portes has attempted to map out the social class structure. His conclusions are startling. He estimates that "the dominant class alone represents no more than 4 per cent of the EAP [economically active population] in any country and no more than 2 per cent, or approximately 1,800,000 persons, for all of Latin America". Taking the middle class and the formal working class (workers in regular, waged employment) together, Portes estimates that these constitute only some 30 per cent of the economically active population. Most striking is his estimate that for Latin America as a whole roughly 60 per cent of the EAP or 80 per cent of all

Poverty Amid Plenty

workers, "can be estimated to be employed outside the formal sector", that is they have no regular, waged employment.[11] Table 1.2, taken from Portes, compares the class structure of Latin America with that of the United States. The striking difference is that three-quarters of the income in Latin America is concentrated among the top 30 per cent of the population whereas in the United States the same amount is spread somewhat more evenly among the top 50 per cent.

Table 1.2 – Income distribution in Latin America and the United States, 1960-1975

Income strata	Share of total income (%)		Income per household (1970 Dollars)	
	1960	1975	1960	1975
Latin America				
Richest 10%	46.6	47.3	11,142	15,829
20% below richest 10%	26.1	26.9	3,110	4,497
30% below richest 10%	35.4	36.0	2,542	3,636
Poorest 60%	18.0	16.7	833	1,095
Poorest 40%	8.7	7.7	520	648
United States				
Richest 10%	28.6	28.3	15,538	21,488
20% below richest 10%	26.7	26.9	13,490	17,807
30% below richest 10%	36.7	36.9	11,577	15,891
Poorest 60%	34.8	34.8	6,099	8,276
Poorest 40%	17.0	17.2	4,976	6,635

Source: Figures for Latin America were adapted from Enrique Iglesias, "Development and Equity, *CEPAL, Review 15* (Dec. 1981): 7-16, table 1. Figures for the two next-to-highest income strata were calculated by interpolation from data provided by CEPAL. Figures for the United States were taken from the U.S. Bureau of the Census, *Statistical Abstract of the United States,* table 730. Figures for the three intervening income strata were calculated by interpolation. *Taken from:* Alejandro Portes: "Latin American class structures" in *Latin American Research Review,* vol. XX, no. 3, 1985, p.25.

It is generally acknowledged that Latin America is the region of the world with the most unequal distribution of wealth though the type of class structure outlined above applies widely throughout the Third World. Yet the global generalisations that can be made about this issue are limited, both because data is simply unavailable for many countries (of the 132 countries listed in the World Bank's world development indicators, the table on income distribution gives data on only 71 countries) and because what data is available is often unreliable. It must also be remembered that the developed world is far from a model of equality with, in most countries, between 35 per cent and 40 per cent of wealth concentrated among the top 20 per cent of the population while the poorest one fifth receive between 5 per cent and 8 per cent of the wealth. For example, the United Nations Development Programme, in measuring poverty in its 1993 *Human Development Report*, showed the way that poverty disproportionately affects blacks in the United States, which it labelled "One country, two nations".[12]

While we live in a starkly divided world, therefore, the divisions between rich and poor are found within each country rather than corresponding to a divide between a rich developed world and a poor underdeveloped one. This calls into question the continuing use of categories such as "developed" and "underdeveloped", "First World" and "Third World". Perhaps a more adequate way of considering these global divisions would be to accept the description of John Cavanagh of the Washington-based Institute for Policy Studies. He has described the world in terms of a global market in which 80 per cent of the people of the developed "North" and 20 per cent of those in the underdeveloped "South" participate (though, of course, some participate far more fully than others). In this "global village", as he calls it, "the rich in the United States and Brazil have much more in common with one another than with the poor in their own countries".[13]

History of development

While the widespread use of terms such as "developed" and "underdeveloped" dates only from the period following the end of the second World War, the reality of the divided world they seek to express has a far longer history. Ever since Christopher Columbus and his band of 87 adventurers waded ashore on what today is Watling Island in the Bahamas on 12 October 1492, Europeans have gone out in ever greater numbers to conquer parts of the wider non-European and non-Christian world. Convinced of their noble mission to civilise barbarians and christianise pagans, they helped mould a global economic and political system in which the western European colonial powers were dominant and eventually controlled much of the rest of the world.

Attempts to understand this world system date from the middle of the 19th century. Marx saw colonial expansion as inherent to the capitalist system as capitalism required both cheap raw materials and an ever-expanding market if it was to continue to grow. Yet, while Marx denounced the excesses of colonialism, in much of his writings he presumed the expansion of capitalism to the peripheral countries would necessarily lead to their industrialisation and development. This would make them more and more like the developed countries, thus exacerbating the contradictions inherent in capitalism and preparing the way for socialism. It was largely due to his examination of the cases of Ireland and India that he began to revise his positive view of colonialism, though he continued to believe that, once these colonies were independent, capitalism would provide the motor-force of their development. In other cases, such as Mexico, he seemed to hold that the "inferior" natures of their people required some kind of semi-colonial tutelage for their development.[14]

Marx, however, lived largely before the major expansion of European colonialism in Africa, Asia and the Pacific from the 1870s onwards. This expansion greatly extended the reaches of European colonial rule so that by 1914, for example, Britain exercised control over a fifth of the world's land surface and a quarter of its people. This new phase of colonialism, usually termed imperialism, was analysed by a group of writers in the first two decades of the twentieth century. The one non-Marxist among them was the English liberal, J.A. Hobson. Writing in 1902, Hobson identified what he called "the social parasitic process" whereby wealth was sucked from the colonised territories "in order to support domestic luxury".[15] This view, that the wealth of the developed world is based on the exploitation of the underdeveloped countries, was to become more influential in the 1960s and 1970s as we shall see.

Hobson's main importance, however, lies in his influence on Lenin's views of imperialism. It was V. I. Lenin who identified the five features of imperialism: the concentration of capital; the emergence of finance capital, merging industrial, commercial and bank capital; the export of capital; the emergence of international monopolies; and the territorial division of the world. In his celebrated phrase, the title of his book written in 1916, imperialism was "the highest stage of capitalism" in which wealth and economic power became more and more concentrated leading to stagnation at home and growing competition for colonies and markets abroad. This, Lenin predicted, would lead to the demise of capitalism and usher in socialism. While Lenin's predictions about the collapse of capitalism have not yet been borne out, his views of monopoly capitalism and the increasing concentration of wealth and economic power at a world level have proved farseeing as is clear from the role of transnational corporations and international banking in contemporary capitalism.

Rosa Luxemburg represents a variant of this Marxist analysis of imperialism. Instead of Lenin's concentration on the export of capital, Luxemburg sees imperialism as resulting from the need to find new markets for the goods over-produced by capitalism. Thus the continuation of capitalism depended on drawing more and more countries into its net, transforming in the process pre-capitalist modes of production such as feudalism. Once this expansion reached its limits, once there were no further non-capitalist countries to be conquered, production could no longer expand and capitalism would collapse.

In all of this, however, the main concern was the impact imperialism had on capitalism in the developed countries. Little or no detailed attention was paid to the peripheral countries themselves and their prospects for development, an issue which was not to come into focus until after the second World War. This was given sharper focus by the process of decolonisation, a major watershed of which was the independence of India in 1947, even though many colonies did not achieve independence until the late 1950s and the 1960s. The emergence of the Cold War between the capitalist and communist systems and, in particular, the victory of the communists in China in 1949, also saw the issue of development being drawn into the intense competition to show which of the two systems was superior. In the developed capitalist world it was a time of optimism as the Keynesian partnership between the state and private capital led to a quarter century of unprecedented economic growth and social wellbeing. This generated considerable optimism about the development prospects of the underdeveloped countries as they emerged from colonial rule.

This was the climate in which was born the terminology which has provided our basic framework for considering these issues. In his seminal essay on the archaeology of the development idea, Wolfgang Sachs dates the introduction of the notion of an underdeveloped world to the inauguration speech of President Harry Truman in January 1949. "For the first time, the new worldview was thus announced: all the peoples of the earth were to move along the same track and aspire to only one goal – development."[16] The key terms of this worldview were popularised by the World Bank and other UN agencies in their division of the world into developed and developing countries. These were later subdivided to include such categories as LDCs (least developed countries, with per capita GNP of $300 or less) and NICs (newly industrialising countries, usually referring to the four east Asian "Tigers" – South Korea, Taiwan, Singapore and Hong Kong though sometimes extended to include such countries as Brazil and Mexico).[17]

These terms still bear the marks of the era in which they were coined. Firstly, they reflect a view of development based on GNP growth as its basic criterion and on modernisation theories which postulate that all countries are somewhere along a spectrum from traditional to modern. These theories promote the view that with more aid, investment and technical advice from the developed world, developing countries can be brought to a stage of "take-off" to self-sustained growth (see Chapter 2). There is therefore an inbuilt optimism in the terms which implies that, despite setbacks, most countries are on a journey to development which is evidenced by growing GNP throughout most of the world.

The second element which marked the birth of these terms was the need to counteract communism. One of the most influential theorists of modernisation, W. W. Rostow, went so far as to give the sub-title *A Non-communist Manifesto* to his major work, published in 1960, *The Stages of Economic Growth*. It is not surprising therefore that some identified a link between the geo-political concerns of the United States and mainstream development policies. An example often cited is the Alliance for Progress, a comprehensive attempt to modernise and develop Latin America which was prompted by the success of the Cuban Revolution in 1959 and the determination of Washington to ensure that this success was not repeated elsewhere in the region. A similar link has been noted in US policies towards El Salvador in the early 1980s when the US promoted a radical land reform and nationalisation of the banking system in order to counter the growing strength of the left, policies which Washington elsewhere resisted. As Sachs puts it: "To talk about development meant nothing more than projecting the American model of society onto the rest of the world."[18] Motivated as it was until the end of the 1980s by the need to combat communism, it now remains to be seen what the fate of development will be in the post-communist world. Reports in the early 1990s of a so-called "development fatigue" throughout the developed world auger badly for its future.[19]

The other principal set of terms to date from the post-War period is "First World" and "Third World". These are the direct offspring of the Cold War as they identify the countries of the underdeveloped world as a third world over and against the first world of developed capitalist states and the second world of developed communist states. Alfred Sauvy claimed he coined the term in 1952 based on the "third estate" at the beginning of the French Revolution in 1789. As such it had more than a geographical connotation as it embodied a sense of the underdeveloped world charting an alternative road of development to the roads offered by the first and second worlds. This found concrete expression in attempts by former colonies not to imitate the developed capitalist or communist countries, attempts for which labels were coined such as African socialism, Arab socialism, even the royal Buddhist socialism of Cambodia.

A collective expression of this "third way" emerged with the Bandung conference of 1955, the forerunner of the non-aligned movement and the first political expression of the underdeveloped countries finding common cause. Out of this emerged the determined attempt in the 1970s to achieve a New International Economic Order, a set of policies promoted by Third World countries to ensure the international financial and trading system gave them more favourable treatment. The active opposition of the United States, coupled with the advent of Reaganism and Thatcherism and the international debt crisis in the 1980s, ensured its complete collapse. With it has gone any attempt to chart a distinctive path towards development and thus the collapse of the distinction that gave the term "Third World" some validity. Mark T. Berger argues that it may now be a term that severely distorts the reality of today's world: "The idea of a 'Third World' now serves an important function in terms of the 'management' of the global political economy and allows for the homogenisation of the history of diverse parts of the world. What began in the 1950s as an attempt to forge a political and diplomatic alliance ostensibly outside the capitalist and socialist 'camps' has now become an all encompassing category reducing the governments, economies and societies of Africa, Asia, Latin America and Oceania to a set of variables distinct from and inferior to the 'First World'... And this 'Third World' is still evaluated in terms of its ability or lack of ability to advance towards a degree and type of economic development similar to the 'First World'".[20]

With the calamitous economic crisis of the 1980s for many underdeveloped countries and the growth of a more radical critique of the development process (thè ecological, cultural and feminist critiques, outlined in Chapter 4), two new sets of terms have become more common, terms which avoid the presuppositions embodied in those already discussed. The most common of these are the simple geographical terms, "North" and "South"; their weakness, however, is that they are not entirely accurate as two of the world's most developed countries, Australia and New Zealand, are at the heart of the South while, as I will argue in part two of this book, a country like Ireland, at the heart of the North, may bear more in common with countries we think of as underdeveloped. The other set of terms now in wider use is "core/periphery" and derives from the Latin American dependency critique of the 1960s. While these terms express more accurately the unequal power relationship between the "developed" and "underdeveloped" part of the world, they fail to do justice to the enormous spread of levels of development which exist among underdeveloped countries.

Impact of development

If we live in a divided world and daily use terms which accept this division, we next need to ask whether we are in any way moving towards a day when such divisions will be eradicated. After almost a half century of development efforts, what is the balance sheet? Are the underdeveloped countries really developing?

The attempt to answer this question raises a deeper question – what is development? The answer given to that question helps determine how we assess the impact of half a century of development efforts. There is therefore little consensus on the impact of development with views ranging from those who see a steady improvement among most developing countries and foresee a bright future ahead to those who paint an apocalyptic scenario of growing environmental destruction, socio-economic breakdown and cultural annihilation. The range of viewpoints can be grouped into the following four positions.

1) *The economic growth position:* This approach can be identified with the major multilateral institutions, the World Bank and the International Monetary Fund. For these institutions, promoting economic growth is the basic requirement for development. As the Bank's 1991 *World Development Report* on "The Challenge of Development" put it: "Growing productivity is the engine of development."[21] This is not to say that poverty, inequality or social services are overlooked by advocates of this position. As the Bank makes clear in its 1991 *Report*: "Any notion of strictly economic progress must, at a

minimum, look beyond growth in per capita incomes to the reduction of poverty and greater equity, to progress in education, health, and nutrition, and to the protection of the environment."[22] However, to achieve these social goals, the Bank promotes what it has called "a new development paradigm ... one that emphasizes market-friendly approaches and stresses the importance of private sector development, the creation of viable enterprises, and the development of domestic capital markets".[23] Following these policies, it believes, will put countries on a sustainable path to development while poverty alleviation can be met by more targeted social spending, especially in poverty safety-nets.

In ranging more widely over the past 40 years of development efforts, the Bank sees success and failure: "During the past forty years many developing countries have achieved progress at an impressive pace. Many have achieved striking gains in health and education. Some have seen their average incomes rise more than fivefold – a rate of progress that is extraordinary by historical standards. So if nothing else were certain, we would know that rapid and sustained development is no hopeless dream, but an achievable reality. Nonetheless, many countries have done poorly, and in some, living standards have actually fallen during the past thirty years. That is why poverty remains such a formidable problem and why substantial economic progress has yet to touch millions of people."[24] The main reason for the persistence of such poverty, the Bank contends, is the inadequate implementation of its "new development paradigm". This is essentially an optimistic position holding that more economic growth will lead to development, provided certain social safety nets be put in place as an essential element in the growth process.

2) *The social wellbeing position:* This is identified with the United Nations Development Programme which has, since 1990, produced an annual human development index (HDI). This is the most ambitious attempt to date to provide a scale of social wellbeing and to measure countries' relative position on it. It is based on three indicators – life expectancy at birth, adult literacy and schooling, and per capita income.[25] This puts the focus on people as the beneficiaries of development and it views the expansion of output and wealth (GNP growth) as a means to development.

Chapter 2 of the 1990 *Human Development Report* makes a comprehensive assessment of the record of development since 1960. This concluded that the gap between developing and developed countries has been greatly narrowed in relation to life expectancy, school enrolment and literacy but a huge GNP per capita gap remains. These findings raise hopes but also a question mark, says the report. "The hope is that the developing world can be taken to a basic level of human development in a fairly short period – if national development efforts and international assistance are properly directed. The question mark relates to the fact that four-fifths of the people in the Third World are leading longer, better educated lives, but they lack opportunities to tap their full potential. Unless economic opportunities are created in the South, more human talent will be wasted, and pressures for international migration are likely to increase dramatically. Moreover, while gaps in basic survival have narrowed, the widening gaps in science and technology threaten the South's future development."[26]

The UNDP, while acknowledging the social gains made, says that for many of the world's people "the reality is continuing exclusion". It stresses, for example, the importance of access to productive and remunerative employment but says that "on present trends, employment's growth will continue to lag far behind that of both output and the labour force". It therefore argues that "new models of sustainable human development are needed" including markets and governments that serve and involve people, especially the poor.[27] While acknowledging the benefits of economic growth, the UNDP realises that on its own it is not sufficient for development and may even exacerbate divisions and instability. Growth must go hand in hand with reforming economic and political structures to ensure that the poor have a better chance to share in its benefits.

3) *Global geopolitical position:* Unlike the two previous approaches which focus primarily on the situation within the Third World, this approach charts how the Third World has fared compared to the First World. It thus looks on the impact of development with rather more scepticism identifying what the Nicaraguan academic, Xavier Gorostiaga, has called "the contradictory, dialectic and global character of the changes taking place".[28] These include a widening gap between the North and South, with the former getting richer and more powerful at the latter's expense.

Giovanni Arrighi has charted the relationship between the income of the developed world and the underdeveloped world in the 50 year period between 1938 and 1988.[29] The overall picture that emerges, he writes, "is one of a major widening of the already large income gap that fifty years ago separated the peoples of the South from the peoples of the organic core of the capitalist world-economy. To be sure, the gap has widened very unevenly in space and time ... Yet, the overall long-term tendency is unmistakable: the vast majority of the world's populations have [sic] fallen increasingly behind the standards of wealth set by the West."[30]

Gorostiaga identifies what this means: "The countries that form the Group of Seven [consisting of the United States, Canada, Japan, Germany, France, Britain and Italy], with their 800 million inhabitants, control more technological, economic, informatics and military power than the rest of the approximately 4 billion people who live in Asia, Africa, Eastern Europe and Latin America ... The underdeveloped countries, with 75 per cent of the world's population, have access to scarcely 19 per cent of the world's gross domestic product, a reduction from the 23 per cent figure of a decade ago, and their participation in foreign stock investment has dropped from 25 per cent to 17 per cent. This is even more serious if we consider that in the same decade the net financial transfers from the South to the North were the equivalent of ten Marshall Plans. In the case of Latin America, according to the April 1991 Latin American Economic System (SELA) report, foreign debt-service payments alone were 80 per cent more than the total amount of foreign investment. If we include Latin American capital in the North (in the order of $160 billion) and the deterioration in the terms of trade (some $100 billion), Latin America's financial and productive debacle in the 1980s could be compared to the worst years of colonial pillage."[31]

Viewed from this perspective, the world capitalist system functions in a way that perpetuates unequal development at a world level. While it is recognised that some of the peripheral countries increase their wealth and show some of the attributes of development, for example a strong industrial base, yet the absolute gap between them and the developed countries continues to grow. If the fault lies in the capitalist system itself, therefore, the means to resolve it lies in promoting a renewed socialism mobilising the excluded sectors and building alliances at regional and world level between, for example, workers and people's movements. Out of this may emerge what Arrighi calls "an intellectual project and a political programme capable of transforming systemic chaos into a more equal and solidary world order".[32]

4) *The sustainable development position:* Unlike the three approaches just outlined all of which accept the need for further growth, this approach sees growth itself as the problem since it is destroying the environment and the human cultures that have sustained biological and social life. As Herman E. Daly has written: "The Earth ecosystem develops (evolves), but does not grow. Its subsystem, the economy, must eventually stop growing, but can continue to develop. The term 'sustainable development' therefore makes sense for the economy, but only if it is understood as 'development without growth' – i.e. qualitative improvement of a physical economic base that is maintained in a steady state by a through-put of matter-energy that is within the regenerative and assimilative capacities of the ecosystem. Currently the term 'sustainable development' is used as a synonym for the oxymoronic 'sustainable growth'. It must be saved from this perdition."[33]

Proponents of this position tend to view the last half-century of development in largely negative terms, emphasising its destructive impact on the environment and on the fragile human cultural systems which had helped sustain and regenerate it. It is, in the words of Ted Trainer, "inappropriate development" using up the earth's finite mineral and energy resources at a rate that is unsustainable. It is thus based on an illusion, that everybody in the world can in principle emulate the lifestyle of the wealthy of the earth.[34]

This critique poses a fundamental philosophical challenge to the notion of development itself as derived from Western, Enlightenment thought, what Dallmayr calls "the aspirations of Western modernity with its bent toward rational universalism".[35] In its search for models of sustainable development, it is "not so much an invention of the future as a rediscovery of the past",[36] discovering in traditional indigenous societies "both a radical cultural critique and a source of alternative vision".[37] This position is emerging in the early 1990s with enough force to call into question the dominant paradigm of the past half-century whether in its conservative, moderate or radical variants (see Chapter 4).

Rescuing development

The term "development" to which we now return following the discussion so far is, then, a rather battered concept, not subject to a precise definition to which all will agree. As we have seen, development not only means different things to different people but it inspires practices which can be diametrically opposed to one another. What is development for one may be destruction for another. Furthermore, the discussion has shown the context within which the terms we use were coined, a context which has inevitably coloured their meaning. The section assessing the impact of 50 years of development shows that the results are very much disputed based to some extent on different understandings of what development means. Before concluding this chapter, therefore, we must clarify how the term "development" is understood in this book and even justify that it is still a term worth rescuing.

In discussing what should constitute development, it is relatively easy to find consensus on a list of basic goals. Such a list would, for example, include: 1) family incomes adequate to meet basic subsistence such as food, shelter and clothing; 2) employment which provides a regular and relatively secure income as well as meeting deeper needs for a sense of social usefulness and participation; 3) levels of education and health care which allow for a satisfying and healthy life; and 4) participation in society through free access to civil organisations, a free press, and a democratic system (not necessarily one modelled on Western systems).[38] Agreeing on such a list, however, raises as many questions as it answers. What levels of subsistence would need to be reached to describe a society as developed? How many of the goals on this list would need to be attained or would they all need to be met? Furthermore, the list involves no consideration of the means used to arrive at such social goals. Is an oil producing country like Kuwait which can boast a higher per capita income than that of Australia or the United Kingdom more developed than these countries?

A better way of capturing the core issues which concern development theorists is to look at what constitutes underdevelopment. This at least will help to clarify some of the core realities which development is trying to eradicate and overcome, though there is little agreement on what are the main causes of these core realities nor on how they can be eradicated and overcome. To many people the term underdevelopment conjures up images of starving children, famine, destitution, drought, particularly in sub-Saharan African countries or in some of the populous Asian countries like Pakistan and Bangladesh. These certainly are images of stark underdevelopment but such conditions do not exhaust what is meant by underdevelopment. For such images often present people in a situation of absolute poverty but while examples do occur (with growing frequency, let it be said) of millions of people pushed to the brink of survival, these situations of absolute poverty affect only a small percentage of the world's people. Most of those we categorise as poor in the world are so because their situation is defined relative to some notion of a basic income level necessary for meeting human needs; in other words, their poverty is relative.

While there may be difficulties in defining just what a basic income level might be in a particular society,[39] the distinction between absolute and relative poverty has important implications for a view of development. Thus, a society can show dramatic increases in per capita income, yet display growing levels of relative poverty (Brazil since the 1950s is a good example). If we make relative poverty a central concept in our view of underdevelopment, then by definition growing equality in income distribution becomes a key criterion of development (since relative poverty is usually defined as a certain percentage of average income). This is recognised in the famous definition of development formulated by Dudley Seers and much quoted in development literature: "The questions to ask about a country's development are therefore: What has been happening to poverty? What has been happening to unemployment? What has been happening to inequality? If all three of these have become less severe, then beyond doubt this has been a period of development for the country concerned. If one or two of these central problems have been growing worse, especially if all three have, it would be strange to call the result 'development', even if per capita income had soared."[40]

This point is an important one to bear in mind when evaluating the undoubted achievements of half a century of development efforts. These were summed up in the 1994 *Human Development Report*: "The record of human development during this period is unprecedented, with the developing countries setting a pace three times faster than the industrial countries did a century ago. Rising life expectancy, falling infant mortality, increasing educational attainment and much improved nutrition are a few of the heartening indicators of this human advance.

"While nearly 70 per cent of humanity survived in abysmal human conditions in 1960 only 32 per cent suffered such conditions in 1992. The share of the world population enjoying fairly satisfactory human development levels increased from 25 per cent in 1960 to 60 per cent in 1992.

"The wealth of nations has multiplied in these 50 years.

Global GDP has increased sevenfold – from about $3 trillion to $22 trillion. Since the world population has more than doubled – from 2.5 billion to 5.5 billion – per capita income has more than tripled."[41]

In assessing the impact of these gains, however, adequate attention must be paid to growing inequality at a world level and within many developing countries (the East Asian NICs provide a counter-example of development progressively reducing inequality). For example, CEPAL (the UN Economic Commission for Latin America) drew attention in its 1995 report on social progress throughout the region to the fact that economic growth was not reducing inequality in income distribution nor generating employment among the poorest 10 per cent.[42] The report expresses particular concerns about two of the region's most successful economies, Brazil and Chile, and provides figures which show growing inequality in both countries.[43]

This draws attention to what must be one of the most disturbing aspects of underdevelopment in the 1990s, often called social exclusion. This refers to the fact that, as John Friedmann has put it, recent changes in the world economy such as globalisation, technological innovation and the centralisation of economic and financial power in huge transnational companies "have resulted in the virtual exclusion of vast numbers of the world's poor from effective economic and political participation. The message sent to them is very clear: for all practical purposes, they have become largely redundant for global capital accumulation." He spells out the sectors to which this applies in particular and its implications for social spending: "Modern capitalism can, for the most part, do without subsistence peasants, landless rural workers, and the so-called popular sectors of rapidly growing urban slums and shantytowns. Some, in fact, perceive them to have negative effects on capital accumulation, on the grounds that the urban poor siphon off capital for relatively unproductive public expenditures on housing, education, and health, and that subsistence peasants obstruct necessary modernization in agricultural production."[44]

These people may be better educated, live relatively more healthy lives and be more integrated into the money economy than were their predecessors but very often the social, communal, cultural and even psychological supports which made life tolerable for those earlier generations have been severely eroded in today's world. The result may often be people living lives of far greater insecurity, fear, meaninglessness and stress than did

40   *Poverty Amid Plenty*

previous generations of the poor. The challenge of integrating these excluded sectors has therefore become one of the great development challenges of the 1990s.[45] It draws attention to the fact that economic growth in itself is not sufficient; greater attention must be devoted to the ways in which the structuring of the economy and its links to society spread the benefits of such growth. As the historian Eric Hobsbawm put it at the end of his history of the 20th century, *Age of Extremes*: "The structures of human societies themselves, including even some of the social foundations of the capitalist economy, are on the point of being destroyed by the erosion of what we have inherited from the human past. Our world risks both explosion and implosion. It must change." [46]

This is the understanding of underdevelopment that informs this book. It can be defined as a process that is generating social exclusion of which some of the key elements are poverty, unemployment and inequality in income distribution. This then allows us to define development as a process characterised primarily by growing social inclusion through rising living standards, meaningful employment, active political and social participation and a satisfying cultural life extending to all sectors of society and thus widening the life choices and possibilities for the great majority. The book will assess development theories according to their success in achieving these goals.

Some argue however that the process of development has itself been a major contributory factor in generating social exclusion through a steady imposition of western economic interests and a western value system on peoples who had over centuries evolved their own means of economic survival. Sachs has described well what this western imposition has often meant in practice: "Traditions of sufficiency have been pushed aside, local exchange relations dissolved, collective forms of ownership broken up, and subsistence economies wiped out."[47] In this view, the problem of development lies not with those defined as "underdeveloped" but with those who seek to develop them, incorporating in a way analogous to a religious crusade the world's peoples into a western economic and value system.[48] It is therefore understandable that some could see development as "another tool of domination".[49] This view cannot lightly be dismissed and has led Susan George to call for the term development to be replaced by the term resistance, thus highlighting the attempts of the poor and marginalised of the world to resist what is imposed on them in the name of development.[50]

Yet, while such a critique may alert us to the ethnocentric

assumptions behind much development thinking, its ultimate target is not development thinking as such but the process of western economic expansionism that is an inherent part of the capitalist system. This expansionism may have cloaked itself in the guise of development over recent decades but it will continue under some other guise even if we end all discussion of development. Indeed, it is the challenge of development that is today stimulating some of the sharpest critique of western capitalist domination and positing development as a dialogue of cultures searching for new, pluralist and sustainable models of human emancipation. It must also be pointed out that not all traditional practices are necessarily more beneficial to society and therefore traditional societies and cultures also need to be critically examined from the point of view of development. We can agree therefore with Colin Leys when he writes that there is "an urgent need to revive development theory, not as a branch of policy-oriented social science within the parameters of an unquestioned capitalist world order, but as a field of critical enquiry about the contemporary dynamics of that order itself, with imperative policy implications for the survival of civilised and decent life, and not just in the ex-colonial countries".[51]

Conclusion

In the quote which opens this chapter, Ruben Zamora, the main opposition candidate in the presidential elections in El Salvador in 1994, predicted that the next century will be marked by naked conflict over the gross inequality in the distribution of the world's resources. This highlights the extent to which the issues under discussion in this book may well be among the most important ones to be addressed by the international community if the foundations are to be laid for a more equitable and stable world. Yet, as this chapter has emphasised, it is not for lack of attempts to resolve them that these problems are still with us. The remainder of Part I will give a broad critical overview of the main theories which informed these attempts at development, placing them in the economic and political context out of which they emerged.

Footnotes
1 In an interview in *The Irish Times*, 12 February 1994
2 *The Irish Times*, 31 January 1994
3 The phraseology used in regard to this target was significantly modified in the text of the White Paper on Foreign Policy entitled *Challenges and Opportunities Abroad*, published by the Department of Foreign Affairs in early 1996. This reads: "...the Government have suggested that the number of

APSO volunteer placements could be increased towards a target figure of 2,000. This figure is, however, subject to the established needs of developing countries, to the availability of qualified nationals and to the interests of sustainability including increased emphasis on local capacity" (p. 242).

4 *World Development Report 1993*, Oxford University Press for the World Bank, 1993

5 The pervasiveness of such images and their role in re-inforcing stereotypes have been the subject of a campaign by Comhlámh, the Irish Association of Returned Development Workers. Entitled "For a Truer Picture of the Majority World", the campaign sought to influence policy in the media and among development agencies to ensure that the realities and complexities of the countries of the South were portrayed and their people respected.

6 *The World Bank Atlas 1996*, The World Bank, 1995, p.33

7 The data is taken from the World Bank's *World Development Report 1995*, pp.162-163 and is based on 1993 per capita GNP figures (with some exceptions).

8 *Human Development Report 1992*, United Nations Development Programme, 1992, p.34

9 *The World Bank Atlas 1994*, The World Bank 1993, p.17

10 Figures from the World Bank, *World Development Report 1995*, p.221

11 Alejandro Portes, "Latin American class structures: the composition and change during the last decades" in *Latin American Research Review*, vol.20, no.3, 1985, pp.7-40

12 *Human Development Report 1993*, United Nations Development Programme, 1993, p.26. It summed up the inequality in living standards between whites and blacks in the US as follows: "Their disadvantage starts at birth. The infant mortality rate for whites is 8 per 1,000 live births, but for blacks it is 19. And black children are much more likely than white children to grow up in single-parent homes – in 1990, 19 per cent of white children were growing up in single-parent households, compared with 54 per cent of black children. Children in black families are also more likely to grow up in poverty. The real GDP per capita for whites in 1990 was around $22,000, but for blacks it was around $17,000."

13 John Cavanagh in a talk on "Global corporate strategies" given in Amsterdam, November 1991, which the author attended.

14 For a comprehensive discussion of Marx's views on development, see Jorge Larrain, *Theories of Development*, Polity Press, 1989, pp.28-62

15 Quoted in Larrain, ibid., p.68

16 Wolfgang Sachs, *On the Archaeology of the Development Idea*, first published in English by Pennsylvania State University Science, Technology and Society Programme, 1989. The quote is from essay 1, p.1. For a fuller discussion of the history of the concept of "development", see Gustavo Esteva, "Development" in Wolfgang Sachs, ed., *The Development Dictionary: A Guide to Knowledge as Power*, Zed, 1992, pp. 6-25.

17 Some scholars also consider Ireland a NIC. See, for example, John Kurt Jacobsen, *Chasing Progress in the Irish Republic*, Cambridge University Press, 1994.

18 Wolfgang Sachs, *On the Archaeology of the Development Idea*, op. cit., essay 1, p. 4.

19 See, for example, "US to Cut Foreign Aid to Latin America" in *The Christian Science Monitor*, World Edition, 28 January-3 February 1994 and "Meeting with poor states abandoned in disagreement" in *The Irish Times*, 17 February 1995.

20 Mark T. Berger, "The End of the 'Third World'?" in *Third World Quarterly*, vol.15, no.2, 1994, p.270

21 *World Development Report 1991*, Oxford University Press for the World Bank, 1991, p.4

22 ibid., p.4

23 *Learning from the Past, Embracing the Future*, The World Bank Group, 1994, p.10

24 *The World Bank Atlas 1994*, The World Bank, 1993, p.17

25 For a discussion of issues relating to HDI and its formulation, see the UNDP's *Human Development Report 1990*, Chapter 1, pp.9-16

26 *Human Development Report 1990*, Oxford University Press for the UNDP, 1990, p.18

27 See the *Human Development Report 1993*. The quotes are taken from the Overview, pp.1-8

28 Xavier Gorostiaga, "Latin America in the 'New World Order'" in *TNIdeas*, November 1992, p.10

29 Giovanni Arrighi, "World income inequalities and the future of socialism" in *New Left Review*, no.189, 1991, pp.39-66

30 ibid., p.48

31 Gorostiaga, op. cit., quotes from pp. 10, 11

32 Arrighi, op. cit., p.66

33 Herman E. Daly, "Sustainable growth: an impossibility theorem" in *Development*, vol. 3, no. 4, 1990, p.45

34 Ted Trainer, *Developed to Death: Rethinking Third World Development*, Green Print, 1989

35 Fred Dallmayr, "Modernization and postmodernization: whither India?" in *Alternatives*, no. 17, 1992, p.421

36 Michael Redclift, *Sustainable Development: Exploring the Contradictions*, Methuen, 1987, p.171

37 Vincent Tucker, *The Myth of Development*, Department of Sociology, UCC, 1992, p.34

38 For a discussion of what constitutes development on which this list is partially based, see David Colman and Frederick Nixson, "The concept and measurement of development" in Anna Farmar, ed, *The Developing World*, DESC, 1988, pp.28-43

39 For a discussion of absolute and relative poverty, see Amartya Sen, "Concepts of poverty" in Anna Farmar, ed, op. cit., pp.22-27

40 Dudley Seers, "Challenges to development theories and strategies" in *International Development*, 1969, p.7

41 *Human Development Report 1994*, Oxford University Press for the UNDP, 1994, pp.1, 2

42 *Panorama Social de America Latina 1995*, CEPAL, 1995; translation by Peadar Kirby

43 ibid. Figures which show growing inequality relate to two issues. Firstly, the report draws attention to the persistence of high unemployment among the poorest 20 per cent. Secondly, among the lower middle class which should be benefiting more from economic growth, the report provides figures showing that the relation between the average income of this sector (which is defined as the 30 per cent of households above the poorest 40 per cent) declining as a percentage of total average income.

44 John Friedmann, *Empowerment: The Politics of Alternative Development*, Blackwell, 1992, p.14

45 See Dharam Ghai and Cynthia Hewitt de Alcantara, *Globalization and Social Integration: Patterns and Processes*, UNDP, 1995

46 Eric Hobsbawm, *Age of Extremes: The Short Twentieth Century 1914-1992*, Michael Joseph, 1994, p.585

47 Wolfgang Sachs, op. cit., essay 4, p.8

48 This, for example, is the view put forward by the anthropologist Fabrizio Sabelli in a talk on "Development as Myth" at a conference in Amsterdam in November 1992 attended by the author.

49 Vincent Tucker, op. cit., p.34

50 Susan George made this point in a talk given at the conference mentioned in note 48 above.

51 Colin Leys, "The crisis in 'development theory'" in *New Political Economy*, vol.1, no.1, 1996, p.56

Chapter 2

From Modernisation to Dependency

"Modernisation theory was unambiguously and directly an expression and agent of the then-hegemonic US imperialism. For its part, dependency theory was, 'in the last instance', a justification and tool of a revolutionary strategy. The failure of both theories was, also, due less to their conceptual inconsistencies than to their collapse as political strategies."

– Ronaldo Munck[1]

Introduction

The allied victory in the second World War unleashed a wave of optimism that progress and prosperity were an achievable goal for the world's people. This found concrete expression first and foremost in the ambitious Marshall Plan to rebuild Europe which, within a few short years, was yielding results regarded as little short of miraculous and ushering in a quarter century of unprecedented consumer prosperity in western Europe and north America. But, for the first time ever in human history, the new order emerging from the ashes of war aspired to be truly global in extent. The Bretton Woods conference in 1944 had prepared the way for the founding the following year of the International Monetary Fund and the World Bank; significantly, the latter was officially titled the International Bank for Reconstruction and Development. More and more these institutions began to devote their attention to the problems of developing countries. The United Nations, founded in 1945, also took upon itself a brief for economic and social development worldwide.

By the early 1950s, parts of the Third World were beginning to assert their presence on the world stage. The process of decolonisation had begun with the independence of Lebanon in 1945, Syria and Jordan in 1946, India and Pakistan in 1947, Ceylon (Sri Lanka) and Burma in 1948, Indonesia in 1949 and Libya in 1951. This led academics from a range of disciplines – economics, sociology, political science, psychology – to turn their attention to the development problems of such countries and to elaborate a body of theory which offered a description of what they saw as the path to development. Inspired by two of the founding fathers of sociology, Emile Durkheim (1858-1917) and Max Weber (1864-1920), this started from a conception of development as a movement from traditional to modern society and laid down what it saw as the necessary conditions to achieve this transition. Though there are many different emphases within this broad theoretical approach, it is usually identified by the term, modernisation theory.

Modernisation

Durkheim: traditional to modern

Durkheim had, as early as 1893, proposed his views on the fundamental difference between traditional and modern society. In the former, life was circumscribed by tradition and by the demands of the community, according to Durkheim and he identified the nature and allocation of social roles as being a major difference between traditional and modern society. In traditional society these were far more diffuse and generalised (for example the role of hunter) and were allocated by the community, usually by the group into which the person was born. By contrast, modern society for Durkheim is characterised by a multiplicity of very specific roles (a teacher, a nuclear physicist) and individuals fill these roles through their personal achievement. Modern society is therefore a much more fluid, open and mobile setting within which individuals can hope to improve their living situation through their own efforts. Motivated by his abiding concern about problems of social stability and integration, Durkheim focused on what binds societies together – in the former "mechanical solidarity" (a solidarity derived from the very structured nature of social life) and in the latter "organic solidarity" (based on the more open but yet interrelated nature of modern society). These concerns also led Durkheim to emphasise the importance ·of common norms and values which hold society together and prevent the social dissolution which he so feared. This emphasis on values was to characterise most modernisation theorists.

Weber: the spirit of capitalism

Unlike the highly speculative basis of Durkheim's theory, Weber developed his theory about the transition from traditional to modern society by examining the emergence of capitalism in western Europe. He identified the principle of rationality which he saw as playing a crucial role in the organisation of economic activity in such a way as to allow a surplus to be accumulated and re-invested thereby contributing to a dynamic economic advance. This principle of rationality he contrasted to those customs which governed the more static life of traditional society and which often led to the spending of economic surplus on, for example, the demands of an extended family or individual consumption. For Weber, then, the principle of rationality (which he particularly equated with the Protestant ethic) is "the spirit of modern capitalism". Again, in the work of Weber can be seen a stress on the importance of values and norms in the process of moving from traditional to modern society, as is obvious from the title of his most famous work *The Protestant Ethic and the Spirit of Capitalism* (1904).

Parsons: evolutionary universals

In the early 1950s, this analytical framework came to be applied to the problems of developing countries by a group of mostly US scholars. Among the most influential, certainly in the field of sociology, was Talcott Parsons who elaborated on the dualistic opposites of Durkheim's mechanical versus organic solidarity or the oft-quoted distinction of Tönnies between *Gemeinschaft* (relationships based on community) and *Gesellschaft* (relationships based on association). For Parsons, these distinctions offered too simplified a picture of social change and in their place he offered a series of five "pattern variables" or value choices – affectivity versus affective neutrality, ascription versus achievement, diffusion versus specificity, particularism versus universalism and collective orientation versus self-orientation. The first of each of these five choices characterises the fundamental value-orientation of traditional society, according to Parsons, while the second choice constitutes that of modern society. Thus the social ties of traditional society are based on affectivity whereas those of modern society are not; social roles in the former are allotted whereas in the latter they are achieved; such roles in modern society have very specific functions which are universally applicable whereas in traditional society they are very diffuse and particular; finally, collective interests predominate in traditional society whereas personal ones are to the fore in modern society.[2]

Parsons went on to elaborate in greater detail the stages through which societies pass on the road to modernity. Central to his theory was the view that societies are complex social systems made up of roles and institutions which are continuously adapting to change. The key to understanding these institutions is their functionality to the wider social system, that is they play a necessary role in the functioning of the whole. From this derives the term structural functionalism, the term by which the work of Parsons is usually identified. Thus, for example, Parsons argued from the evidence of biology that successful evolution happens when organisms furnish themselves with the means to adjust and adapt to their environment and in so doing "break out" from lower forms of life to higher; a similar process happens in social evolution, he contended. An example in the life of societies is the move from an authority system based on kinship (tribal or clan society) to one based on a legitimate and independent political system. If societies fail to make this transition they remain stuck, unable to evolve. In this way, Parsons identified what he called "evolutionary universals" such as bureaucratic organisation, money and markets, a universalistic legal system and democratic association with elective leadership in both government and private organisations. These, he contended, constitute "the main outline of the structural foundations of modern society".[3]

For Parsons, as for most modernisation theorists, the ever growing differentiation of social roles and institutions is what characterises the move from traditional to modern society. For example, what characterises the transition from primitive societies such as the Australian aborigines to advanced primitive societies such as ancient Egypt or the Inca empire is the differentiation of the political function and its structuring in the form of a religio-political elite of ruler and court. The next transition to historic societies such as Confucian China or the Roman Empire involves cultural differentiation and a more complex class structure of a politico-military elite, a cultural religious elite and urban and peasant lower classes. Next came "seedbed" societies such as Greece and Israel with the development of a judiciary; the final stage in social evolution is constituted by modern societies with economic and technological differentiation structured in a high level of occupational differentiation.[4]

It is difficult in a brief account to do justice to the complexity of Parsons' theoretical framework. This was to exercise a major influence on modernisation theorists so much so that Harrison writes that "it was from the soil of Parsonian sociology that modernisation theories sprouted".[5] Yet, it must also be borne in mind that Parsons' theories are highly abstract and speculative though they may give the impression that they have been derived from a detailed historical examination of the evolution of societies. Instead, they are deductive, based on grand theories for which useful illustrations are found. Indeed in one revealing comment, Parsons implied that concrete evidence should not be allowed interfere with his grand theoretical scheme. Urging his readers to pay attention to the soundness of the idea of the evolutionary universal rather than his illustrations of it, he wrote: "If this idea is sound, empirical shortcomings in its application can be remedied by research and criticism."[6]

Rostow: stages of growth

Among economists, the principal modernisation theorist was Walt Rostow whose book *The Stages of Economic Growth* identified five stages through which societies pass to achieve economic "take-off" as he called it.[7] The first stage is that of traditional society in which subsistence agriculture provides the economic base for the poor mass of the population. The second stage he calls the "preconditions for take-off" in which an increasing population provides the pressure for greater agricultural productivity and economic diversification. Stage three offers the take-off into economic growth through the growth of manufacturing industry thus generating the dynamic for stage four, the drive to maturity, in which the wealth produced generates further economic growth and social development. Stage five, the stage of mass high consumption, marks the arrival at a state of sustained growth in which a diversified economy can support a constant increase in living standards. Rostow therefore offers an outline of the economic stages on the path from traditional to modern society and he has no qualms in placing the societies of Asia, the Middle East, Africa and Latin America at "the stages of preconditions and take-off of other societies, in the late eighteenth, nineteenth and early twentieth centuries".[8] The implication is that they are all well on the route to becoming advanced industrial societies if they follow the example of the developed world. To help them on their way, he advocates the injection of capital and technology from the developed world.

McClelland: need for achievement

Like Weber, Rostow places great emphasis on the importance of a new elite emerging which internalises the value system of advanced capitalist society characterised by individualism and a spirit of competitive entrepreneurship. The importance placed on the acquisition of such values within the modernisation perspective, led David McClelland to study the conditions which gave rise to individuals acquiring these values. Through examining children's stories and other writings, he identified what he called the "need for achievement" or N-ach and claimed that he found high levels of this present in societies as diverse as Athenian Greece, Spain in the sixteenth century and modern Japan.[9] For McClelland, it is the business entrepreneur who translates high N-ach into economic growth in particular societies and it is the task of formal education to develop this trait so that more children acquire an entrepreneurial drive.

Modernisation theory therefore presented development as a relatively painless evolution from a static and custom-bound traditional society to a dynamic and achievement-oriented modern society. Some theorists tried to make the strict polarisation between these two opposites a little more nuanced, such as David Lerner who proposed what he termed a "transitional society", that is a society permeated by the aspiration to modernity.[10] However, for modernisation theory, the key to achieving modernity lay in the diffusion of modern values and the increasing role differentiation that would result, leading gradually to the more complex institutional make-up that characterises modern industrial society. It was thus permeated by the developmental optimism of the times in which enlightened elites, internalising the values of the US and other developed societies, would gradually bring enlightenment and development to their own societies.

Challenges

Revolution or social struggle had no place in modernisation theory. Such major social and political upheavals as the Cuban revolution in 1959 and the Vietnam War, both of which had a profound impact on political consciousness in the 1960s, challenged therefore the easy assumptions of evolutionary progress under the leadership of benign elites following the US example. By 1968, the challenge reached the heart of the developed world itself as student uprisings showed the alienation of that very social sector which for modernisation theorists embodied their hopes for modernity. This helped highlight just how deductive was modernisation theory, based not on an examination of actual attempts at development in Third World societies, but rather on abstract theoretical assumptions from which universal norms were derived.

Huntington: political authoritarianism

The growing evidence that the path to development was not as smooth and evolutionary as envisaged, led a number of modernisation theorists to examine the difficulties of integration. The influential US political scientist, Samuel Huntington, turned his attention to the breakdown of the political systems of some newly independent states acknowledging that they were proving too weak for the demands being placed upon them.[11] Huntington's answer was to argue that what was important was not the particular form of the political system – whether democratic or not – but the system's ability successfully to manage the strains of modernisation. Thus, for Huntington, democracy could be sacrificed for the sake of stability and he argued, for example, that in Latin America the military intervened to protect the stability of a modernising middle class against the incursions of the masses. As Lehmann points out, Huntington was "one of the first conservative thinkers to challenge the optimistic nostrums of the liberal modernisation theory which underlay the 'aid optimism' of the time" and, not surprisingly, he was both an adviser to the Pentagon and a friend of senior members of the Brazilian military.[12]

Eisenstadt: breakdown of modernisation

S. N. Eisenstadt examined the roots of the theoretical problems being encountered by modernisation theory. He pointed out, for example, that while modernisation theory offered a description of the transition from a traditional to a modern society, it did not offer an explanation of why this transition happened. He wrote: "We do not know exactly what conditions facilitate or precipitate these different types of change in different societies."[13] Therefore the process of integrating more differentiated institutions into modern society was not properly understood, he argued, and, as well as a successful modern society emerging, what could emerge would be "a breakdown of modernisation" or "constricted development".[14] Crucial to such a breakdown, he wrote, was the absence of "an active group of special 'entrepreneurs' or an elite able to offer solutions".[15]

Ethnocentric and elitist

Modernisation theory provided the theoretical apparatus for the West's development drive of the 1950s and 1960s. The diffusion of Western advice through sending advisors and educating local elites, through Western aid and investment and through Western technology would provide the motor-force for drawing traditional societies towards economic "take-off", a modern class structure and the complex social and political institutions of a modern society. Much of this was in the West's self-interest but hidden within its abstract theoretical constructs was a strong ethnocentric bias, an assumption that the economy, social structure and political system of advanced Western societies embodied the ideal that all societies could reach if only they followed the same evolutionary route. Societies were treated as a series of similar interdependent units placed at different stages along an evolutionary spectrum. No attention was paid to the ways in which there might be a structured interaction between societies benefiting one at the expense of the other, what was later to be identified as the exploitation of the periphery by the core countries.[16]

Indeed, the very vocabulary of modernisation theory, with its emphasis on terms such as role, norm, diffusion, institution and specialisation, conspired against any analysis of the actual economic and social conditions in underdeveloped countries. Thus some of the fundamental realities of development are theorised into virtual meaninglessness. Bernstein offers a good example of this in quoting how one modernisation theorist described the exploitation of his tenants by a hacienda owner (large Latin American landowner), referring to it as "a Case IV situation of conflictual goal-seeking involving representatives of different organisational structures".[17]

Another assumption which had major consequences was the elitism of modernisation theory. It identified the elites, both foreign and local, as the key actors in promoting development, elites which had internalised the necessary values of individualism, achievement-orientation and economic rationality. Other social sectors were written out of the picture, expected passively and unquestioningly to accept the advice of these Westernised elites and act accordingly. As Bernstein asks: "What becomes of the rural capitalists, peasants and share-croppers, the artisans and industrial workers, the labour migrants and urban unemployed, the traders and money-lenders?" As he says, these are lumped into a single category of "non-elite" which "can then be forgotten except when it gives rise to social protest (headache for the elite) or serves as the raw material of 'mobilisation' (support for the elite)".[18]

These criticisms of modernisation theory draw attention to the fact that it was not as politically disinterested as it claimed to be. As we have seen, W.W. Rostow subtitled his *The Stages of Economic Growth* a "Non-Communist Manifesto" and the leading dependency theorist, André Gunder Frank says that Rostow once told him that from the age of 18 he had understood his mission in life as being to offer the world a better alternative to that offered by Karl Marx.[19] Rostow went on to play a key role at the State Department during the Kennedy presidency and was chief adviser on Vietnam to President Johnson. Allusion has also been made to the political uses to which the work of Samuel Huntington was put in giving a theoretical basis to US support for authoritarian regimes throughout the Third World. Thus, in the context of the Cold War, modernisation theory and some of its main proponents can be seen as promoting a Western model of development for the Third World in opposition to the alternative being offered by communism.

In the words of Hulme and Turner, "Eisenstadt's work was an appropriate obituary for the modernisation paradigm. The miraculous transformations of traditional societies into modern ones had not taken place. Increased poverty, growing indebtedness, political repression and stagnating economies were all too evident – and they were not supposed to happen".[20] And, in drawing attention to the fact that "a given social sphere contains not one but several, often competing, possible orientations and potentialities for development",[21] Eisenstadt was acknowledging that development could be a more conflictual process than modernisation theorists had allowed for, foreshadowing the emergence of a fundamental theoretical challenge in the form of dependency theory.

Dependency

CEPAL and structuralism

It was appropriate that the first elements of a new development paradigm challenging the dominance of modernisation theory were to emerge from the Third World. In 1947 the United Nations established its Economic Commission for Latin America (called ECLA in English but usually referred to as CEPAL from its Spanish acronym) with its headquarters in the Chilean capital, Santiago. Under the inspired leadership of the Argentine economist, Raul Prebisch, it quickly emerged as a major centre of social and economic thought, seeking to understand the nature and processes of Latin American underdevelopment, what Kay calls "the first genuine Third World development school".[22]

Through its reports and studies in the 1950s, CEPAL challenged the dominant neo-classical view that free trade benefited both developed and underdeveloped countries and that countries should concentrate in trading goods in which they had a comparative advantage, the "law of comparative advantage". Instead, CEPAL formulated a theory of unequal development between the "centre" or developed countries and the "periphery" or underdeveloped countries. According to this theory, the fruits of development are appropriated by the core at the expense of the periphery which falls further and further behind. This happens, for example, in the tendency for the prices of Third World products, primary food products or minerals for the most part, to decline while the prices of First World products, mostly manufactured goods, increase. Therefore the Third World gets less and less for its exports while having to pay more and more for its imports.

CEPAL went on to formulate a strategy for development in this unequal international context. Instead of an "outward-looking" development based on export growth, it proposed an "inward-looking" process of import-substitution industrialisation behind tariff barriers which would protect infant industries. Prebisch, however, cautioned against excessive protectionism which would damage competitiveness. The state would play an active role in this process though again Prebisch was wary of too much state intervention. To strengthen this process of inward-looking development, CEPAL by the early 1960s was recommending a policy of regional common markets thus increasing the market for the goods being produced by these new industries.[23]

The work of CEPAL is usually credited with marking the beginning of what is called "structuralism", a focus on the structural conditions for economic growth as distinct from the emphasis of neo-classical economics on the efficient allocation of resources through prices within a market economy.[24] By the early 1960s, this emphasis on the structural obstacles to development provided the context for the emergence of a more radical group of theorists exploring the dependent nature of development in the Third World. Since much of this work was emerging from Latin America, they were known in Spanish as *dependentistas* or in English as dependency theorists. The key figure in bringing this perspective to a wider public was André Gunder Frank.

Frank: the development of underdevelopment

Frank was of German extraction; his father had fled from Nazi Germany to the US when André (then called Andreas) was four. His intellectual formation was that of a classical modernisationist – he studied economics at the University of Chicago with Milton Freedman and was briefly a colleague of Walt Rostow at the Massachusetts Institute of Technology. Some of his earliest work was done for the World Bank. Through his work on social change, he came to the conclusion that the truly important factors in development were political. "It became increasingly clear to me that all American, including my own, development studies and thinking therefore were not at all part of the solution to development problems. Instead they were themselves really part of the problem, since they sought to deny and obscure both the real problem and the real solution, which lay in politics."[25] This growing sense of dissatisfaction led Frank to visit some of the main revolutionary states of the time, Cuba, Ghana and Guinea, and in 1962 to move to Latin America. The following decade, during which he worked in Mexico, Brazil but mostly Chile, was to see his major work in formulating and bringing to international attention a new development paradigm.[26]

Frank came to Latin America at a time when the "inward-looking" development model pioneered by CEPAL was running into crisis. He soon took issue with CEPAL's view that foreign investment could help Latin America make up the gap between what it earned from its exports and what it needed to import in order to further industrialisation. On the contrary, Frank concluded that foreign investment was leading to a net outflow of funds from Latin America through profit repatriation and interest payments. This led Frank into what was to be his major contribution to development theory; this can be summarised in two points.

The first was the denial of the dominant progressive position that Latin American economies were dualistic, made up of two sectors co-existing side by side, a feudal agricultural system and a capitalist industrial system. Instead, Frank argued that the European conquest in the sixteenth century had incorporated Latin America into a world capitalist system. This view led him, in his first major work *Capitalism and Underdevelopment in Latin America* published in English in 1967, to take issue with the position of communist parties in the region that the survival of a feudal landed aristocracy was the major cause of Latin American underdevelopment. This position led such parties to propose an alliance with so-called progressive sectors of the bourgeoisie (industrialists) and the working class in an inward-oriented capitalist drive to break this stranglehold of feudal landed sectors on economic progress. Frank took issue: "My reading of Chilean history and my analysis of capitalism oblige me to reject both this premise and conclusion. Because of capitalism, Chile's economy was already underdeveloping throughout the three centuries before independence. And, if the innate contradictions of capitalism continue to operate in Chile today, as my analysis contends that they must and my observation that they do, then no kind of capitalist development, be it toward the outside or toward the inside, can save Chile from further underdevelopment."[27]

His second contribution was to elaborate mechanisms by which capitalism leads to underdevelopment in the periphery. This involved taking Marx's view of the appropriation by capitalists of the surplus value created by workers and extending this view to the relationship between the developed capitalist countries (the centre or core) and the underdeveloped (the periphery). Frank likened this to a chain-like "metropolis-satellite" relationship "which extends the capitalist link between the capitalist world and national metropolises to the regional centres (part of whose surplus they appropriate); and from these to local centres, and so on to large landowners or merchants who expropriate surplus from small peasants or tenants, and sometimes even from these latter to landless labourers exploited by them in turn. At each step along the way, the relatively few capitalists above exercise monopoly power over the many below, expropriating some or all of their economic surplus and, to the extent that they are not expropriated in turn by the still fewer above them, appropriating it for their own use. Thus at each point, the international, national, and local capitalist system generates economic development for the few and underdevelopment for the many".[28] Though elements of this relationship may change over time, there is a fundamental continuity, according to Frank, which characterises the nature of international capitalism.

Frank's writings therefore constituted a radical position within development theory. The conclusion was that capitalism itself generates underdevelopment on the periphery and, within this international system, the only possibilities for peripheral countries to develop occur either when countries are weakly integrated into the system or else when the system itself is in crisis (as in the 1930s). Thus could Frank's key phrase "the development of underdevelopment" be understood. The only solution lay in breaking the links with capitalism through a socialist revolution.

Frank was not the first dependency theorist; he himself mentions the work of Paul Baran as a major influence on his thinking. Baran is important because he was the first Marxist to challenge the accepted Marxist notion that capitalism is a progressive force for development in the Third World (see Chapter 1). Instead, Baran argued, underdevelopment is not due to pre-capitalist structures or modes of production; rather, it is a product of capitalism itself under which developed countries siphon off part of the economic surplus from the Third World while local elites squander another part of it.[29] Baran has been called "the hinge which joins or articulates the theory of imperialism with, and marks the beginning of, dependency theory".[30] Neither was Frank the most sophisticated of the dependency theorists; Foster-Carter's verdict that "Frank's formulations are extremely crude"[31] would be widely accepted.[32] But, again in the words of Foster-Carter, "Frank's great merit is to have, at a certain place and time, stated the new paradigm with such brute force that no one could possibly confuse it with anything else".[33]

Cardoso and Faletto: associated-dependent development

Part of the problem with Frank that soon became clear, however, was that his theories denied the possibility of any development happening under capitalism. It was, therefore, all or nothing – either achieve socialism or be condemned forever to deepening underdevelopment. With the publication of *Dependency and Development in Latin America* by Fernando Henrique Cardoso and Enzo Faletto in Spanish in 1969 and in English in 1979 (the latter with a specially written preface clarifying their thinking on dependency) came a more subtle variant of dependency theory acknowledging that a form of "associated dependent development" was possible for peripheral countries within capitalism. By this they mean a form of development dependent on foreign capital which leads to the expansion of productive forces but which also increases poverty and marginalisation. This work was to prove perhaps the most enduring legacy of dependency theory as the authors provide an analysis of "how development is possible in the Latin American countries"[34] identifying through concrete examination the ways in which "subordinated social groups and classes, as well as dominated countries, try to counter-attack dominant interests that sustain structures of domination".[35]

Cardoso and Faletto refuse to accept a concept of dependency that would seem to trap peripheral countries, and they refer therefore to "'situations of dependency' rather than to the 'category' or to the 'theory' of dependency".[36] These situations of dependency which characterise the position of peripheral countries under capitalism severely limit the freedom of action of such countries, acknowledge Cardoso and Faletto; yet, they argue that a national society can achieve a certain autonomy of decision-making and that this can be identified through examining the relationship of internal social classes both to one another and to the international forces which keep their society in a dependent position. "We conceive the relationship between external and internal forces as forming a complex whole whose structural links are not based on mere external forms of exploitation and coercion, but are rooted in coincidences of interests between local dominant classes and international ones, and, on the other side, are challenged by local dominated groups and classes," they write.[37] If external dependence condemned all peripheral countries to deepening underdevelopment, how does one explain the great differences in levels of development between various countries in Latin America, they ask. The explanation cannot lie entirely in differences in natural resources nor in the different periods they were incorporated into international capitalism but also must lie "in the different moments at which sectors of local classes allied or clashed with foreign interests, organized different forms of state, sustained distinct ideologies, or tried to implement various policies or defined alternative strategies to cope with imperialist challenges in diverse moments of history".[38] This variant of dependency theory therefore gives central importance to social actors in determining how to create possibilities for development on the periphery. Yet, such development, Cardoso and Faletto caution, will always be capitalist development which "produces as it evolves, in a cyclical way, wealth and poverty, accumulation and shortage of capital, employment for some and unemployment for others. So, we do not mean by the notion of 'development' the achievement of a more egalitarian or more just society ... In the end what has to be discussed as an alternative is not the consolidation of the state and the fulfillment of 'autonomous capitalism', but how to supersede them. The important question, then, is how to construct paths toward socialism".[39]

Fernando Henrique Cardoso is the only one of the major dependency theorists to have achieved prominence more recently through his political involvement. He was successively Brazil's foreign and finance minister in the early 1990s and took office as President of Brazil in January 1995.

Wallerstein: world-systems theory

Though world-systems theory is usually distinguished from dependency theory, Immanuel Wallerstein in many ways takes over where Frank left off and the latter wrote an editorial note for

Poverty Amid Plenty

publication with the first volume of Wallerstein's three-volume work *The Modern World System* in 1974 predicting that it would become a classic.[40] For Wallerstein, the subject of analysis is the capitalist economy that emerged in the 16th century in north-west Europe as the core area of a world economy and by the 19th century had become the unique world system. This leads Wallerstein to support Frank's view that Latin America had become capitalist in the 16th century; though slave or other forms of forced labour may have persisted in Latin America, these do not constitute remnants of feudalism, he writes, as these areas do not have a separate mode of production but have been integrated into the world capitalist system. Similarly, he denies the existence of a separate socialist world system and sees the socialist countries as forming part of the capitalist world system; indeed, he views the 1917 revolution as reversing Russia's decline to peripheral status within the world system, re-instating it as a very strong member of the semi-periphery and even making possible its advance to full core status.

The categories of core and periphery Wallerstein takes from Frank with whom he agrees that the core countries appropriate the surplus produced by the periphery, the principal mechanism of the latters' underdevelopment. But he modifies Frank's view in a very important way by introducing the notion of semi-periphery, likening its role in the world system to that of those social sectors within any individual country (be they bureaucrats, intellectuals, merchants) who "feel that their own well-being is wrapped up in the survival of the system as such and the competence of its leaders. It is this staff which not only propagates the myths; it is they who believe them".[41] If such an intermediate group between the rulers of the system and its victims is necessary for the system's survival so too, he says, "the semi-periphery is needed to make a capitalist world-economy run smoothly".[42] These are countries, then, which manage a form of dependent development (such as the newly industrialising countries of Latin America and East Asia) offering the illusion to the peripheral countries that all could follow the same route. Within this world system of centre, semi-periphery and periphery, some individual states may move their position from one to another category (as Japan moved to the core and perhaps Britain may be moving in the other direction to the semi-periphery) but the existence of these categories is a fundamental part of the system. In other words, there will always be developed, developing and underdeveloped countries; it is just the countries which fill these categories that may change.[43] Finally, it is worth noting that Wallerstein's categories offer a useful way of situating a country like Ireland within the capitalist world system. Thus Brian Girvin entitles his study of politics and economy in independent Ireland *Between Two Worlds*, situating Ireland on the semi-periphery.[44]

Emmanuel and Amin: unequal exchange

Two theorists, Arghiri Emmanuel and Samir Amin, examined in more detail the central mechanism by which core countries extracted surplus from the peripheral ones thereby condemning them to be underdeveloping. In his work *Unequal Exchange*, Emmanuel developed a theory which identified the differences in wage levels between core and peripheral countries as "the elementary transfer mechanism"[45] through which the surplus is taken from workers in underdeveloped countries and given to workers in developed ones. For Emmanuel, this happens as the low prices at which Third World goods are sold depend on the fact that workers who have produced, picked or extracted them are paid a lot less; in effect, therefore, the core country gains as a result and part of this gain is passed on in the form of higher wages to workers there. Significant political consequences flow from this conclusion for Emmanuel; since workers in the core countries realise their living standards depend in some measure on this continuing exploitation of the periphery, they acquiesce in this situation. The key struggle, therefore, he argues, is not between worker and capitalist but between poor and rich countries.

The Egyptian, Samir Amin, disagreed with Emmanuel's emphasis on unequal wages and on the political conclusions he drew from it. But, in a series of works,[46] Amin developed some of the theoretical positions of Emmanuel into a more nuanced analysis of the differences between development in the core and in the periphery and the consequences of this for political action. Indeed, Hoogvelt finds in Amin's prolific work "a genuine attempt to synthesise all that was good and lasting in the dependency and underdevelopment literature from Baran onwards".[47] For Amin, the level of wages paid to workers in underdeveloped economies cannot be divorced from the nature of the productive processes in these countries as their products are exported cheaply to the developed countries by those who make high profits as a result. In this way, capital is drawn out of the peripheral countries to the ever expanding benefit of the core countries.

Amin, therefore, focuses his attention on the fundamental difference in the nature of development at the core of the capitalist system and on the periphery. The former is a self-centred type of

Poverty Amid Plenty

development, whereby the countries at the core have the capacity for self-generated capital accumulation based on their own productive forces. Eventually through the growth of trade union power, workers were able to improve their conditions and living standards thereby stimulating the consumer demand that further developed the productive forces, especially industry. In countries on the periphery, however, an entirely different form of development happened, dependent on capital from overseas which was invested in the export of goods rather than in production for the internal market. While much of the surplus flowed out with the goods, that which was accumulated in the peripheral countries was not distributed to the workers but remained largely in the hands of those small sectors of local people who co-operated with foreign capital; this wealth they used for luxury consumption and not for productive investment, according to Amin. Similar to many of the dependency theorists, therefore, Amin sees capitalist development as leading to more unequal distribution of wealth and more poverty in peripheral countries.

Again Amin draws different political conclusions from those of Emmanuel. Instead of seeing the key struggle as being between rich and poor countries, Amin sees that the main focus of the class struggle between capitalists and workers is no longer at a national level but at a global level, between the world's capitalists (mostly but not exclusively nationals of the core capitalist countries) and the workers (mostly but not exclusively in peripheral countries). This means that the Third World has now become the key place where the struggle for world socialist transformation is taking place. However, Amin does allow for the possibility of development under capitalism and urges a selective "de-linking" to allow for the building up of capital accumulation at a national level combined with internal redistribution of wealth to stimulate consumer demand.

Impact of dependency theory

While it would be too much to claim that dependency theory caused the emergence of revolutionary states throughout the Third World (many of them pre-dated the emergence of dependency theory in the late 1960s), it did make a significant contribution to the emergence of a new development paradigm which gained ascendency in the 1960s and was the development orthodoxy of the 1970s. This has been loosely called "Third Worldism" by Harris[48] and found various forms of expression, some relatively moderate, some more radical. Among the former can be included a number of progressive military regimes in Latin America, often called "military socialism" – General Juan Velasco in Peru (1968-75), General Omar Torrijos in Panama (1968-78), General J. J. Torres in Bolivia (1970-71) and General Guillermo Rodriguez Lara in Ecuador (1972-76) – or Michael Manley's "democratic socialism" in Jamaica. The Allende government in Chile (1970-73) and the emergence of liberation theology can be numbered among more radical expressions.[49]

The essential contribution of dependency theory was to apply categories of Marxism to the contemporary problem of world underdevelopment in a way that gave a basis for the underdeveloped countries and the marginalised social sectors within them to fashion their own counter-project. No longer were they simply to follow the advice of the developed countries, advice that often laid the blame for underdevelopment at least implicitly on the underdeveloped countries themselves and on their peoples. Instead, dependency theory offered a rich theoretical basis for turning accepted views on their head, laying the blame for underdevelopment on the developed countries and their draining of the wealth and resources of the Third World. This led to governments and social groups within the Third World taking their own steps to development, often in opposition to the developed world. Though broadly socialist in orientation, dependency theory also embodied an alternative to the dominant socialist model of the time, that of the Soviet Union.

The clearest expression of Third World attempts to develop their economies from within was import substitution industrialisation (ISI). Though initially this policy of fostering a native industrial base behind high tariff barriers was due to the closing of international markets at the time of the Great Depression in the early 1930s, the work of CEPAL later gave it a theoretical coherence. It involved the state in a very active way in the marketplace through establishing a highly protected home market, through setting multiple exchange rates to facilitate the import of technology and machinery for the new industries being established and through taking a direct role in production by establishing state industries in key sectors such as mining, oil, transport and various forms of manufacturing. ISI succeeded in transforming many countries (particularly in Latin America) from being predominantly rural and agricultural to being predominantly urban and industrial but it ran into a major contradiction. This lay in the fact that a policy designed to achieve greater economic independence for Third World states in

Poverty Amid Plenty

fact created a new form of dependence due to the reliance of local industries on importing the machinery they needed. To earn the foreign exchange to pay for this meant exporting more and more of the traditional raw materials though the policy was intended to lessen dependence on these.[50]

The most significant international expression of "Third Worldism" was the coming together of most Third World governments in the early 1970s around the demand for a New International Economic Order (NIEO). The NIEO was the most concerted attempt yet made to reform the international trading and financial system for the benefit of the Third World. It demanded structures to stabilise and guarantee prices for Third World commodity exports, better access for Third World goods to the markets of the developed world, the provision of more financial resources for the developing world, debt relief and the transfer of technology. Meeting concerted opposition from much of the developed world, especially the United States, this was doggedly pursued by the so-called Group of 77 (grouping virtually all Third World states) through numerous international fora throughout the 1970s.[51] Theoretically, the North-South dialogue continues still but, by the early 1980s, it had run out of steam partly due to the negotiating tactics of the US in particular which insisted on dealing with issues separately and on stringing the negotiations along endlessly. Perhaps its major contribution to world development was to raise awareness of the inequalities of the world trading and financial system, weighted as it is against the development of the South. In practice, however, a decade of negotiations managed to change this system little.

Assessment of dependency theory

In assessing dependency theory itself, a similar point can be made. Frank puts it starkly: "In terms of their practical application, *all* of these theories failed the test of history in the 1970s and 1980s".[52] While it may have correctly identified some central elements of the international economic system and the ways these operate as obstacles to the development of the South or, worse, serve to underdevelop it even more, dependency theory led to few specific policy prescriptions to help overcome this situation. At worst, it relegated the possibility for development to some vague socialist future; at best, development was to emerge from a radical redistribution of wealth and power within the South and its delinking from the world economy. How to carry out such an ambitious programme was far from clear. As O'Brien puts it: "Much writing on dependency seems to leave one with the vision of the desirability of an anti-imperialist, populist leader uniting his people under a technocratic state."[53]

This central weakness of dependency theory stems from the failure to spell out in concrete terms the actual mechanisms of dependency or how these necessarily lead to underdevelopment. As some writers have pointed out, for example, Canada is a highly dependent country but could hardly be called underdeveloped. At the other end of the spectrum, Albania was during this time virtually cut off from the outside world yet this did not mean that it was a shining example of self-sufficient development. Where mechanisms were spelt out, as in the various versions of the extraction of the surplus wealth of the South and its siphoning off to the North, these assumed rather too easily that such wealth would otherwise have been available for development within the underdeveloped countries. However, as Kitching has pointed out in his examination of these arguments, it often takes foreign capital to utilise resources which would otherwise have lain unused; many benefits may accrue to the underdeveloped country as a result. "For example if the initial investment was in a railway, one has to attempt to assess the extent to which other monetary benefits – increased internal production and trade along the railway, or increased exports of other commodities – have been 'indirectly' a result of the railway. It is clear that similar considerations may apply to foreign loans, depending upon what the loans have been used for".[54] Indeed, so general is the argument often advanced by dependency theory that one critic has accused it of adopting premises and hypotheses that are unfalsifiable, in other words that empirical data cannot be used to confirm or deny them.[55]

One can accept many of these criticisms and still hold to the validity of some of the core insights of dependency theory. Even such a trenchant critic as Packenham admits to the positive contribution of dependency theory to development studies. He lists, for example, its emphasis on external sources of development or underdevelopment, on class linkages across national boundaries, on equality as well as productivity and on the merging of economics and politics.[56] Ultimately, dependency theory contributed, in O'Brien's words, a "higher level or general hypothesis"[57] and, contrary to Packenham's assertion, much empirical data would still validate some of the central elements of that hypothesis. As outlined in Chapter 1, the income gap between core and periphery (in terms of per capita GDP) continues to grow and Wallerstein's categories of core, semi-periphery and periphery serve to describe far more accurately where countries stand in terms of development than any easy notion of countries moving from traditional and underdeveloped to modern and developed. It is far from clear that the painful adjustment many Third World countries have made in the 1980s and early 1990s from protectionism to liberalisation is putting them on the path of development or is lessening poverty and inequality.[58] And, looking at the internal situation of many countries of the South in the 1980s, the stark evidence is one of greatly deepening poverty and inequality.[59]

Of course, none of this evidence can "prove" the validity of dependency theory, just as no conclusive evidence exists to "prove" that the tenets of modernisation theory will lead to the emergence of modern societies. To seek such a level of verifiability, as Packenham does, is to misunderstand the nature of a general hypothesis or paradigm, to use Kuhn's term.[60] As Foster-Carter has written, applying Kuhn's term to development theory: "... there is never a complete fit between 'the facts' and a dominant paradigm, but at first it will be assumed that an otherwise successful paradigm will in time solve any remaining puzzles ... whereas at a later stage there is decreasing confidence that anomalies will constitute puzzles ever soluble within the paradigm".[61]

Conclusion

Many theoretical anomalies were shown to exist within dependency theory.[62] In its predominant focus on external dependence as the main cause of continuing underdevelopment, it also left itself open to the accusation that it conveniently overlooked many internally generated causes such as endemic corruption, political authoritarianism and gross bureaucratic inefficiency. But Frank is correct in stating that dependency theory was not defeated by argument. "Rather, these 'theories' and their associated policies have been defeated by more powerful opponents. Politically, General Pinochet has done this by force of arms in Chile, the main locus of the germination, birth, development, and application of both structuralism and dependence [sic] theory. Economically, the world economic crisis and especially its severe 1973-1975 and 1979-1982 recessions have rendered these theories inapplicable as recipes for practical political policy".[63] To these practical challenges and the crisis they engendered in development theory, we next turn.

Footnotes

1 Ronaldo Munck, "Political programmes and development: the transformative potential of social democracy" in Frans J. Schuurman, ed., *Beyond the Impasse: New Directions in Development Theory*, Zed Books, 1993, pp.113, 114
2 Talcott Parsons, *The Social System*, The Free Press, 1951
3 Talcott Parsons, "Evolutionary universals in society" in *American Sociological Review*, vol.29, no.3, June 1964, p.357
4 For two useful figures illustrating the states of social evolution and the structure of modern societies as elaborated by Parsons, see Ankie M. M. Hoogvelt, *The Third World in Global Development*, Macmillan, 1982, pp.112, 114
5 David Harrison, *The Sociology of Modernization and Development*, Unwin Hyman, 1988, p.8
6 Talcott Parsons, "Evolutionary universals in society", op. cit., p.357
7 W.W. Rostow, *The Stages of Economic Growth*, Cambridge University Press, 1960
8 Rostow, quoted in Larrain, op. cit., p.97
9 David McClelland, *The Achieving Society*, Van Nostrand, 1961
10 David Lerner, *The Passing of Traditional Society*, The Free Press, 1964
11 Samuel Huntington, *Political Order in Changing Societies*, Yale, 1968
12 David Lehmann, *Democracy and Development in Latin America*, Polity Press, 1990, p.25
13 S. N. Eisenstadt, "Social change, differentiation and evolution" in *American Sociological Review*, vol. 29, no. 3, 1964, p.378
14 ibid., p.382
15 ibid., p.384
16 The point is well made by Cardoso and Faletto: "Superficial or apologetic analysts, in order to minimize exploitative aspects of the international economy, have merely assumed that 'modern' economies are 'interdependent'. By stating this platitude, they often forget that the important question is what forms that 'interdependency' takes. While some national economies need raw material produced by unskilled labour, or industrial goods produced by cheap labour, others need to import equipment and capital goods in general. While some economies become indebted to the financial capital cities of the world, others are creditors. Of course, bankers need clients, as much as clients need bankers. But the 'interrelationship' between the two is qualitatively distinct because of the position held by each partner in the structure of the relationship. The same is true for the analysis of 'interdependent' economies in world markets." See F. H. Cardoso and E. Faletto, *Dependency and Development in Latin America*, University of California Press, 1971, p.xxi
17 H. Bernstein, "Breakdowns of modernization" in *Journal of Development Studies*, vol. 8, no. 2, 1972, p.315. He is quoting from an essay·by D. B. Macklin.
18 ibid., p.312
19 A. G. Frank, "The underdevelopment of development" in *Scandinavian Journal of Development Alternatives*, vol.X, no.3, September 1991, p.17
20 D. Hulme and Mark M. Turner, *Sociology and Development*, Harvester Wheatsheaf, 1990, p.42
21 S. N. Eisenstadt, op. cit., p.384
22 Cristóbal Kay, *Latin American Theories of Development and Underdevelopment*, Routledge, 1989, p.26
23 For a critical, though largely sympathetic, assessment of CEPAL's contribution to development thinking, see Fernando Henrique Cardoso, "The originality of a copy: CEPAL and the ideas of development" in *Cepal*

Review, no.2, 1977, pp.7-36.

24 For an overview of the key components of structuralism and how this school has developed in Latin America, see Nora Lustig, "From structuralism to neostructuralism: the search for a heterodox paradigm" in Patricio Meller, ed., *The Latin American Development Debate: Neostructuralism, Neomonetarism and Adjustment Processes*, Westview Press, 1991, pp.27-42.

25 A. G. Frank, op. cit., p.18

26 See the influential essay by Aidan Foster-Carter, "From Rostow to Gunder Frank: Conflicting paradigms in the analysis of underdevelopment" in *World Development*, vol.4, no.3, 1976, pp.167-80.

27 A. G. Frank, *Capitalism and Underdevelopment in Latin America: Historical Studies of Chile and Brazil*, Monthly Review Press, 1967, pp.5, 6

28 ibid., pp.7, 8

29 Paul A. Baran, *The Political Economy of Growth*, Monthly Review Press, 1957

30 J. Larrain, op. cit., p.115

31 A. Foster-Carter, op. cit., p.176

32 The main criticisms of Frank have centred on his definition of capitalism as primarily a system of exchange (so that, for example, the exchange of goods between Latin America and Spain in colonial times meant that Latin America had been integrated into a capitalist world system). This, of course, runs counter to the Marxist conception of capitalism as being primarily defined by a certain mode of production which involves relations of production through which a worker sells his or her labour power to a capitalist who appropriates the surplus value from this labour. Lively debate therefore raged over whether Frank was a Marxist or not and to what extent his theories minimised the importance of internal class relations and therefore class struggle. Laclau is regarded as perhaps his most trenchant critic. See E. Laclau, "Feudalism and capitalism in Latin America", *New Left Review*, no.67, May/June 1971, pp.19-38.

33 A. Foster-Carter, op. cit., p.175

34 Cardoso and Faletto, op. cit., p.7

35 ibid., p. xi

36 ibid., p. xxiii

37 ibid., p. xvi

38 ibid., p. xvii

39 ibid., pp. xxiii, xxiv

40 Immanuel Wallerstein, *The Modern World System: Capitalist Agriculture and the Origins of the European World-Economy in the Sixteenth Century*, Academic Press, 1974; *The Modern World System II: Mercantilism and the Consolidation of the European World-Economy 1600-1750*, Academic Press, 1980; *The Modern World System III: The Second Era of Great Expansion of the Capitalist World-Economy 1730s-1840s*, Academic Press, 1989. For an introduction to world systems theory, see Thomas Richard Shannon, *An Introduction to the World-System Perspective*, Westview Press, 1989.

41 I. Wallerstein, "The rise and future demise of the world capitalist system: concepts for comparative analysis" in *Comparative Studies in Society and History*, vol.16, no.4, January 1974, p.404

42 ibid., p.403

43 World systems analysis continues to get a certain attention from the mainstream media. See, for example, the contributions of Wallerstein reproduced in two supplements of *The Irish Times* – "Into the slump: Europe stands alone" in "Europe/An *Irish Times*/World Media Special Supplement" published with *The Irish Times*, 31 December 1992, p.8; and "The new world order is already dead – but what will rise from its ashes?" in "Networks of Power", published with *The Irish Times*, 29 December 1993, p.9

44 Brian Girvin, *Between Two Worlds: Politics and Economy in Independent Ireland*, Gill & Macmillan, 1989, pp.9, 10. Girvin refers to the study by Nicos P. Mouzelis entitled *Politics in the Semi-Periphery* as his source for the concept of semi-periphery. However, Mouzelis, in a lengthy footnote, acknowledges its origins in the work of Wallerstein. See Nicos P. Mouzelis, *Politics in the Semi-Periphery*, Macmillan, 1989, pp.224, 225, footnote no 6.

45 Arghiri Emmanuel, *Unequal Exchange*, New Left Books, 1972, p.265
46 See Samir Amin, *Accumulation on a World Scale*, Monthly Review Press, 1974; *Unequal Development*, Monthly Review Press, 1976; *The Law of Value and Historical Materialism*, Monthly Review Press, 1978; *Eurocentrism*, Monthly Review Press, 1989; *Delinking*, Zed Books, 1990; *Empire of Chaos*, Monthly Review Press, 1992.
47 A. Hoogvelt, op. cit., p.199
48 N. Harris, *The End of the Third World*, Pelican, 1987. "Third Worldism" is the title of the first chapter.
49 On the connection between dependency theory and liberation theology, Frank has the following to say: "Dependence [sic] theory and writing, including mine, also made a notable impact on and through the 'theology of liberation,' which was and still is spread through Catholic Church groups in Latin America. Although we have never met, the Peruvian 'founder' of liberation theology, Gustavo Gutierrez, acknowledged this influence in writing." See Frank, "The underdevelopment of development", op. cit., p.35.
50 For a balanced description and assessment of ISI, see Duncan Green, *Silent Revolution: The Rise of Market Economics in Latin America*, LAB, 1995, pp.16-20.
51 For a good overview of the NIEO, see Charles A. Jones, *The North-South Dialogue: A Brief History*, Francis Pinter, 1983.
52 A. G. Frank, "Latin American development theories revisited: a participant review" in *Latin American Perspectives*, issue 73, vol.19, no.2, 1992, p.134
53 Philip J. O'Brien, "A critique of Latin American theories of dependency" in Oxaal, Barnett, Booth, eds, *Beyond the Sociology of Development*, Routledge Kegan Paul, 1975, p.25
54 Gavin Kitching, *Development and Underdevelopment in Historical Perspective: Populism, Nationalism and Industrialization*, Routledge, second edition, 1989, p.167. See pp.157-75 for his detailed critique of mechanisms of surplus extraction.
55 Robert A. Packenham, *The Dependency Movement: Scholarship and Politics in Development Studies*, Harvard University Press, 1992, p.41
56 ibid., chapter 12
57 O'Brien, op. cit., p.11
58 See, for example, the evidence assembled by Walden Bello in his *Dark Victory: United States, Structural Adjustment and Global Poverty*, Pluto Press, 1994, chapters 5, 6, 7, 8.
59 For a good summary of the evidence for Latin America throughout the 1980s, see Jorge G. Castañeda, *Utopia Unarmed: The Latin American Left after the Cold War*, Knopf, 1993, pp.255-64.
60 Thomas Kuhn, *The Structure of Scientific Revolutions*, University of Chicago Press, 1970
61 A. Foster-Carter, op. cit., p. 169. Foster-Carter emphasises the vital importance of a paradigm for any scientific work: "Research is inconceivable without a paradigm, since the latter imposes a minimal orderliness on what would otherwise be a hopeless and endlessly confusing myriad of sheer data ... There is no science except from within a paradigm." pp.169 and 175.
62 For example, F. H. Cardoso, in "The originality of a copy", op. cit., discusses some of the main criticisms levelled against CEPAL theories of unequal development. Or Ian Roxborough, in discussing Cardoso and Faletto's own work, finds fault with both its empirical assertions and its lack of conceptual clarity yet commends its theoretical framework. See I Roxborough, "Dependency and development: Cardoso and Faletto: Multiple Paths" in Eduardo P. Archetti, Paul Cammack and Bryan Roberts, eds, *Sociology of 'Developing Societies': Latin America*, Macmillan, 1987, pp.7, 8.
63 A. G. Frank, "Latin American development theories revisited", op. cit., p.132

Chapter 3

Development in Crisis

"The South must recognize that the sterile dialogue of the 1970s must give way to a more enlightened dialogue on new patterns of development cooperation in a changing world – mutual interests, not unilateral concessions; two-sided responsibility, not one-sided accusations; more equitable access to global opportunities, not massive transfer of financial resources; more open markets, not more managed markets."

– Mahbub ul Haq, UNDP[1]

The 1970s marked the high-point of attempts by the developing countries to chart their own model of development and to achieve basic reforms to the international trading and financial system. By the end of the decade, many of the countries which had shown most determination in rejecting the Western development model and fashioning an alternative route to development were in crisis.

Perhaps the most dramatic examples were in Asia. China, after a decade of cultural revolution from 1966 to 1976 which had caught the imagination of the West's alienated youth, was beginning to turn its back on its Maoist past. The Vietnamese invasion of Cambodia (then called Kampuchea) in January 1979 laid bare for the world the horrors of the Pol Pot experiment in social engineering while China's invasion of Vietnam a month later showed that national self-interest remained stronger than socialist internationalism. In Africa, the early promise of Kwame Nkrumah's Ghana and of Ahmed Sekou Touré's Guinea had long since faded while even Julius Nyerere's Tanzania was encountering major difficulties. In Latin America, the hopes raised by Salvador Allende's Chile had been snuffed out and most of the larger countries were under brutal military dictatorships. The hope of an alternative path to development was being kept alive in only small pockets – in Central America, with the Sandinista victory in Nicaragua in July 1979 and expectations that El Salvador and Guatemala would soon follow its example; in Africa with the radical governments which took power in the former Portuguese colonies of Mozambique, Angola and Guinea-Bissau in the mid 1970s, and in Asia with the Vietnamese victory over the US in 1975.

Similarly, the determined attempts by the developing countries as a block to push through major reforms of the international trading and financial system, had also run out of steam by the end of the 1970s. Again, the promise of such reforms which ran high following the dramatic success of the oil exporting countries in 1973 in quadrupling the price of oil and their own income overnight, proved largely illusory. Despite determined attempts throughout the 1970s and the remarkable unity of the developing world on an agreed set of demands (on stabilising commodity prices, on financial flows, on transfer of technology and on preferential access for Third World goods to First World markets), the achievements were meagre in the extreme.[2]

The most ominous sign for the developing countries that the tide was turning decisively against their agenda was the coming to power of Margaret Thatcher in Britain in 1979 and Ronald Reagan in the United States in 1981, both of them crusaders for a new conservatism in economic thinking. This sought to reactivate economic growth through drastically scaling down government intervention in the economy and to stimulate private initiative through lightening the tax burden on corporations and on individuals. Behind these economic policies lay a philosophy of individual self-help as the only effective way to combat poverty. Such a philosophy was hostile to the sorts of government intervention and structural reforms for social development which formed the basis for the North-South dialogue of the 1970s. The symbol of this radically changed international environment was the Cancun summit of leaders of North and South held in the Mexican resort in October 1981.

This grew out of a recommendation of the Brandt Commission and was conceived as a forum to move forward the dialogue on a new international economic order. Yet Ronald Reagan used it as a platform to underline the emerging new orthodoxy in his "magic of the market" address. The summit ended with a communique that was vague and non-commital, accurately reflecting the lack of any basis for continuing the dialogue between developed and underdeveloped. Instead, as Walden Bello summed it up, Cancun "turned out to be the prelude to a global economic counter-revolution carried out in the name of the free market".[3]

This chapter firstly examines the economic counter-revolution of the 1980s and critically assesses its content and impact. The second section outlines the lively debate raging over the East Asian economic miracle and the ways it focuses critical attention on some of the key prescriptions of the new economic orthodoxy. Following this is a section which details the basic needs approach which has come to dominate much development practice among the NGO sector. The final section looks at the crisis in development theory and the ways this is being addressed by theorists.

The neo-classical counter-revolution

The 1980s witnessed a dramatic reversal of the main principles which had guided development theory in the 1970s. Central to these was a focus on the international economic system as a basic cause of the underdevelopment of the South and the need therefore for the state to take an active role in promoting an inward-oriented national development. The laws of neo-classical economics were assumed not to apply in the South in the same ways as they did in the North due to the dependent and unequal position of the countries of the South in the international economy.[4] Within a few years in the early 1980s, however, these ideas had undergone a complete reversal as the countries of the South vied with one another to follow the prescriptions of neo-classical economics, opening their economies, stimulating exports, privatising their large nationalised sectors and generally cutting back state involvement in the economy. The reason for this dramatic about-turn demands consideration before we look in more detail at the content of the new economic orthodoxy sweeping the Third World.

Undoubtedly one of the major reasons for this about-turn lay in the huge changes taking place in the world economy. The structuralist ideas which were dominant in the 1970s presumed the ability of the nation state to govern and direct the national economy to serve the goal of national development. Yet, even while this effort was going on, the world economy itself was becoming more and more globalised as transnational companies formed chains of production that spanned not only countries but continents. Technological developments further fuelled this potential for global production through innovative transportation and communications technologies which shrank both space and time. World trade expanded nearly 30-fold in the three decades after 1960 and manufactured goods, as a percentage of total exports, increased from 55 per cent in 1964 to 75 per cent in 1990.[5] This had a number of consequences. Firstly, the traditional profile of Third World countries exporting unprocessed raw materials to earn foreign exchange underwent dramatic change as they were incorporated more and more into the production chains of transnational companies. Indeed by the 1980s, about a third of all trade between countries had come to consist of the movement of goods between the branches of the same transnational companies located in different countries.[6] Secondly, the very dynamism of world trade undermined more and more the viability of an inward-oriented project of national development. Alongside the growth of chains of transnational production, the financial system was also becoming more globalised and liberalised, further eroding the ability of the nation state to control capital movements. As Colin Leys sums up the impact on many regions of the South: "Most Third World countries, then, found themselves more vulnerable than at any time since they were first colonized. Their economies were least well placed to prosper in the new 'global' market place. Primary commodity exports, other than oil, became steadily less significant as manufacturing became less commodity-intensive, and the overall share of the Third World in world trade fell dramatically."[7]

To try to stave off the growing crisis, many Third World countries resorted to foreign borrowing which was readily available because of the inflow of "petrodollars" into Western banks following the oil price rises of the early and late 1970s. But the low interest rates of the 1970s dramatically changed in the early 1980s after Ronald Reagan's monetarist response to recession sent international interest rates to record highs, thus triggering off the international debt crisis with Mexico's effective default in August 1982.[8] This hit the countries of Latin America hard since they were the largest debtors but, in Africa also, a collapse in commodity prices, meant their smaller debt burdens became unsupportable. This "system-wide shock"[9] led to a major re-think in economic policy throughout the developing world. A belief grew that the inward-looking, protectionist policies of the past had not worked, that nationalised industries had led to inefficiency and that the much sought-after goal of national self-reliance was illusory. Amid the gloom of the 1980s in development circles, the example of one group of countries which had managed to prosper and develop through actively engaging in international trade seemed to show a new way forward. These were the East Asian NICs (or Newly Industrialising Countries) of South Korea, Taiwan, Hong Kong and Singapore in which per capita income rose dramatically, industry diversified into more technologically sophisticated products and these were able to compete with success against the products of the advanced industrial countries.[10]

The criticisms of past failures and the example of the East Asian NICs seemed to give validity to the prescriptions of a group of economists whose writings since the 1970s had been arguing for the benefits of a market-led path to development. The leading writers of the neo-classical counter-revolution as it came to be called were Lord Peter Bauer, Deepak Lal, Ian Little, Harry Johnson and Bela Balassa; their central message was that underdevelopment is caused not by factors external to developing countries such as the structure of the international economy but by factors internal such as too much state intervention in the economy and a poor allocation of resources due to incorrect pricing policies. This has led to inefficiency, corruption and a lack of economic incentives which has resulted in slower economic growth than would otherwise take place, they argued. The "new vision of growth" propounded by these economists has been summarised as consisting of three main elements: the benefits of markets and the danger that government action will negate these benefits; the relative unimportance of physical capital compared with human resource development; and the distorting effects of government economic policies.[11] This held out the promise therefore of a new path to development through counteracting the causes of underdevelopment which lay in 1) an overextended public sector; 2) an overemphasis on accumulating physical assets for production while neglecting the improvement of human abilities and skills, and 3) the proliferation of economic controls which lead to inefficiency.[12]

One of the most significant results of the crisis of the early 1980s for development theory was, in Adams' words, that the countries of the South emerged "chastened and greatly weakened, drained of any fighting spirit".[13] This made them turn to the World Bank and the International Monetary Fund for credit but also for advice, a situation which gave the multilateral institutions an enhanced influence over what policies developing countries should follow. The policy mix strongly promoted by the Bank and the Fund was greatly influenced by the neo-classical counter-revolution. The policy advice given has been called "the Washington consensus" by John Williamson and consists of ten items: fiscal discipline (keep budget deficits small); public expenditure priorities (re-direction from administration, defence and subsidies to health, education and infrastructure); tax reform (broaden the tax base and cut marginal tax rates); financial liberalization (move to market-determined interest rates); exchange rates (a competitive rate to induce a rapid growth in non-traditional exports); trade liberalization; direct foreign investment (abolish barriers to entry); privatization of state enterprises; deregulation (abolish regulations that restrict competition; and property rights (legal backing for secure property rights).[14] The impact of this advice has been nicely expressed by Stallings: "One of the most fascinating aspects of the late 1980s was the list of third world governments that became outspoken advocates for privatization, free trade, and fiscal austerity, even though they or their political parties had long followed a different path."[15]

The neo-classical counter-revolution addressed some widely recognised problems that had for long dogged the more state-led protectionist model of the 1970s. Among these was inefficiency as the state took on a wide range of tasks beyond its capability, corruption as public officials abused the extensive power placed in their hands, and the politicization of price and exchange fixing as the state made decisions on such things as interest rates and exchange rates on political grounds often with little consideration for the market or competitiveness. But, as Toye puts it, the neo-classical solution "having over-simplified the problem, matches it up with a correspondingly over-simplified 'solution'. As a result, the new vision of growth is made both blinkered and myopic."[16]

By way of example, this can be illustrated with regard to three issues central to the neo-classical counter-revolution. The first is the assumption that markets, when left to themselves, will operate in an efficient and competitive manner so that all state intervention is counter-productive by definition. Yet, as Todaro has put it, "the problem is that many Third World economies are so different in structure and organization from their Western counterparts that ... competitive markets simply do not exist." His conclusion is: "The ideal of competition is typically just that – an ideal with little relation to reality."[17] A second issue discussed by Todaro is a confusion of free markets with price allocation. While he acknowledges that neo-classical theory has a lot to teach with regard to the importance of elementary supply-and-demand analysis in arriving at "correct" prices, he argues "enlightened governments can also make effective use of prices as signals and incentives for influencing socially optimal resource allocations",[18] a point that takes on added importance in the context of the need to ensure greater equality in the distribution of the benefits of economic growth. A third issue central to the neo-classical counter-revolution is free trade. While Todaro agrees that "where opportunities for profitable exchange arise, foreign trade can provide an important stimulus to aggregate economic growth", he cautions that "an export-oriented strategy of growth, particularly when a large proportion of export earnings accrue to foreigners, may not only bias the structure of the economy in the wrong directions (by not catering to the real needs of local people) but also reinforce the internal and external dualistic and inegalitarian character of that growth."[19]

In arriving at a policy mix suitable to promote development, therefore, Todaro concludes: "In an environment of widespread institutional rigidity and severe socioeconomic inequality, *both* markets and governments will typically fail. It is not simply an either-or question based on ideological leaning; rather it is a matter of assessing each individual country's situation on a case-by-case basis."[20]

Apart from a theoretical assessment of the adequacy of the neo-classical prescriptions for underdeveloped countries, enough time has now elapsed to make an empirical assessment of what impact they are having in different regions of the world. Stallings summarises the evidence from the four main regions of the South. For Latin America, she says, growth remains anaemic in comparision with Asian growth rates and is subject to serious problems of volatility. Added to this continuing low growth are increases in inequality. Sub-Saharan Africa shows by far the most serious problems with per capita incomes declining by 1.2 per cent a year during the 1980s, gross investment falling sharply and exports contracting. This situation has further deteriorated in the 1990s. Asia is the one region where the picture looks more positive (and it is, of course, the most populous region in the world). The countries of Southeast Asia have benefited from the shifting by Japan of its production offshore and from generous Japanese official development assistance which is helping to improve social indicators. This has bound these countries more tightly to Asian production and trade networks. Finally, the countries of East Asia, being already export-oriented, were in a position to benefit from the changes of the 1980s and have established a much stronger position for themselves in the international marketplace.[21]

If all these regions were following the same policy mix, then at least the success of the Asian countries could be held up as evidence for the potential of neo-classical-inspired policies to lead to successful development. But Stallings makes two important qualifications in this regard. Though all these regions claim to be opening their economies and following market-oriented policies, by the early 1990s it had become clear that this meant different things to different countries, she writes. Thus Asia may be export-oriented but it is not necessarily open to imports, and state capacity has been maintained there while it has been severely weakened in Latin America and in Africa.[22] This has opened up what is now perhaps the most lively and potentially far-reaching debate in mainstream development theory.

The East Asian miracle and its lessons

Amid the many relatively failed development efforts in many parts of the world, one group of countries increasingly began to attract attention for its remarkable success both in sustaining economic growth over a long period and in reducing inequality. These were the countries of East Asia, led by Japan and followed by the four "Tigers" of South Korea, Taiwan, Singapore and Hong Kong. Through the 1980s Thailand, Malaysia and Indonesia were added to the list and by the early 1990s China itself was recognised as part of the East Asian miracle. As a World Bank study described it: "The success of development in East Asia is legendary. No other group of developing countries has done as well in fostering growth, reducing poverty, integrating with world markets, or raising standards of living. Over the past twenty-five years, per capita incomes in the region almost quadrupled. Absolute poverty fell by about two-thirds on average, population growth rates declined rapidly, and health and education improved markedly".[23]

Yet, while the success was widely recognised, debate raged about the means used to achieve it. This was a crucial question as it touched centrally on the advice being given by the World Bank and the International Monetary Fund, backed by most Western governments, to developing countries throughout the world. The free market model they promote – opening domestic markets to foreign imports and reducing the state's role to one of facilitating a positive environment for private enterprise – has been accepted by many Third World governments on the understanding that it could lead their countries to emulate the East Asian success story. However, many proponents of the East

Asian miracle claim that these countries achieved their success by following policies directly opposed on some crucial points to those of the World Bank, involving active state intervention in the economy and selective protection of domestic industries until they were strong enough to compete abroad. If this was true then it served to undermine what the Bank was promoting as a "new development paradigm"[24] while at the same time drawing attention to a set of policies that *had* led to successful development. Barbara Stallings suggests that the distinction between what she calls the "Japanese model of development" and the US/IFI [International Financial Institutions] model may be crucial to development in the 1990s. She puts forward the premise that "the Japanese model of development is more conducive than its US/IFI counterpart to producing rapid growth with equity.... The US/IFI model has yet to prove it can produce high growth rates on a long-term basis, and some evidence indicates it generates increasing concentration of income and wealth."[25]

By the late 1980s, Japan was beginning to express openly its disagreements with the World Bank's approach. As a result, it proposed that the Bank undertake a major study of East Asian development and offered to fund it. This study, entitled *The East Asian Miracle* was announced in 1991 and published in 1993.[26] Its findings emphasised that the East Asian countries succeeded by "getting the basics right" meaning sound macroeconomic policy through stable fiscal policies, competitive exchange rates and control of inflation. It also emphasised policies entailing "shared growth" especially bringing education widely to all groups, thereby developing human capital resources which had positive effects on the quality of the civil service and the skills of the workforce. In terms of economic growth strategy, the study placed a lot of emphasis on export promotion which helped raise productivity and allowed more rapid access to advanced skills and technology. All of these could be expected from a World Bank study. But the Bank went further, in acknowledging the role of government intervention to develop specific industries which were identified as having a high potential for growth and for job creation. Such intervention, through such instruments as restrictions on imports and foreign investment, tax incentives, subsidised loans and exemption from antimonopoly laws, "resulted in higher and more equal growth than otherwise would have occurred", said the study.[27] Such an acknowledgement, however, runs counter to the orthodoxy promoted by the World Bank so the study goes on to add that the impact of such policies on industrial development was limited and concludes that "the prerequisites for success were so rigorous that policymakers seeking to follow similar paths in other developing economies have often met with failure".[28] Despite trying to downplay its significance and warn other countries off trying the same, the Bank has had to acknowledge that heresy has worked. As Albert Fishlow and Catherine Gwin wrote about the importance of systematic government intervention in their analysis of *The East Asian Miracle*: "That experience clearly challenges the teachings of neoclassical economic theory and the prevailing policy wisdom advanced by the Bank itself and by its industrial country member governments, except Japan".[29]

Yet, even if the World Bank did timidly admit to the unthinkable in terms of its economic orthodoxy, in the view of some leading scholars of the East Asian success the World Bank study failed to do this success justice. As Dani Rodrik, an economics and international affairs professor at Columbia University, wrote: "The Bank emerges bloodied but as the self-declared victor of the encounter".[30] But it does so, he adds, because the study poses "too few questions and provides too many but misleading answers".[31] This, he says, is particularly true in the Bank's analysis of the significance of interventionist industrial policies where he finds major flaws in the methodology used which undermine the credibility of the conclusions, particularly the conclusion that such intervention had little impact on industrial development.

The development fellow, Robert Wade, whose book *Governing the Market: Economic Theory and the role of Government in East Asian Industrialization* won acclaim when published in 1990, also rejects the conclusions of the World Bank study. From an examination of the way the study deals with selective government intervention, he concludes that "there is scope for such policy, and it is not limited to Asia alone, as historical experience and some recent theoretical work suggests".[32] In the light of this conclusion, Wade trenchantly criticises the refusal of the World Bank to countenance such selective industrial policies for potential growth industries throughout the developing world. The result is, he says, that countries must remain dependent on Western and Japanese multinationals over which they have little bargaining power. These very policies ensure they can never emulate the success of the East Asian Tigers.

While reiterating the World Bank report's emphasis on sound marcroeconomic policy and on a form of government intervention that is selective and targeted at managing the market rather than dominating it, these experts fault the Bank severely for its refusal to fully acknowledge the importance of a strong, activist and developmental state to the East Asian success. Though there were differences between the measures used by different countries, state intervention was crucial in the success of Japan, South Korea, Taiwan and Singapore. Hong Kong, as a British colony, is a rather different case, as are the more recent success stories of Thailand, Malaysia and Indonesia, partly because here growth is driven by investment from their more developed neighbours.

If we acknowledge then that East Asia provides an example of the success of what by the dominant economic policies of the West are rather heretical approaches, what are the chances for other developing countries to emulate this success? Apart from the role and nature of selective state intervention, two other key points emerge from the World Bank's study and its critics. The first is the relative social equality with which the East Asian countries began their success, largely due to such factors as the sweeping land reforms introduced by the US occupying forces in Japan and South Korea and by the Kuomintang in Taiwan. This ensures that the benefits of development are shared widely throughout society. However, unequal distribution of wealth and resources is far greater in much of the developing world and is getting worse. The second point is the authoritarian and repressive nature of many of the East Asian states. The lessons here "constitute somewhat of an embarrassment", writes Stephan Haggard.[33]

Another set of issues relevant to whether such success can be emulated elsewhere relates to the wider geopolitical and international economic environment. Japan, South Korea and Taiwan received massive US aid and preferential access to US markets because they were situated in the front line of the struggle against communism in the post-War era. Such conditions have never been matched elsewhere and certainly will not be in future. Furthermore, the current globalisation of the world economy and the more active efforts of the US to open foreign markets and undercut the various forms of domestic protectionism that were central to the East Asian success make their replication far more difficult. At the end of the day, however, the issue may be one of political will. As Haggard puts it, "The central question is whether international politics will allow a replication of the East Asian strategy".[34] The admission of the World Bank, timid and all as it is, that the East Asian success was not due to free market economics may help provide the basis for a wider acknowledgement of the policy mix that did lead to such success and generate the political will to allow others follow the same route.

Basic needs and sustainable development

As the great debates over development paradigms and marcoeconomic policy raged during the past quarter century, however, a more immediate approach to development was formulated which has guided a lot of development practice on the ground, particularly the work of NGOs. This approach, concentrating on providing communities with the minimum requirements for survival – from schools and health centres to clean drinking water and basic foodstuffs – is often called a "basic needs strategy". With the impact of the environmental critique in the 1980s, this strategy has become part of what is loosely called "sustainable development".[35]

Basic needs arose out of the growing awareness in the early 1970s that poverty was worsening despite over two decades of development efforts. One influential voice was that of the then president of the World Bank, Robert McNamara (1968-81) who pioneered the concept of "absolute poverty" and brought a moral fervour to the task of eradicating "the extremes of privilege and deprivation [that] are simply no longer acceptable".[36] Rejecting an emphasis on the redistribution of income and wealth, however, McNamara, instead urged that a major part of development efforts be directed at the poorest 40 per cent of the population. During his term of office, he greatly increased World Bank lending in order to increase "the productivity of the poor, thereby providing for a more equitable sharing of the benefits of growth".[37]

It was, however, the World Employment Conference of the International Labour Organisation in 1975 which explicitly formulated the basic needs strategy. The conference document stated that "it is no longer acceptable in human terms or responsible in political terms to wait several generations for the benefits of development to trickle down until they finally reach the poorest groups" and it recommended the adoption by each country of "a basic needs approach aiming at the achievement of a certain minimum standard of living before the end of the century".[38]

This launched basic needs (sometimes referred to simply as

BN) which, as Grindle points out, "is an approach to development, not a single strategy in the sense that it gives priority to certain development objectives, but does not dictate the means by which these objectives are to be achieved".[39] However, the objectives themselves have generated considerable debate. The ILO document listed a wide range of basic needs from minimum requirements of food, shelter, clothing and access to essential services such as transport, sanitation, education and health care to an adequately remunerated job, a healthy environment and popular participation in decision-making. In practice, however, the basic needs approach has tended to limit itself to what Stewart calls a "minimalist approach" relating to basic standards of health care and education while postponing the satisfaction of wider needs until resources allow.[40]

The basic needs approach was rejected by many developing countries in the 1970s when first formulated since it was seen as a way of telling developing countries they could never hope to aspire to true modernisation, industrialisation and all the benefits of development and would have to remain satisfied with resolving the most basic needs of their people. Instead, at this time, many countries saw in the demands of the New International Economic Order (NIEO) a way of fashioning a more just international system; in this context, basic needs were seen as a way of avoiding fundamental reforms by the developed countries. Leaders in underdeveloped countries also resented what seemed like outside interference in dictating ways that aid and resources should be directed primarily to the poorest. Despite such opposition, a basic needs approach was adopted by many governments as a way of trying to improve the lot of the poorest of their people and some countries showed that quite a lot could be achieved through decisive government action.[41]

The impact of structural adjustment programmes[42] on the poor served to focus attention again on the basic needs approach from the mid-1980s on. The acknowledgement of the need to ensure poverty alleviation while economies were undergoing adjustment, often called "adjustment with a human face", was one example of this. The 1980s also saw the emergence of the term "sustainable development" largely as a result of the growing awareness of the destructive impact of development on the environment and the limits this imposes upon growth. The report of the World Commission on Environment and Development, usually known as the Brundtland Report, was one of the most influential formulations of this view and it also adopted a concept of basic needs as a central element of sustainable development.[43] One of the advantages of this formulation is that it has the potential for uniting many diverse interests since it bases itself upon both ethical concerns and pure self-interest. Thus, for example, poverty is identified as an environmental hazard since poor people are forced to deplete limited natural resources (such a wood, water and soil). Poverty eradication is therefore presented as a necessary element in any programme of environmental protection. As Lélé puts it, sustainable development "has become a bundle of neat fixes ... that will unite everybody from the profit-minded industrialist and risk-minimizing subsistence farmer to the equity-seeking social worker, the pollution-concerned or wildlife-loving First Worlder, the growth-maximising policy maker, the goal-oriented bureaucrat, and therefore, the vote-counting politician".[44]

This, however, is the great weakness of basic needs as well as of sustainable development. Wide consensus has been built around these approaches because of their very vagueness. What is being done in the name of basic needs and of sustainable development may be helping local communities throughout the underdeveloped world but there are larger forces at play which are marginalising virtually whole societies (as is the case in many sub-Saharan African countries) or sections of the population (as in many Latin American countries) and destroying the environment. It is in confronting these larger forces that basic needs and sustainable development are inadequate.

Lélé identifies three key issues on which this approach has failed to define a coherent position. The first is the issue of poverty and environmental degradation on which mainstream sustainable development thinking concentrates on technical and managerial questions ignoring the need for deeper socio-political changes such as land reform or cultural changes such as reducing overconsumption in the developed world. The second issue is the relationship between economic growth and sustainability on which sustainable development thinking is riddled with vagueness and muddled thinking, says Lélé, confusing ecological and social sustainability and refusing to define the conditions in which economic growth might help to achieve the goal of sustainability.

The third issue is that of participation which, Lélé argues, is understood in sustainable development thinking as a substitute for equity and social justice. Neither is the link between these and sustainability clear, he adds.[45] Furthermore, argues Lélé, many of the accepted dominant approaches towards development today contradict ecological sustainability and social well-being. He takes as an example the current encouragement of intensive and specialised agriculture to the detriment of species variation and ecological sustainability; this ignores the evidence that weaker economies tend to lose out as free trade benefits the stronger ones. He also highlights the contradiction inherent in the Brundtland Commission's acknowledgement that the increased production resulting from the Green Revolution is at the cost of significant soil salination and pollution due to the intensive use of chemical fertilizers.

The impasse in development theory

We have already seen how modernisation theory and dependency theory mirrored and influenced the competing development paradigms followed by policymakers in developing countries in the post-War era. As one would expect, therefore, the development crisis of the 1980s had a major impact on development theory leading to a fundamental re-evaluation of its content and of its relationship to the practice of development on the ground.

By the early 1980s the twin grand paradigms that had dominated development theory since its inception – modernisation theory with its evolutionary path of gradual modernisation and westernisation, and dependency theory with its revolutionary path of breaking the links of dependence on the capitalist core countries and following a policy of socialist self-reliance – had lost both their explanatory and their prescriptive power. Quite simply, events in the real world were not following the paths laid out by either theory. The result, in the words of Frans Schuurman, was a "theoretical vacuum".[46]

David Booth, in a famous article published in 1985, analysed the roots of this vacuum and gave the name by which discussion of the problems of development theory was to be known for most of the following decade – the impasse.[47] For Booth, the grand theories that had dominated development theory "were either simply wrong (untenable empirically, conceptually unstable or redundant) or else pitched at a level of generality that made them irrelevant to the most important practical issues facing developing countries".[48] He confined his critique to the Marxist-inspired development theories (often labelled neo-Marxist), partly because these were the dominant critical theories of the time and partly because they were the ones with which he himself identified.

The crisis in these theories was a generalised one, he argued, and not confined to particular variants. It lay in the central commitment of radical development theory to establish that patterns of exploitation under capitalism were not only explicable but were necessary. This "necessicist" bias of Marxism took two main forms. The first was the belief that the significant characteristics of capitalist economies anywhere in the world could be identified and understood from the underlying capitalist mode of production. This led to a "blindness to systematic variation in development experience between countries," he argued.[49] The second, and in Booth's eyes more persistent and fundamental weakness in Marxist development theory, is what he calls its system-teleology or functionalism. By this he means its tendency to ascribe development problems to the nature of Third World countries' insertion into the world capitalist system. This he says is no explanation for underdevelopment as it simply asserts that underdevelopment is a function of the international capitalist system. "It has not been established, and there are strong reasons for doubting that it ever will, that there are 'feedback' mechanisms in the social order of the type whose existence is necessarily presupposed by a strictly functional statement which purports to be an explanation. Given this, to persist in advancing such statements is not only unscientific but pernicious."[50] This form of analysis is often called teleological, meaning that an object is analysed in terms of what is seen as its purpose. Therefore if capitalism is a system of exploitation, the analysis of any capitalist social process is governed by the need to identify how this exploitation operates in the concrete circumstances being analysed.

Booth argues that Marxism has an ulterior interest not in explaining why the world is as it is and how it may be changed but "in proving that within given limits the world *has* to be the way it is".[51] This, he says, has forced theorising along certain rather restricted lines and led to a failure to explore some of the more urgent empirical issues. He concludes that there is an pressing need, not to free development theory from Marxism, but from the functionalist and necessicist tendencies in Marxism, so that it can return to a central focus on explaining the nature of underdevelopment and on ways to change it.

Booth's article sparked a lively debate in the pages of the leading development journals. His criticisms of Marxist development theory were by and large sympathetically received and contributors to the debate sought to find ways of moving beyond the impasse. Some argued that Marxism remained a valid analytical tool for developing societies. In a forceful expression of this view, Nicos P. Mouzelis argued in defence of Marxism that "as a holistic, historically oriented approach, capable of examining overall societal transformations ... it offers conceptual tools that are quite indispensable and that alternative paradigms do not seem to provide"[52] though he did agree that Marxism needed to shed its reductionist and economistic tendencies, that is, its tendency to reduce the causes of all social phenomena to the economic sphere. He urged a greater acknowledgement of the wide diversity of societies grouped under the label "developing" and suggested that what was needed were far more concrete comparative studies of particular societies and their development. These studies could then provide the basis for building up "typologies and theories about different types of development routes within the third world".[53]

While acknowledging the important contribution of neo-Marxism to development studies, Wandergeest and Buttel argued that recent work in the tradition of Max Weber, which they called neo-Weberianism, could help to move development theory beyond its impasse. The version of Weber appropriated by modernisation theory, particularly by Parsons (see Chapter 2 above), reflected fundamental misunderstandings of Weberian theory and method, they argue, and point to "various correctives"[54] incorporated more recently by such scholars as E. P. Thompson and Charles Tilly through grounding their theoretical work in the study of concrete historical processes. They identify two areas in which the insights of neo-Weberianism may help contribute badly needed new perspectives to development theory – the study of the Third World state and its constitutive organisations, particularly the ways in which these may enable development; and the study of culture as an active process generating meaning which orients social action.[55] On both these subjects, neo-Marxists have been particularly weak, viewing the state as an instrument of factions of the ruling class and viewing culture as a product of economic factors rather than as a variable in its own right. Vandergeest and Buttel deny that neo-Weberianism tends to be too abstract, scholarly and esoteric to be of use to development theory. "When empirical study deals with power relations in the contexts of class, the state, cultural interpretation, and so on, the work quickly leads to strategies for the empowerment of the less powerful – strategies which emerge from the case itself, not from the dictates of teleological theory," they write.[56]

In these, as in other contributions, what was common was an acknowledgement that development theory had concentrated far too much on generalised theories of development but lacked the concrete studies of the development paths of specific societies which could give substance to (or in many cases disprove) the generalised theories. There was general agreement on the need to study the diversity of development experience as it had actually happened, from there drawing insights that could inform theory. Thus a path out of the impasse was mapped out and Booth himself subsequently identified in the range of development literature since the late 1970s three broad categories, all of which he grouped under the title "Rediscovering diversity".[57] The first of these categories concerned macro-studies of particular countries or groups of countries such as the East Asian "Tigers" or various Latin American countries, as well as studies comparing different countries, for example East Asian or Southern European with Latin American cases. These studies helped "to undermine the once common notion that socio-political development conforms to a pre-written script," wrote Booth.[58] His second category concerned what he called "meso-diversity", specifically studies of gender and class. The study of gender within development, he wrote, "has successfully disentangled itself from the universalist and functionalist pretensions with which it was initially encumbered"[59] while studies of class are beginning to emerge which examine the actually existing class structure of particular societies rather than applying a pre-determined analytical framework. Booth's final category relates to micro-diversity, especially the emergence of studies of rural development which again examine the diversity of agrarian structures and farming systems instead of being limited by the established theoretical constructs of how agrarian change happens.[60]

This new generation of historically grounded studies of how development actually happens entails a number of important consequences. Where both modernisation and dependency theoretical approaches are quite deterministic, these new approaches emphasise the room for manoeuvre that does exist for actors in the development process to influence its path and outcome. These actors include states on the international stage, social classes within particular societies or grass-roots movements at local level. What Booth wrote of the impact of rural development research on rural people can be applied more generally to a wide variety of actors in that this new generation of studies reveals that the well-being of people is "the result of complex interactions between individuals and groups endowed with different and changing amounts of knowledge and power".[61] It therefore serves to empower those involved in development, helping identify the constraints but also the possibilities for real advance.

In this way it also addresses the concerns of those who have questioned the relevance of development theory to the actual practice of development. This view was expressed in an influential and hard-hitting article by Michael Edwards of Save the Children Fund in which he juxtaposed the continued existence and in many cases worsening of poverty in the Third World with the ever increasing amounts of development research, and wrote: "The fact that this immense outpouring of information and advice is having little demonstrable effect on the problems it seeks to address should at least give us cause for concern."[62] Edwards concluded that "general solutions manufactured from the outside are offered to problems which are highly localised";[63] he argued that the purpose of development research is the development of poor and powerless people around the world and that, to do this, it must involve these people in constructing both the process of the research and its output. Not all development theorists agree with Edwards' call for a greater unity of development research with development practice,[64] but the issue of relevance he raised is of ongoing concern.

While the rediscovery of diversity in development studies has offered a way of moving beyond the impasse in development theory, it does not in itself help to reconstitute theory. As Booth has emphasised, the great variety involved in this examination of diversity raises the question of what unifies it, of whether it is helping develop a coherent theoretical or methodological framework. The fear, in Booth's memorable word, is that post-impasse development research could become simply a "mish-mash".[65]

Even the very validity of aspiring to reconstitute development theory and its ability to offer valid generalisations about processes of development is under challenge from post-modernists. These argue that the era of modernity which began with the Enlightenment, characterised by the belief that rationality and scientific knowledge would lead to greater control by people over nature and society and the progressive ability to eradicate poverty, slavery and ignorance throughout the world, is at an end. Post-modernists such as Lyotard argue that Auschwitz and Stalin heralded the end of modernity since they undermined the fundamental optimism it embodies. As Boyne and Rattansi summarise Lyotard's position: "All of the grand discourses of

Western society, which is to say all of the legitimating narratives which purport to provide valid and definitive principles, in any sphere, across all societies, can now be seen to be defunct".[66] A plurality of perspectives replaces truth, individual actors replace social structures and even the existence of a single reality is in doubt. On this reading, any generalised theory of social and economic development is no longer valid since knowledge and power are too fragmented and diffused; the most one can aspire to is local mobilisation to resist the encroachments of the dominant system of power and knowledge. From a developmental point of view, Schuurman's critique of post-modernism is telling: "... however relevant it may be to characterise the industrial North as post-modern or post-industrial, the developing countries in the South cannot be characterised as such. On the contrary, what typifies those countries is an aborted modernity project whereby the Ideals of Enlightenment such as Freedom, Equality and Fraternity are further out of reach than they ever were in the North. The equating of the failure of the modernity project in the South to a post-modern situation exhibits a far-reaching naivety and leads to a political demobilisation and conservatism".[67]

If the validity of reconstituting development theory is asserted in the face of the post-modernist challenge, Booth sees the way forward as being to map out those areas of agreement and disagreement on some fundamental theoretical points. The first he mentions is the importance of translating the findings of empirical studies into theoretical formulations so as to achieve a sufficient level of generality to be of interest and relevance to wider audiences whether of academics or of development practitioners. He then goes on to look at some specific questions within social theory such as achieving a balance between an approach that emphasises the primacy of actors as against one that emphasises structures, or the need to reconcile insights about development at local level with the wider national or international structural situation that constrains and influences this. The detailed theoretical points need not detain us here but Booth's approach does indicate the painstaking way in which development theory and its ability to offer valid generalisations about how development happens is being reconstituted from the ground up as it were.[68] To further this process, he suggests that organising social development research in the form of co-ordinated collaborative projects around a coherent analytical theme is an obvious next step. He finally makes the point in relation to the relevance of development theory and its link to the empowerment of the poor that "the key thing is the illumination of alternatives".[69] This is probably the single greatest challenge facing development theory.[70]

Conclusion

Discussion of development issues in the 1990s displays far greater realism than was the case two decades earlier. The promises held out by alternative development paths have proved largely illusory and their demise has resulted in an acknowledgement of the importance of the market and of sound macroeconomic management. But that is not to say that the great issues of development have been resolved and the underdeveloped countries of the world put on a path towards gradual poverty reduction and sustainable development. A new development paradigm based on neo-liberal economic policies may have achieved dominance but fierce debate rages about its impact, whether it provides a basis for equitable and broadly based development and, in particular, whether it exacerbates poverty and social dislocation. But the alternatives espoused have more to do with the timing and the means of insertion into the global capitalist economy rather than with any attempt to delink from it.

Just when the realities of the global marketplace appear to be widely accepted for the first time in development circles, however, voices are emerging which pose fundamental questions about the nature of economic growth itself. These questions are being posed with ever greater insistence by environmentalists worried about the impact of economic growth on the world's delicate ecosystem, by women recognising that economic growth is placing ever greater burdens on their shoulders in many parts of the world, and by indigenous peoples seeing the integrity of their cultures destroyed by economic development. These questions are challenging development theory, forcing it to look more deeply at its presuppositions and stimulating fresh and radical perspectives on the future.

Footnotes
1 Quoted in Thomas J. Biersteker, "The 'triumph' of liberal economic ideas" in Barbara Stallings, ed., *Global Change, Regional Response: The New International Context of Development,* Cambridge University Press, 1995, p.180
2 For an assessment of what was achieved, see Nassau A. Adams, *Worlds Apart: The North-South Divide and the International System,* Zed Books, 1993, pp.131-141

3 Walden Bello, *Dark Victory: The United States, Structural Adjustment and Global Poverty*, Pluto Press, 1994, p.24.

4 For example, Duncan Green quotes Humberto Vega, chief of the Chilean Treasury: "In the 1960s the economics department taught you Keynes and *Cepalismo*. Classical economics was only taught in economic history! The role of the state was obvious, no one argued with it, not even the right, which was very protectionist." Duncan Green, *Silent Revolution: The Rise of Market Economics in Latin America*, LAB, 1995, p.16

5 Gary Gereffi: "Global production systems and third world development" in Barbara Stallings, ed., op. cit., p.106

6 Colin Leys, *The Rise and Fall of Development Theory*, Indiana University Press, 1996, p.20

7 ibid., p.22

8 For an overview of the international debt crisis with particular attention to the various solutions both tried and proposed, see Mary R. McCarthy and Thomas G. McCarthy, *Third World Debt: Towards an Equitable Solution*, Trócaire and Gill & Macmillan, 1994.

9 Thomas J. Biersteker: op. cit., p.185

10 See Yun-Han Chu, "The East Asian NICs: a state-led path to the developed world" in Barbara Stallings, ed., op. cit., pp.199-237.

11 John Toye, *Dilemmas of Development*, Blackwell, second edition, 1993, p.69

12 ibid., p.70

13 N. A. Adams, op. cit., p.150

14 See John Williamson, *Latin American Adjustment: How Much Has Happened?*, Institute for International Economics, 1990.

15 Barbara Stallings, "Introduction" in Barbara Stallings, ed: op. cit., p.13

16 John Toye, op. cit., p.74

17 Michael P. Todaro, *Economic Development*, Longman, fifth edition, 1994, p.87. Among the reasons he gives why competitive markets do not exist are limited information, fragmented markets, widespread externalities of both production and consumption, discontinuities in production and indivisibilities in technology.

18 ibid, p.87

19 ibid., p.437

20 ibid., pp.87-88

21 Barbara Stallings, op. cit., pp.14-22

22 ibid., p.22

23 Danny M. Leipziger and Vinod Thomas, *The Lessons of East Asia: An Overview of Country Experience*, World Bank, 1994, p.10

24 The term is used, for example, in the document issued by the World Bank to mark its 50th anniversary, *Learning from the Past, Embracing the Future*, World Bank, 1994, p.10

25 Barbara Stallings: "Introduction" in Barbara Stallings, ed., op. cit., p.3

26 For a fascinating account of the attempts by Japan to get the World Bank to take seriously the lessons of its own development experience and of the Bank's difficulties in learning those lessons, see Robert Wade. "Japan, the World Bank, and the art of paradigm maintenance: 'The East Asian miracle' in political perspective" in *New Left Review*, 217, 1996, pp.3-36. Wade's account of the Bank's efforts to ensure its study of Japan did not yield conclusions that might contradict its own theoretical paradigm puts even the Vatican's guardianship of dogma in the shade.

27 The World Bank, *The East Asian Miracle: Economic Growth and Public Policy*, Oxford University Press, 1993, p.6

28 ibid., p.6

29 Albert Fishlow, et al, *Miracle or Design? Lessons from the East Asian Experience*, Overseas Development Council, 1994, p.2

30 Dani Rodrik, "King Kong meets Godzilla: The World Bank and 'The East Asian miracle'" in Fishlow, et al, op. cit., p.14

31 ibid., p.48

32 Robert Wade, "Selective industrial policies in East Asia: Is 'the East Asian miracle' right?" in Fishlow, et al, op. cit., p.57

33 Stephen Haggard, "Politics and institutions in the World Bank's East Asia", in Fishlow et al, op. cit., p.100

34 ibid., p.108

35 This, for example, is the strategy that informs the Irish Government's overseas development programme. See *Irish Aid: Consolidation and Growth, A Strategy Plan*, Department of Foreign Affairs, Dublin, 1993, pp.7-9.

36 Quoted in Susan George and Fabrizio Sabelli, *Faith and Credit: The World Bank's Secular Empire*, Penguin, 1994, p.38

37 Quoted in H. W. Arndt, *Economic Development: The History of an Idea*, University of Chicago Press, 1987, p.99

38 Quoted in Arndt, ibid., p.102

39 John Grindle, *Bread and Freedom: Basic Human Needs and Human Rights*, Trócaire and Gill & Macmillan, 1992, p.32

40 Frances Stewart, *Planning to Meet Basic Needs*, Macmillan, 1985, p.4

41 Stewart (1985) examines how such success cuts across the wider socio-economic policies being followed by governments and shows cases of success and failure existed among socialist countries, countries following market-oriented development and countries with a more mixed welfare-type intervention.

42 Structural adjustment programmes refer to those policies implemented by Third World governments, usually with strong encouragement from the World Bank and the IMF, to open their economies to foreign competition, to balance budgets by cutting back on state spending and by laying off workers, to privatise state companies and, in general, to allow market forces set prices, and exchange and interest rates.

43 World Commission on Environment and Development, *Our Common Future*, Oxford, 1987, p 49

44 Sharachchandra M. Lélé, "Sustainable development: a critical review" in *World Development*, vol.19, no.6, 1991, p.613

45 ibid., pp.613-616

46 Frans J. Schuurman, "Introduction: development theory in the 1990s" in Schuurman, ed., *Beyond the Impasse: New Directions in Development Theory*, Zed Books, 1993, p.9

47 David Booth, "Marxism and development sociology: interpreting the impasse" in *World Development*, vol.13, no. 7, 1985, pp.761-87

48 This is how Booth put his 1985 argument in a later review of the debate on the "impasse". See D. Booth, "Rethinking social development: an overview" in D. Booth, ed., *Rethinking Social Development: Theory, Research and Practice*, Longman, 1994, p.5.

49 D. Booth, op. cit., p.773

50 ibid., p.775

51 ibid., p.777

52 Nicos P. Mouzelis, "Sociology of development: reflections on the present crisis" in *Sociology*, vol.22, no.1, 1988, p.40

53 ibid., pp.39-40

54 Peter Wandergeest and Frederick H. Buttel, "Marx, Weber, and development sociology: beyond the impasse" in *World Development*, vol.16, no.6, 1988, p.686

55 ibid., pp.689-90

56 ibid., p.691

57 D. Booth, 1994, op. cit., pp.7-11

58 ibid., p.8

59 ibid., p.9

60 For a comprehensive overview of developments in the literature and the insights they offer, see Peter B. Evans and John D. Stephens, "Development and the world economy" in Neil Smelser, ed., *Handbook of Sociology*, Sage, 1988, pp. 739-773.

61 D. Booth, 1994, op. cit., p.11
62 Michael Edwards, "The irrelevance of development studies" in *Third World Quarterly*, vol.11, no.1, 1989, p.116
63 ibid., p.120
64 For example, Buttel and McMichael argue that the need felt by development theorists to be relevant to development practice has placed a straitjacket on the intellectual growth of the discipline. See Frederick H. Buttel and Philip McMichael, "Reconsidering the explanandum and scope of development studies: Towards a comparative sociology of state-economy relations" in D. Booth, ed., op. cit., pp.42-61
65 D. Booth, op. cit, p.12
66 Quoted in Booth, op. cit., p.13
67 F Schuurman, op. cit., p.26
68 Booth outlines his analysis in some detail in D. Booth, op. cit., 1994, pp.11-26
69 D. Booth: "How far beyond the impasse?" in D. Booth, ed., 1994, op. cit., pp.308 and 310
70 For an example of the sharp critique which development studies can offer to the current practice of neo-liberalism, see Cristóbal Kay, "For a renewal of development studies: Latin American theories and neoliberalism in the era of structural adjustment" in *Third World Quarterly*, vol.14, no.4, 1993, pp.691-702.

Chapter 4

New Questions

"The poor are not the problem, they are the solution."

– Robert Chambers[1]

The 1980s witnessed the collapse of alternative paths to development and the acceptance by governments throughout the South of free market discipline. All of this served to reinforce the dominant capitalist understanding and practice of development. But the 1980s also witnessed a series of events and movements which emerged unexpectedly and which, more starkly than ever before, posed radical questions about the nature of development as it had been practised up to then. These have prompted important and even subversive new insights into what development might and should be.

Some of these, like the rise of what is usually called Islamic fundamentalism or the huge and recurring famines in parts of sub-Saharan Africa, were dark and threatening, at least to Western public opinion. Others, like the UN conference on women and development in Nairobi in 1985 or the growing recognition of the strength of grassroots movements throughout the South, were seen as more positive. But the questions all of them raised complemented one another and, for some, marked the emergence of a new people-centred, bottom-up and more human alternative to the dominant development model.[2] Attempts have been made to incorporate some elements of this alternative, such as environmental and women's concerns, into mainstream development thinking, but for others it embodies a radical critique of such development and, in particular, the rationality that underlies it and gives it form. As well as proposing a new form of people-centred development in radical distinction to today's model, it identifies sectors of society which carry the potential to implement this alternative development. In terms of development theory, it needs to be asked whether such an alternative constitutes a new development paradigm. These issues form the subject of this chapter.

Disturbing realities

1) Culture

The 1979 Iranian revolution profoundly shocked the West. Not only had Iran been a model of Western-style modernisation in the Middle East and Washington's closest ally in the region, but the Shah was replaced by a fundamentalist Islamic cleric, the Ayatollah Khomeini, who publicly advocated a society based exclusively on a literal interpretation of Islamic law, the Sharia, and ruled by the clergy. His writings made not the slightest reference to basic Western concepts such as democracy, nationalism or socialism.[3] Furthermore, as was visibly demonstrated again and again from his return to Iran in 1979 to his death in 1989, he commanded enormous popular support and adulation, of a kind unknown to any Western leader.

Events in Iran have been called "an extreme riposte to economistic development policies ... a revenge"[4] but it was the form this took that was especially disturbing. The post-War era had witnessed a succession of revolutions expressing the urge for a more autonomous and egalitarian form of development – from China in 1949 through Vietnam, Cuba, Cambodia, Ethiopia, Mozambique and Angola, to Nicaragua and Grenada. The West may not have liked these, but at least they found expression in terms it understood. Instead, the Iranian revolution focused attention on a rising political tide of revolt throughout the Muslim world expressed in terms the West very definitely did not understand and found frightening.[5]

An indication of this lack of understanding is the tendency in the Western media to speak of Islamic fundamentalism and to highlight the more distasteful features of it such as barbaric physical punishments or the subordination of women. The term "fundamentalism", however, comes from Christianity and holds little meaning for Muslims. In the words of one Western journalist who has written of the application of the term to those espousing Islamic political ideas: "Across the Middle East, these people have taken such diverse approaches to achieving their goals and developed such a broad range of political habits, that the label seems misleading".[6] What it hides also is any appreciation of the positive reasons motivating the Islamic resurgence – the desire for true independence and a way of life based on indigenous cultural traditions, free of Western domination.[7]

This example highlights the emergence of cultural diversity as a challenge to the dominant Western paradigms of development, whether of left or of right. The reaction against Western models and the return to indigenous traditions, respecting traditional knowledge and practices and finding there sources on which to draw for the task of development, is now widespread. Islamic activism is only one very visible form. In his well-known book *Small is Beautiful*, the British economist, E. F. Schumacher advocated a Buddhist economics whose aim would be "the maximum of well-being with the minimum of consumption".[8] Another example is the resurgence of indigenous peoples throughout both the North and the South; a recognition of this resurgence was the awarding of the Nobel Peace Prize to the Guatemalan indigenous woman, Rigoberta Menchu in 1992, the year of the quincentenary of the first arrival of Europeans to the shores of the Americas.

2) Women

The award to Rigoberta Menchu also honoured women who have, over the past two decades, become much more visible on the development stage. This initially happened through the impact on development thinking of the women's movement in the North and the growing awareness during the 1960s of the need for action to counter discrimination against women, both at national level and through the United Nations. This led the UN to nominate 1975 as International Women's Year and a major UN conference held that year in Mexico City established the UN Decade for Women (1975-85). Activities during this decade helped to give greater visibility to women's role in development. As a mid-decade UN conference in Copenhagen in 1980 put it: "Although women represent half of the world's population and one third of the official labour force, they receive only one per cent of the world's income and own less than one per cent of the world's property".[9]

This decade saw a number of important shifts in the focus of action programmes for women. Initially these had a very restricted view of women, concentrating on their domestic and reproductive roles and assisting them through welfare and family planning programmes. A study of women's role in economic development by Esther Boserup, published in 1970, had a major influence in widening the focus to take into account women's productive roles in subsistence agriculture or low-wage industrial work.[10] Boserup's work drew attention to the fact that the process of development had often worsened women's status and economic position, adding economic tasks outside the home, whether in tending the family plot as the men were drawn into waged labour in commercialised agriculture or in low-wage, insecure jobs in the new processing industries being set up.

Out of this appreciation of women's marginalised economic role grew an emphasis on the need for equality with men, an approach often called Women In Development or WID. With the advent of the debt crisis and structural adjustment programmes in the 1980s, women's position worsened further as reduced job opportunities and cuts in social budgets usually hit women worse than men. In this situation, concern for equality gave way to anti-poverty schemes, targeting aid on women's most urgent needs but avoiding the profound changes needed to address inequality between men and women. Another approach that emerged during the 1980s, promoted by the World Bank and other development agencies, emphasised efficiency and sought to integrate women into the labour force on the understanding that this increased equity. Yet, as Moser emphasised, this has also served to worsen the plight of women as it simply adds another (usually very poorly) paid productive role on to women's many unpaid roles in caring for children, gathering fuel, processing food, preparing meals and nursing the sick.[11]

The UN Conference on Women and Development in Nairobi in 1985, which marked the end of the UN Decade, witnessed the emergence of autonomous women's groups in the South with their own distinct agenda, critical of the assumptions underlying the WID approach. These were usually groups of women who had come together in the struggle for survival and who based their critique on their own experiences.[12] Third World women had been critical of the fact that their experiences were being voiced by Northern women researchers, experiences that shaped the determination of policy towards them.[13] This new-found assertiveness of Third World women Moser labelled the empowerment approach as Southern women's movements resisted being integrated into what they considered a Western and patriarchal model of development.[14] Instead, as one India-based network of women activists called Development Alternatives with Women for a New Era (DAWN) put it, "it is the experiences lived by poor women throughout the Third World in their struggles to ensure the basic survival of their families and themselves that provide the clearest lens for an understanding of development processes. And it is *their* aspirations and struggles for a future free of the multiple oppressions of gender, class, race and nation that can form the basis for the new visions and strategies that the world now needs".[15]

96

This new agenda found expression in a number of conferences organised by women before the Rio Earth Summit in 1992 as well as in a women's conference which took place in Rio during the Summit. In the words of Braidotti et al, these "represent a major breakthrough because for the first time ever women across political/geographical, class, race, professional and institutional divides came up with a critique of development and a collective position on the environmental crisis, arrived at in a participatory and democratic process".[16] A similar comment could be applied to the way women mobilised and participated in the UN summits on population in Cairo in 1994 and on women in Beijing in 1995.[17]

3) Environment

Apart from the cultural and feminist challenges to dominant development thinking, a third challenge took on particular force in the 1980s and early 1990s – the environmental challenge. Chapter 3 has already discussed attempts to integrate environmental concerns into mainstream development thinking, particularly through the concept of sustainable development. But these concerns have also resulted in more radical critiques of the dominant forms of development and in what Adams calls "'greener' models of development".[18]

Already in the 1970s grim warnings had been sounded about the carrying capacity of the earth if the present rate of resource depletion and population growth were to continue. The book *Only One Earth* by Barbara Ward and René Dubos, written for the first UN conference on the environment held in Stockholm in 1972, quickly became a classic. Another influential voice was that of the US economist, Herman Daly, who said that present levels of consumption are unsustainable and argued for a "steady state economics" in which Northern consumption and Southern population would be reduced to reach a common level of capital stock per person.[19]

Events in the 1980s seemed to bring home for the first time to public opinion in the North the reality of the environmental limits on which these critiques were based. A series of major famines in sub-Saharan Africa, particularly the Ethiopian famine of 1984-85, focused attention on the severe effects of soil erosion and desertification[20] and made horrifying images of their effects on African women and children virtual icons of contemporary black Africa. But for the affluent North, these were distant problems, touching consciences and evoking moral concern. Before the end of the decade, however, environmental limits had become an issue of self-interest to the North as the depletion of the ozone layer and the effects of global warming led some to predict catastrophic consequences for life on earth within the lifetime of people already alive.[21] Public opinion was therefore ready for the conclusions of the Brundtland report, *Our Common Future* published in 1987. This report brought together for the first time the issues of environment and development, arguing that both are inseparable. Up to then, much of the focus of environmental concern had been on the conservation of the diversity of animal and plant species and on how resources could be used in such a way as not to exhaust them.[22] Brundtland began instead with the threat of poverty and underdevelopment to the environment and urged that "the international economy must speed up world growth while respecting environmental constraints".[23] But, as Adams put it, Brundtland "hopes to have its cake and eat it". It does not say how the balancing act between the demands of growth for greater energy and raw materials and the limits imposed by nature itself is going to be achieved.[24]

These tensions between environmental concerns and the urgent imperatives of development came into sharp focus at the UN Conference on Environment and Development, or the Earth Summit as it was called, in Rio de Janeiro in 1992. Here a Northern environmental agenda clashed with a Southern developmental agenda. As Middleton et al. put it, as far as the conference convenors were concerned, such issues as the ozone layer, polluted seas, increasing deserts and the loss of biodiversity were the main problems facing the world.[25] This agenda "effectively marginalised the case that Northern industry made the environmental mess and that any Southern contribution to global pollution is largely a consequence of the uneven patterns of development forced on the South by Northern finance and protectionism".[26] Leaders of the South were suspicious that this agenda would have the effect of preventing their development and they sought large financial transfers in their favour if they were to agree to some of the conservation measures being sought. The end result for Middleton et al. was "an immense document of good intentions, made toothless by the rigid exclusion of timetables, serious financial targets, consideration of the terms of international trade and, above all, the role and unaccountability of the multinationals".[27] However disappointing the conclusions of Rio it was clear that the issue of environmental limits was now firmly at the heart of the development agenda.

Differing approaches

These various challenges have been recognised by mainstream advocates of development and attempts made to respond. Thus the World Bank established an environmentally sustainable development vice-presidency to help incorporate "environmentally appropriate management and sustainability into the design of development policies and projects".[28] The Bank also adopted a strategy "to reduce gender disparities and enhance women's participation in the economic development of their countries by integrating gender consideration in country-assistance programmes".[29] The Bank committed itself to poverty reduction and human resource development, both of them the responsibility of the Human Resources Development and Operations vice-presidency.[30] Finally, the Bank has sought to take the cultural challenge seriously through incorporating concerns such as indigenous peoples and the preservation of cultural heritage.[31]

Yet, critics have found the Bank's practice in these matters seriously wanting. On environmental issues, Susan George concludes: "While reinforcing its environmental staff, capacity, et cetera with one hand, it continues to lend to expensive impending environmental disasters with the other".[32] On women, Braidotti et al. describe the World Bank's approach as one that "addresses women's problems only partially.... The feminist concern for changes in the sexual division of labour is evaded.... Women's lives and problems are rarely seen in their full complexity. If they are, it would be obvious that they cannot be addressed effectively within the confines of development projects; to so address them would imply more radical changes in society at large".[33] On poverty reduction, the development agency Oxfam argues on the basis of the experience of its workers that the World Bank's policies are "a recipe for even greater levels of economic insecurity, poverty, and inequality".[34] On culture, Goulet argues that one effect of development has been the destruction or dilution of cultures, including the fragmentation of patterns of living and ways of being.[35]

Some theorists claim that the fault lies in the dominant model of development that is actively promoted by the Bank which, in regard to environmental matters, they categorise as a technocratic approach involving management of the ecosystem and the rational utilisation of resources and land. This approach is essentially reformist in contrast to what they call an ecocentrist approach which is much more radical and takes seriously such notions as bioethics and biorights.[36] This latter approach often espouses a form of decentralised development from below, drawing on indigenous knowledge as, for example, in development practices of Gandhian inspiration.

While there is a clear theoretical distinction between these two approaches, this, as Adams points out, is often blurred in the real-life practice of development. This may be because the ecocentrist approach, being largely based on concerns about the conservation of nature, lacks a clear framework for analysing political economy. For example, it has little or nothing to say about the implications for the wider economy and society of the radical conservation measures it promotes and neither does it examine the structures of wealth and power that constrain their implementation. This weakness in the ecocentrist approach leads Redclift to look at the ways in which capitalist development has undermined environmental sustainability. He argues that "conventional economic development identifies the optimal conditions for exploiting resources, a rather different process from considering sustainable development" with the result that "resource depletion and unsustainable development are a direct consequence of growth itself".[37]

In fact, Redclift goes further in arguing that the environment is itself socially constructed and environmental change is a social process. He points out how, ever since colonial times, the environment throughout the world has been shaped to satisfy the needs of the dominant classes in the North while marginalising the local population. "Just as consumer preferences in the North help determine present-day forms of resource exploitation in the South so, in the eighteenth and nineteenth centuries, the environment in the South was being restructured around changing social patterns and behaviour in the industrializing countries".[38] In this process, the relationship of local peoples to nature has been changed so that what was formerly valued for its use-value (for consumption, for example) is now primarily valued for its exchange value (to sell). "Whether they are willing or unwilling agents in the irrecoverable destruction of the environment, the rural poor are resocialized in the process, often lending credibility by their actions to the view that development is an inevitable, progressive process which is most successful when it is least sustainable".[39]

Thus, concludes Redclift, "whether or not development is *necessarily* unsustainable ... it is clearly unsustainable on current models for many of those whose livelihoods are made in the South, and for reasons that lie outside their control".[40] He

Poverty Amid Plenty

identifies what he calls "a clash of rationalities" in which one person's world of resource depletion is another person's world of resource abundance[41] and he urges us "to interrogate our assumptions about both development and the environment and give political effect to the conclusions we reach" if we are to avoid growing ecological destruction.[42] A similar interrogation of our assumptions is called for by feminist and cultural critics of development.[43]

Interrogating assumptions

The emergence of rationality (as distinct from tradition or custom) as the governing principle of public affairs has been accepted by all forms of development theory as being fundamental to the emergence of the modern world. But, as Lovett puts it, what needs to be analysed is what *kind* of rationality it is that has moulded the world as we know it.[44] Identifying the assumptions on which this rationality rests allows us to become critically aware of the assumptions underlying the dominant model of development.

Lovett traces the emergence of empirical rationality (also called scientific or instrumental rationality) to the 17th century revolution in science through the work of such figures as Copernicus, Galileo, Kepler, Descartes, Bacon, Hobbes, Locke, Newton, Pascal, Boyle and Leibnitz. This rationality he distinguishes from the rationality of the classical world in that it refuses to accept any form of meaning or value as valid until subject to verification in the material world. While this led to enormously positive gains in our understanding of the physical world, it also came to govern our understanding of human consciousness, of society and of history, resulting in "a spreading reductionism, materialism, positivism, relativism and historicism".[45]

Lovett traces some of the ways in which empirical rationality was formative in the emergence of economics as a distinct discipline thus throwing light on some key characteristics of the discipline. He identifies in the political philosophy of Hobbes, Locke and Hume an economic theory that makes human freedom and the value of the individual dependent on possessions. "Locke removed any limitations on the acquisition of property – henceforth, the 'value' of individuals would be measured by how much they possessed".[46] The founding work of economics – *The Wealth of Nations* published in 1776 by Adam

Smith – "marked the breakthrough of empirical rationality in determining economic value," writes Lovett.[47] Smith divorced economics from morality, basing it instead on the presumed natural instincts of human beings and society. Indeed, the very language of morality itself was redefined in quantitative ways: as the Chilean economist, Manfred A. Max-Neef puts it, "'good' became a synonym for 'more and more'" with the result that "social justice became confused with growth itself".[48] For Lovett, economics has developed through ever more sophisticated methods of quantification but he draws attention to "the contrast between technical brilliance and poverty of perspective" inherent in most economic thinking.[49] As an example, he takes economic thinking about human labour which reduces the labourer to a producer for the market and a consumer of commodities; production and consumption are assumed to be among the primary purposes of life. As Lovett sums up the impact of empirical rationality: " … reductionist methodologies cannot do justice to the increasingly complex levels of intelligibility to be found in our evolving universe. We are still a staggeringly long way from anything like an adequate science of the human".[50]

Feminist theoreticians have also been highly critical of the Western rational and scientific worldview as it has developed since the Enlightenment. They question its claims to universality, to being value-free and to pursuing truth for its own sake. Instead they link it to patriarchal power relations and view it as a discourse "that systematically devalues every category that is 'other' than the male, Western, bourgeois self: women, children, other races, foreign cultures, lower classes, handicapped people and nature".[51] Some feminist theorists see this male rationality as intrinsically violent and dominating, and draw a connection between its domination of women, of nature and of Third World peoples.[52]

Friberg and Hettne apply the critique of empirical rationality to development theory. For example, they examine the identification of growth with progress seeing it as a most significant shift. They point out that for the Greeks growth was a cyclical process while for the medieval mind it was conceived of in terms of degeneration, decay and "with a sense of doom".[53] Modern ideas of development are instead suffused with the "optimistic mechanical worldview" of scientific rationality: "The dynamics of society follow natural laws. Infinite human progress is assured by the application of scientific knowledge about these laws in the governance and regulation of society".[54] Max-Neef draws attention to some of the implications of this mechanical worldview and its assumptions about endless growth which hold that "one of the unavoidable means of achieving a superior human destiny lies in the domination and control of nature".[55] The view that growth is an end in itself and the failure of all dominant economic theories to include the costs of the destruction of nature in their development projections has given rise to what he calls a "vandalic style" of development[56] which is causing the irreversible destruction of the earth's resources at an accelerating rate.[57]

Conceptions of development based on scientific rationality therefore objectify both nature (as an object of measurement and use) and the human person, often also treated as an object in the endless urge for growth. They furthermore embody the evolutionism of 19th century science. Based on these considerations, Friberg and Hettne isolate four basic axioms which are operative in all forms of development theory – modernisation, dependency and the world-system approach. These are:

1) direction: that historical change is directed and cumulative, being seen as a process of growth, expansion or evolution;

2) determinism: that this evolution is predetermined and irreversible, with humanity having an influence in only minor details;

3) progress: that this evolution is progressive and we are moving towards a better world;

4) immanence: that this progressive movement of history is inherent in every society in the world.

All the principal theories of development, therefore, though they purport to be based on fundamentally opposed paradigms of capitalism and socialism are "moved by theories of predetermined change that provide little scope for alternative futures based on autonomous choices and diverse perspective". To this, Friberg and Hettne contrast a view of development as "building autonomy, freedom, well-being, and justice at a number of levels so that ordinary men and women can realize these values".[58]

The dominant Western view of progress has, however, made this task very difficult as it has been imposed on peoples throughout the world, providing a conceptual and moral basis for colonialism and imperialism, writes Tucker.[59] Confronting other societies and cultures with totally different rationalities, the "myth of development" invented the category "traditional", thereby ruling out the possibility that anything of value to the task of development could be learned from these societies and conceiving of them largely as obstacles to development. "The notion of other societies as simple and unchanging by contrast with the complexity and dynamism of 'western' societies was a convenient fiction which legitimised the right, and even the duty, of 'modern' societies to transform them in its image and likeness".[60] Development has therefore become something akin to a religious crusade which continues in new forms even though the societies being developed have virtually all achieved independence. It is being used to mask the process of economic, political, military, even ecological domination of the "Third World" by the West. "The development discourse is part of an imperial process whereby other peoples are appropriated and turned into objects. It is an essential part of the process whereby the so-called 'developed countries' manage, control and even create the 'Third World' economically, politically, sociologically and culturally. It is a process whereby their lives, their plans, their hopes, their imagination are shaped by others who frequently share neither their lifestyles, hopes nor their values".[61] Thus empirical rationality, reducing peoples and nature to the status of objects, reducing value and meaning to what can be verified by reference to material things, divorcing morality from economics and politics, has come to universal dominance.

These are some of the key defining characteristics of what is often called "the modern project" – characterised by a scientific worldview, by the modern, organised state and by the capitalist world economy, all of which have led to incredible advances in human wellbeing over recent centuries. Yet, on the other hand, the late 20th century is being forced towards awareness about the darker side of this modern project – severe and some would say fatal damage to the earth's fragile ecosystem, growing disparities between rich and poor, the sundering of the bonds which tied people to communities and which gave them identity and security.

The various events and movements outlined at the beginning of this chapter are attempts to respond to this historic crisis, to contribute to change. These constitute a highly diverse collection and treating them together runs the risk of implying that a common cause unites them when this is often far from true. Response from some can come in the form of retreating from the gains of modernity and embracing irrationality as seems to be happening in the re-emergence of virulent racism in western

European societies or in some forms of Islamicism. But being critical of empirical rationality is not to embrace irrationality; instead, as Azay Mehmet argues, "abandoning reductionism would reintegrate ends and means in a more holistic framework going beyond Eurocentric rationalism, and would recognize the relevance of group, as opposed to private, benefits and costs .... Such a broader agenda would incorporate indigenous cultures and institutions within an endogenous development theorizing".[62] The challenge therefore is not to abandon rationality and the gains of modernity but to move beyond its limits and find "a wisdom to match our sciences".[63]

A wisdom to match our sciences

Max-Neef, himself an economist, regards economics as a discipline "deprived of arguments and tools with which to tackle what is truly new".[64] Yet, the present crisis, which he regards as being without analogies, calls for us to move beyond the technical questions of economics to the deeper normative questions of ethics, questions with which our dominant Western civilization feels so uneasy: what is the good life? what is a just society? what is a respectful relationship with nature? and, crucial to the concerns of this book, what is the desired goal of development? These are the questions raised by the events and movements with which this chapter began. They are questions which overflow the boundaries of empirical rationality and tend instead to a "revolution in consciousness".[65] For some, they lead to the search for Utopia, for a society that is not only possible but desirable, for conceiving of radically different possibilities. This search involves a return to the traditions of Utopian socialism or anarchism which were influential up to the time of the Russian revolution but which were then overshadowed by scientific socialism (Marxism) which became the main alternative to capitalism. As Hobsbawm has remarked, these earlier traditions corresponded far more closely than did Marxism to the actual ideas of most student rebels of the 1960s and 1970s.[66] Contemporary manifestations of this Utopianism include "humanist eco-anarchism"[67] and "ecofeminism".[68]

Friberg and Hettne see in this return to a Utopian way of thinking the emergence of a new alternative to both the "Blue" development option (market, liberal, capitalist) and the "Red" (state, socialist, planning) option, and to this they give the name "the Green alternative".[69] Though they acknowledge that this is far less articulated, discussed or politically organised than the other two options, they present it as a coherent alternative and argue that the structural and historical conditions exist in the crisis of the dominant models for the Green alternative to advance.

The Green alternative is based on two fundamental principles. The first is that society should be at the service of human self-realisation rather than moulding human beings to fit society's needs. This includes meeting not only material needs which industrial society does very well for a part of the human race but, more importantly, meeting second-order needs for meaning and identity which industrial society fails so singularly to satisfy. Among these they include cultural identity, self-reliance, social justice and ecological balance. The second principle underlying the Green alternative is that "human beings or small communities of human beings are the ultimate actors".[70] They thus see it as profoundly non-deterministic, following no universal paths but drawing upon the richness of human cultures, valuing diversity and recreating the world from the bottom up through a process of self-reliance at all levels, particularly regional and local. It would involve a reconceptualisation of the relationship between humanity and nature, substituting a partnership between both for the exploitative relationship deriving from empirical rationality. As Max-Neef puts it: "I personally do not believe in any type of permanent solution. My proposal is geared to current conditions only; long-term flexibility and the willingness to change is built into my philosophy".[71]

This then provides a sketch of the Utopian future desired and the values underlying it. But is it not hopelessly unrealistic and utterly incapable of being realised? Friberg and Hettne acknowledge that Utopian thinking is often very voluntarist and that what is needed is a "realistic Utopianism" embedded in a "theory about the structural and historical conditions for a Green development",[72] with a clear sense of actors who are the bearers of this alternative and how the dominant system opens possibilities for them to promote it. This is perhaps the most original contribution of Friberg and Hettne. In examining the dominant capitalist system today, they identify two orders – the large-scale, depersonalised corporate actors such as companies, bureaucracies, trade unions and political parties side by side with more personalised actors such as the family, work-teams, local communities or the networks of informal relationships which constitute such vital links between individuals and their societies.

Poverty Amid Plenty

The Red or socialist alternative is focused on taking power within the former system of large corporate bodies in order to implement its vision of the just and humane society. The Green alternative, on the other hand, is focused on the second, more personalised order where the more humane values it espouses are predominant.

The future lies in strengthening this order so that local communities, both urban and rural, re-take power over their own lives and re-create the ability to shape their futures. The emergence of the corporate order as part of the modern project of capitalist expansion over the past 500 years has killed off much of the second order of more personalised natural communities. But Friberg and Hettne argue that the process of capitalist expansionism is now reaching its limits both because it is exhausting or destroying the natural resources it has so barbarously exploited and because the corporate order is no longer able to cope with the demands on it to provide for the basic material needs of most of humanity. Even in the most developed societies the welfare state is being cut back while the formal sector will never be able to create enough jobs to satisfy the demand worldwide. The result increasingly is, even in the most developed countries, that societies are divided between a modern corporate sector of well-paid jobs integrated into the international economy side by side with a marginalised informal sector in which people scrape together a meagre income in whatever way they can. In most of the world's countries, the majority of the population inhabits this second order and, even in the West, particularly in semi-peripheral countries like Ireland, it is the defining life experience of significant minorities. This may be a sign that, after growing and expanding for the past 500 years, the capitalist system has begun a slow but steady process of decline as it proves less and less able to meet even the most basic needs of most of humanity, as Friberg and Hettne suggest.[73]

Empowering the poor: social movements

For Friberg and Hettne, not only are the conditions for the Green alternative present but such an alternative already exists in the burgeoning social movements through which the poor and marginalised come together in the struggle for survival at the edge of the dominant system. In the developed North, the most influential form of social movements has been the ecological, women's and peace movements which, since the 1960s, have been recognised as important actors for social change. But these are largely middle-class movements; in the South (and increasingly among the marginalised of the North) the predominant form these movements take is as apparently spontaneous local urban or rural organisations seeking to defend members' survival through co-operative consumption, distribution and production. Examples are soup kitchens, distributors and producers of basic necessities like bread, organisers, petitioners or negotiators and sometimes fighters for community infrastructure like agricultural and urban land, water, electricity, transport, etc.[74] But, as Friberg and Hettne conclude, both the movements' of the North and of the South "should be analysed with two main ideas in mind, the concept of socio-economic dualism between modern and non-modern institutions and the idea of periphery mobilisation as a reaction to penetration from a modernising centre".[75] These social movements then are the bearers of the Green alternative, rather like the working class was seen in Marxist politics as the vanguard class of socialist revolution. Max-Neef expresses the political challenge of these movements: "Most important changes do not come from official power but from small movements that bother and bother. That's what I call 'the cloud of mosquitoes strategy'. If one is confronting a rhinoceros the most stupid thing is to act like a rhinoceros because it will obliterate you. But if you act like a cloud of mosquitoes it won't be able to do anything about you. That is the power we have".[76]

In this very optimistic scenario, Friberg and Hettne see a counter-culture growing within the entrails of the dominant system. This they argue is born out of an alliance between three different groups in reaction against the impact of that dominant system on their lives. The first are traditionalists defending a non-modern way of life – non-Western civilisations and religions, indigenous nations, small independent producers, etc. The second group is made up of all those marginalised by the dominant system – the poor and unemployed, part-time workers, women, young people, the low-paid, the handicapped, etc. The third group are the post-materialists, those who are consciously reacting against the alienation and dehumanisation of the system. These are often the sons and daughters of the elites, the young and well-educated who have experienced the emptiness of what the system can offer. Friberg and Hettne characterise the activities of these groups as constituting "a non-elite counter mobilisation",[77] revitalising suppressed value systems and traditions and weakening the state through withdrawal from it rather than by frontal attack. Theirs is a non-party horizontal politics creating links of self-reliance between local communities in contrast to a vertical representative politics through which the marginalised elect representatives to win favours on their behalf from the centralised state.[78] This alternative does not therefore envisage a revolutionary moment in which the dominant power is smashed and power relations inverted as was the principal expectation of radical political change for much of the 19th and 20th centuries. Instead, it envisages a long drawn-out process of communities taking charge of their own personal and social development as much as possible and thus constituting a sort of "liberated zone" which will be gradually extended through decentralised networks of small primary groups Friberg and Hettne claim that what the Green alternative offers is "a new project and a new destination for humankind.... The important thing is that the Green project catches people's imagination and inspires their daily actions. There is no right historical moment to begin the struggle for a decent life. It has to start right now".[79]

The Green alternative, as outlined by Friberg and Hettne therefore gives to what often seem insignificant, spontaneous local initiatives a value in wider historical and systemic terms, seeing in them the seeds of a new world. Does this not run the risk of overstating the case? For example, do they draw rather too strong a distinction between the dominant system and the counter culture since in practice the creation of alternatives usually depends to some degree on the dominant system through, for example, the provision of grants or credit, or through trading networks? Furthermore there seems little basis for believing that an alliance is possible between the traditionalists, the marginalised and the post-materialists except perhaps on very specific issues at specific times.[80]

It is also significant that in their examination of social movements, Fuentes and Gunder Frank draw rather less sanguine conclusions. They write that such movements tend to be cyclical, developing in response to particular crises and needs but then often waning; they are defensive and "leave few permanent and cumulative marks on history";[81] very few of them are anti-systemic, wanting to destroy the system and replace it by another one or none at all; and there are significant areas of conflict and competition among them. On this last point, Fuentes and Gunder Frank point to the tensions between women's movements and national liberation movements in, for example, Iran, Vietnam and Nicaragua, and they argue that "most religious or strongly religiously oriented movements seem to contain important seeds of internal conflict between progressive and regressive, and sometimes also escapist, aims".[82] This is consistent with the conclusions of other theorists of social movements. For example, Alan Scott concludes: "Social movements are agents of social change but not, as their theorists often suggest, necessarily or usually of total social transformation. Social movements typically bring about change, or attempt to bring it about, not by challenging society as a whole, though they may appear to do so, but by opposing specific forms of social closure and exclusion."[83]

A new paradigm?

"A new development paradigm is now in gestation," wrote Denis Goulet in his critique of how the dominant model of development breeds injustice, destroys cultures, damages environments and generalises *anomie*.[84] But can the alternative emerging from the cultural, feminist and environmental critiques of development that we have, following Friberg and Hettne, labelled the Green alternative, properly be described as a new development paradigm in the same way that Aidan Foster-Carter in 1976 was able to describe dependency theory as an alternative paradigm to modernisation theory?[85] (see Chapter 2). Is it accurate to say that the dominance of the capitalist development paradigm, now in a neo-liberal version, is being contested by the emergence of a new paradigm?

These questions take us back to the work of Thomas Kuhn which provides the philosophical basis for understanding all scientific work as taking place within a paradigm or a pre-theoretical set of assumptions which serve to define the field of study.[86] Thus data are chosen for study according to a particular paradigm which gives significance to some facts over others. These assumptions are taken so much for granted that most of those who operate within them are simply unaware of the assumptions which define their study; it is often only when a paradigm is in crisis that its existence is adverted to. Thus, in the natural sciences, the Ptolemaic solar system gave way to a Copernican one or Newtonian physics has been superseded by Einsteinian physics. These paradigmatic shifts in the natural sciences, called "scientific revolutions" by Kuhn, happen when a number of anomalies accumulate that seem to cast in doubt the dominant paradigm. Resisting attempts to be assimilated within that paradigm, these anomalies lead to a growing suspicion with the paradigm and to its eventual demise. This change Kuhn likens to a conversion experience.

In applying Kuhn's model to the field of development theory, Foster-Carter identified the continuing lack of development as the major anomaly of the then dominant modernisation paradigm; for Americans he points to the Cuban revolution and the Vietnam war as events which, in different ways, "proved exceedingly anomalous for the old paradigm".[87] Within the emerging paradigm of dependency, however, these events were in no way puzzling but rather confirmed its central tenets that development of the core stimulated underdevelopment on the periphery and that only by breaking these links could the periphery hope to develop.

But can we similarly identify anomalies that are currently undermining the dominant development paradigm? There are certainly trenchant criticisms of the dominant development paradigm as have been outlined in Part I of this book but a paradigm implies that a completely new theoretical view is emerging informed by values directly contrary to those informing mainsteam development. To claim that this is happening would appear to be giving too much coherence to the many disparate movements covered in this chapter and to the critique of the Enlightenment project which not all of them equally share. Furthermore it would seem to overlook the major weaknesses of this critique as embodying an alternative project. These weaknesses have been identified as:

1) the issue of strategy: how grassroots organisations are going to shape a global strategy;

2) the state: how the grassroots organisations relate to the state in a way that reinforces and advances their project, and

3) the global economy: how does a programme of alternative development link in with the global (and, let it be said, globalising) economy.[88]

Where Kuhn's analysis may relate to the present situation is in his references to the fact that the dominant causal factors in the emergence of a new paradigm are not logic but rather incompatible modes of community life and social psychology.[89] More than any coherent alternative project, these are what the cultural, feminist and environmental critiques of development often rest upon – affirming modes of community life and social psychology that are incompatible with the dominant capitalist model of development. For, at grassroots level throughout the South (as among the marginalised in the North), this affirmation of differing social values seems widespread.

Conclusion

The cultural, environmental and feminist critiques being insistently made of the dominant model of development pose fundamental challenges for that model with which it has difficulty dealing. But a basic question about these critiques is whether they are seeking a reform of that dominant system or whether they are seeking some alternative to it. For example, is a resurgent Islam turning its back on capitalism and modernity in favour of some Islamic alternative or is it rather a different route towards the benefits of capitalism and modernity?[90] It may be that what is finding expression in many versions of these critiques is a cry for inclusion rather than a cry for some totally alternative future. This, of course, does not lessen the challenge to the dominant model of development; in some ways it makes that challenge greater since the dominant model is being asked to change enough to give women, diverse cultures and the environment a fair deal. More than a challenge from any alternative, this plea for inclusion is surely the greatest challenge to the dominant model.

Footnotes

1   Robert Chambers, "Sustainable rural livelihoods: a key strategy for people, environment and development" in C. Conroy and M. Litvinoff, eds, *The Greening of Aid: Sustainable Livelihoods in Practice*, Earthscan, London, 1988, p.3
2   For a useful discussion of the origin and nature of alternative development, see John Friedmann, *Empowerment: The Politics of Alternative Development*, Blackwell, 1992.
3   Dilip Hiro, *Iran under the Ayatollahs*, Routledge and Kegan Paul, 1987, p.357
4   C. A. O. van Nieuwenhuijze, "Does development have anything to do with culture?" in C. A. O van Nieuwenhuijze, ed., *Development Regardless of Culture?*, E. J. Brill, 1984, p.19
5   NATO's then secretary general, Willy Claes identified Islamic fundamentalism as one of the most important challenges facing the West after the end of the Cold War. See "NATO plan for new North Africa pact", *The Independent*, 8 February 1995.
6   Peter Ford, "What to call those pushing political Islam" in *The Christian Science Monitor*, Weekly Edition, 23-29 April, 1993, p.11
7   As part of the series on Islam and democracy for *The Christian Science Monitor*, Peter Ford interviewed Abel Hussein, an Egyptian newspaper editor who began his political life as a Marxist admirer of the Soviet Union, later converted to Arab nationalism under the influence of Abdel Nasser and more

recently has discovered Islam. As Ford writes: "What Hussein found in Islam was a new way of rooting his anti-imperialist principles. The stress on 'authenticity' recast an old preoccupation of Arab political thinkers: the desire to ensure 'the dignity of Muslims, their right to establish their own way of life, their ambition to develop a different civilization,' free of Western domination.

"In Islam, Abel Hussein found an approach to life that embodies his ideas of social justice and cooperation, puts human values above economic ones, and makes him feel that the materialistic philosophies to which he used to subscribe were shallow." See "A marxist comes home to Islam" in *The Christian Science Monitor*, Weekly Edition, 30 April-6 May 1993. See also the series "Islam on the March" in *The Irish Times*, 4-11 February 1995.

For an alternative and more positive interpretation of the position of women in Islam to the largely negative and condemnatory one usually given in the West, see Rana Kabbani, *Woman in Muslim Society*, Occasional Paper Series no.3, Department of Sociology, UCC, 1992. The author describes the practice of Muslim women taking the veil as "a form of militant feminism" (p.4).

8 Quoted in Thierry G. Verhelst, *No Life Without Roots*, Zed Books, 1990, p.29

9 Quoted in Irene Dankelman and Joan Davidson, *Women and Environment in the Third World: Alliance for the Future*, Earthscan with IUCN, 1988, p.5

10 Esther Boserup, *Women's Role in Economic Development*, Allen & Unwin, 1970

11 Caroline O. N. Moser, "Gender planning in the Third World: meeting practical and strategic gender needs" in *World Development*, vol.17, no.11, 1989, p.1814. The various approaches to women and development outlined in this section are based on this article.

12 See Georgina Waylen, "Women's movements and democratisation in Latin America", in *Third World Quarterly*, vol.14, no.3, 1993, pp.573-87 for examples of women's movements in Latin America and their political impact.

13 See, for example, Marta Zabaleta who wrote that Latin American women are "in the strange position of making their own acquaintance through the medium of an internationally-projected, internationally-recognised image of themselves which they played little part in constructing." M. Zabaleta, "Research on Latin American women: in search of our political independence" in *Bulletin of Latin American Research*, vol.5, no.2, 1986, p.97

14 Rosi Braidotti, et al: *Women, the Environment and Sustainable Development*, Zed Books, 1994, p.81

15 Gita Sen and Caren Grown, *Development, Crises and Alternative Visions*, Earthscan, 1988, pp.9-10

16 R. Braidotti et al., op. cit., p.103

17 For a journalistic account of the participation of women in the Beijing conference, see Lorna Siggins, "The Fourth World Conference on Women: beyond the headlines" in Mary van Lieshout, ed., *A Woman's World: Beyond the Headlines*, Oxfam and Attic Press, 1996, pp.17-26

18 W. M. Adams, *Green Development: Environment and Sustainability in the Third World*, Routledge, 1990, p.65

19 See Herman Daly, *Steady-state Economics: The Economics of Biophysical Equilibrium and Moral Growth*, W. H. Freeman, 1977

20 These issues are comprehensively covered in Lloyd Timberlake, *Africa in Crisis: The Causes, the Cures of Environmental Bankruptcy*, Earthscan, 1988.

21 Following serious flooding in the Netherlands in early 1995, a British scientist, Dr Mike Hulme, was quoted as saying: "At the moment there is no evidence that the current weather conditions are caused by global warming, but the intense rain and early snowfall melting which we have seen in Europe this winter are consistent with a warming scenario." This seems to sum up the present, rather tentative, state of scientific knowledge on the issue. See *The Irish Times*, 2 February 1995.

22 For example, the World Conservation Strategy of 1980, promoted by the International Union for the Conservation of Nature (IUCN), the World

Wildlife Fund (WWF) and the UN Environment Programme (UNEP), in the words of Adams, "bears the hallmarks of much earlier conservation thinking" and reflects "the shallowness of the conversion of the conservation camp after 1972 to any really new way of thinking." See W. M. Adams, op. cit., p.46.

23 World Commission on Environment and Development, *Our Common Future*, Oxford, 1987, p.89

24 W. M. Adams, "Sustainable development and the greening of development theory" in Frans J. Schuurman, ed., *Beyond the Impasse: New Directions in Development Theory*, Zed Books, 1993, p.212

25 Neil Middleton, Phil O'Keefe and Sam Moyo, *Tears of the Crocodile: From Rio to Reality in the Developing World*, Pluto, 1993, p.4

26 ibid., p.6

27 ibid., p.2

28 *The World Bank Annual Report 1994*, The World Bank, 1994, p 42

29 ibid., p.37

30 ibid., p.33

31 See David Wigg, *Of Mosaics and Mosques: A Look at the Campaign to Preserve Cultural Heritage*, World Bank Development Essays, no.3, World Bank, 1994, and George Psacharopoulos and Harry Anthony Patrinos, *Indigenous People and Poverty in Latin America: An Empirical Analysis*, World Bank, 1994.

32 Susan George and Fabrizio Sabelli, *Faith and Credit: The World Bank's Secular Empire*, Penguin, 1994, p.182. See also Michael Redclift, *Sustainable Development: Exploring the Contradictions*, Methuen, 1987, pp.145-6 for a more dated but equally devastating indictment of the World Bank's record on environmental sustainability.

33 R. Braidotti et al, op. cit., p.83

34 *Structural Adjustment and Inequality in Latin America: How IMF and World Bank Policies have Failed the Poor*, Oxfam UK and Ireland Policy Department, 1994, p.7. While this relates to Latin America, Oxfam makes a similarly critical judgment on the activities of the World Bank worldwide: "Since the 1960s, World Bank project interventions have, in many cases, become synonymous with the worst forms of development practice. Insensitivity to local people, indifference to economic realities, and a propensity to disinformation, have combined to produce a litany of development disasters. All too often local elites have been the main beneficiaries while the poor have seen their livelihoods undermined, and suffered displacement. Women have been adversely affected by the failure of project planners to consider the gender implications of their actions." This quote is from *Embracing the Future ... Avoiding the Challenge of World Poverty: Oxfam's response to the World Bank's 'vision' for the Bretton Woods System*, An Oxfam Report, 1994, p. 19.

35 Denis Goulet, "Development: creator and destroyer of values" in *World Development*, vol.20, no.3, 1992, p.471

36 W. M. Adams, *Green Development*, op. cit., pp.12, 201

37 M. Redclift, op. cit., pp.56, 57

38 ibid., p.82

39 ibid., p.119

40 ibid., p.201

41 ibid., p.202

42 ibid., p.204

43 See, for example, R. Braidotti et al, op. cit., chapter 3; Maria Mies and Vandana Shiva, *Ecofeminism*, Fernwood Publications and Zed Books, 1993; V. Tucker, *The Myth of Development*, Occasional Paper Series no.6, Department of Sociology, UCC, 1992; D. Goulet, op. cit.

44 Brendan Lovett, *Life Before Death: Inculturating Hope*, Claretian Publications, 1986, p.39

45 ibid., p.40

46 ibid., p.42

47 ibid., p.43

48 Manfred A. Max-Neef, *From the Outside Looking In: Experiences in 'Barefoot Economics'*, Zed Books, 1992, p.51

49 Lovett, op. cit., p.44

50 ibid., p.46

51 R. Braidotti et al, op. cit., p.31

52 Maxine Molyneux and Deborah Lynn Steinberg, "Mies and Shiva's 'Ecofeminism': A New Testament?" in *Feminist Review*, no.49, spring 1995, p.89

53 Mats Friberg and Bjorn Hettne, "The greening of the world – towards a non-deterministic model of global processes" in Herb Addo et al., *Development as Social Transformation: Reflections on the Global Problematique*, Hodder and Stoughton, 1985, p.209. For a contemporary African view on this issue, see Paul Theroux, "The lepers of Moyo" in *Granta* 48, Penguin, 1994. Theroux writes: "The leper village had an air of being industrious and yet nothing seemed to change .... The people were sustained, and the achievement of the work was that life continued. All this effort was to hang on to life and remain the same" (p 149).

54 Friberg and Hettne, op. cit., p.209

55 Max-Neef, op. cit., p.40

56 ibid., p.44

57 Max-Neef argues that economics, because based on a mechanical worldview of constant repeatability, is unable to grasp the concept of entropy, namely that certain things are irreversible. Thus, he argues, that "the last link of the economic process is not consumption but the generation of waste" since the impact of economic processes on natural resources is to exhaust them. "The generation of increasingly large amounts of unnecessary waste is sealing the fate – destitute poverty – of the world's economically 'invisible' sectors," he writes. See Max-Neef, op. cit., pp.48, 50.

58 Friberg and Hettne, op. cit., p.204

59 Tucker, op. cit., p.5

60 ibid., p.12

61 ibid., p.2

62 Ozay Mehmet, *Westernizing the Third World: The Eurocentricity of Economic Development Theories*, Routledge, 1995, p.146

63 Denis Goulet, op. cit., p.472

64 Max-Neef, op. cit., p.49

65 Friberg and Hettne, op. cit., p.216

66 Eric Hobsbawm, *The Age of Extremes: The Short Twentieth Century 1914-1992*, Michael Joseph, 1994, footnote p.334

67 Max-Neef, op. cit., p.55

68 Braidotti et al, op. cit., p.161

69 Friberg and Hettne, op. cit., p.205

70 ibid., p.221

71 Max-Neef, op. cit., p.55

72 Friberg and Hettne, op. cit., p.226

73 ibid., p.234

74 See Marta Fuentes and André Gunder Frank, "Ten theses on social movements" in *World Development*, vol.17, no.2, 1989, p.184.

75 Friberg and Hettne, op. cit., p.248

76 Interview in *Latinamerica Press*, 10 June 1993, p.5

77 Friberg and Hettne, op. cit., p.242

78 For a detailed description of how these different kinds of politics can operate side-by-side in a Lima shantytown, see Susan C. Stokes, "Politics and Latin America's urban poor: Reflections from a Lima Shantytown" in *Latin American Research Review*, vol.26, no.2, 1991, pp.75-101

79 Friberg and Hettne, op. cit., pp.258-9

80 An example of this in Ireland might be the fact that traditionalist, marginalised and post-materialist groups could all be identified among those

who opposed the referenda on the Single European Act and on the Maastricht Treaty. However their very suspicion of one another even when they found themselves campaigning for the same result indicates the fundamental opposition between them.

81 Fuentes and Gunder Frank, op. cit., p.184
82 ibid., p.190
83 Alan Scott, *Ideology and the New Social Movements*, Routledge, 1990, p.150
84 Goulet, op. cit., p.469
85 Aidan Foster-Carter, "From Rostow to Gunder Frank: conflicting paradigms in the analysis of underdevelopment" in *World Development*, vol.4, no.3, 1976, pp.167-80
86 Thomas Kuhn, *The Structure of Scientific Revolutions*, University of Chicago Press, 1970
87 Foster-Carter, op. cit., p.173
88 See Gerardo L. Munck in "Book Reviews", *Journal of Development Amid Studies*, vol.29, no.2, 1993, pp.179-80.
89 See, for example, the following: "Like the choice between competing political institutions, that between competing paradigms proves to be a choice between incompatible modes of community life" (Kuhn, 1970, p.94) and the point made by Barry Barnes: "Kuhn is insistent that changes of paradigm must be made intelligible in terms of the social psychology of the scientific group, not in terms of purely logical considerations" (in Quentin Skinner, *The Return of Grand Theory in the Human Sciences*, Cambridge, 1990, p.91).
90 This is a question posed by Fred Halliday in his writing on Islam. See, for example, *Islam and the Myth of Confrontation: Religion and Politics in the Middle East*, I. B. Tauris, 1996

Interchapter

"We were more like Third World supplicants than a sovereign · European power. The questions go deep, very deep."

– comment by *Irish Times* columnist, Drapier, on government reaction to the announcement of the closure of the Digital plant in Galway, 1993[1]

Part I of this book has given an overview of development worldwide. This has shown how the categories of "First World/Third World", "developed/developing" that are so widespread in discussion of the world today are seriously misleading since they lump together into one category countries that are vastly different in their levels of development. These differences, as we have seen, have grown over recent decades so that what we class as developing countries today includes sub-Saharan African countries some of which hardly exist any more as functioning states and highly successful developers such as the East Asian "Tigers" of South Korea, Taiwan, Singapore and Hong Kong, or Chile, countries which are on the verge of being classified as developed. We badly need new classifications, therefore, to make sense of the wide diversity of levels of development that characterise today's world.

Development theory has also changed in fundamental ways, as was outlined in Part I. From the antagonistic claims of modernisation and dependency theories, both mirroring to an extent the divisions of the Cold War, a greater consensus has emerged, accepting the disciplines of the market and the challenges of competing in the international marketplace. This is not to say, however, that neo-classical economics is accepted without question. As we saw in Chapter 3, one of the most significant debates happening in mainstream development theory concerns such issues as the role of the state, the use of selective protectionism and the need for social equality so that the benefits of development can be widely shared. Meanwhile, other issues have come to the fore that challenge mainstream development theory in fundamental ways, issues such as the environmental costs of development, the fact that women are often victims of

117

development as much as its beneficiaries and the impact of development on cultural identity. These issues do not yet constitute an alternative paradigm of development and perhaps they never will but they are forcing themselves on to the agenda of mainstream development, both at the level of theory and of practical policy.

This therefore sets the scene for consideration of Irish development. Ireland's development history is similar to that of many countries that are classed as developing – it has a colonial past and it had up until 30 years ago an economic structure closer to that of many developing countries with a large proportion of its population engaged in subsistence agriculture, a relatively weak industrial base and low living standards. The two main development strategies followed since independence parallel those of many developing countries, particularly those of Latin America. The first, which ran from the early 1930s to the late 1950s involved an attempt to develop an indigenous industrial base behind tariff barriers, a model of development motivated by the belief that through one's own resources one could develop a society capable of meeting the basic material and social needs of its citizens. This effort had its successes, though it is fashionable now to discredit it.[2] The second strategy has been one of liberalising the economy, opening it to foreign investment which is seen as the engine of industrial growth, and seeking to win markets abroad for goods manufactured at home. This strategy is sometimes called neo-liberalism, particularly in Latin America. Though the Irish strategy shares some key elements of this, the state has maintained a more active role in the economy in Ireland than would be consistent with a thorough neo-liberal strategy.[3]

In broad outlines therefore, Ireland seems to be a good example of an underdeveloped country which has tried different strategies to develop. Because it changed over from an inward-oriented to an outward-oriented development strategy long before most countries in the so-called developing world, the results of that strategy should now be of interest to countries following a similar route. Yet Ireland has been little discussed in development theory. This may be due to the fact that, being a founder member of the Organisation for Economic Co-operation and Development (OECD) in 1961 and being on the periphery of a developed region of the world, it has been widely regarded as a developed country.

This neglect of Ireland by development theory has greatly impoverished the quality of thought here in Ireland about our development problems. Instead of interrogating our

Poverty Amid Plenty

development, most social scientific study assumes that Ireland is a developed country and treats it accordingly. Meanwhile consideration of Ireland's development is left to economists, most of whom are neo-classical in their outlook; therefore the theoretical perspectives of neo-classical economics are very evident in thinking on Irish development. One of the consequences of this situation is that Ireland has come to be seen in much social scientific literature as being quite *sui generis* and as not conforming to the normal patterns of development which are judged to be those of our nearest neighbours. What John Hutchinson has written about Irish historiography on the subject of nationalism could well be applied to social scientific writing on Ireland's development: "An 'internationalisation' of historical practice may achieve considerably more than a corrosive scepticism by lessening the claustrophobic intensity with which the Irish are wont to examine themselves."[4] Thus issues in economics such as the persistence of unemployment in a time of high economic growth rates, issues in sociology such as the problem of entrenched social exclusion or issues in political science such as the nature of populist politics in an underdeveloped society may all be more readily understood from the standpoint of development theory. The conclusion may be that Ireland is not so much *sui generis* as that its experience approximates more to that of countries we think of as being underdeveloped (especially some peripheral European ones and some of the more developed Latin American ones). What makes it appear unique is viewing it through theoretical perspectives derived from countries with a very different (and more successful) history of development than Ireland's.

Part II then applies development to the case of Ireland. Chapter 5 asks whether we can describe Ireland as developed or underdeveloped and is largely a descriptive chapter about the nature of Irish development. It draws on development theory to draw attention to aspects of Irish development that may not be adequately treated in mainstream economic or sociological literature. Chapter 6 is more interpretative as it critically outlines the main theoretical explanations for Ireland's development problems, situating these explanations within the main categories derived from development theory – modernisation, dependency, new political economy – as explained in Part I. The two final chapters are entitled "Resources for Development". These examine aspects of the Irish case which have been relatively neglected in recent literature but to which development theory directs attention. Chapter 7 looks at Irish nationalism and argues that it could be a resource to draw on for a more vigorous development effort. Chapter 8 looks at the nature of the Irish state and its adequacy to the tasks of development and argues that the emergence of a vigorous community sector could provide the potential to assert a more developmental agenda and help transform the state as a more adequate agency for development.

Thus civil society, which emerged as a major force in the final chapter of Part I, also emerges as a central theme in the final chapter of Part II. This emphasis on the importance of civil society is derived not only from a sense of the significance of its emergence at this time in human history but also from a sense that underdevelopment is not a technical problem to be left to elite experts to resolve. One of the main lessons to be learnt from both Part I and Part II of this work is that such elitist technocratic solutions have often made matters worse, particularly in allowing the institutionalisation of social exclusion as perhaps the greatest developmental and political challenge we now face. In this situation, it is vital that development be seen as a process that demands the mobilisation of people to empower themselves and to become actors for social and community development. Situating Ireland in the context of development theory reminds us that our challenges are very similar to those throughout the world. Realising this might prompt us to share what we have learnt and also to learn from experiences elsewhere in the developing world in a more active and effective way.

Footnotes

1   *The Irish Times*, 27 February 1993. His reference was to government ministers who travelled to Digital headquarters in Boston appealing to management to keep the plant open.

2   For a balanced assessment, see Brian Girvin, *Between Two Worlds: Politics and Economy in Independent Ireland*, Gill & Macmillan, 1989.

3   For a discussion of the tenets of neo-liberalism and how it differs from import substitution and neo-structuralism, see Duncan Green, *Silent Revolution: The Rise of Market Economics in Latin America*, LAB, 1995, pp.244-49.

4   John Hutchinson, "Irish nationalism" in D. George Boyce and Alan O'Day, eds, *The Making of Modern Irish History: Revisionism and the Revisionist Controversy*, Routledge, 1996, p.117

Part II

Irish Development

Chapter 5

Ireland: Developed or Underdeveloped?

"The Irish situation differs in important respects from that of other Western countries. It is in the large part a long-standing problem of underdevelopment. True, we could tackle it more effectively if other countries were more buoyant, but it will not go away even if other countries solve their unemployment problem. It is a problem we ourselves must solve unless we are content to remain a backwater of Europe."

– Professor Kieran A. Kennedy, ESRI[1]

In observing the stance of successive Irish governments towards the European Union, a certain ambivalence can be detected on the issue of Irish development. When funds for the less developed regions of the Union are being allocated, Dublin has waged a strong diplomatic offensive to secure a share disproportionate to our size. At such times, reference is made to our high unemployment rate and our relatively low living standards compared to those of other EU members to give substance to our claim that we need such funds to help us "catch up" with the more developed regions. In discussions on European Monetary Union and a single currency, however, Irish officials have emphasised a different set of statistics, arguing that our low inflation rate, our current account surplus and our falling debt/GDP ratio entitle us to be considered as one of the select group of "hard core" countries which will join monetary union from day one.[2]

The ambivalence expressed in these differing positions reflects a lack of clarity in some sectors of Irish society about our level of development. On the one hand, such indicators as average per capita income, the percentage of the workforce in industry and services as against agriculture, and levels of education and health place the Republic of Ireland in the ranks of the world's developed countries. In the World Bank's classifications, Ireland appears towards the bottom of the "high-income economies"[3] while, within the 25-member Organization for Economic Co-operation and Development (OECD), it appears fifth from the bottom, ahead of Portugal, Greece, Mexico and Turkey.[4] It may thus be thought of as being among the poorer of the developed countries but securely within that category.

Ireland's position on these tables gives us a snapshot of its level of development, but nothing more. As any snapshot, it is a static picture based on one partial view. It does not tell us how we have got to this position and whether we are likely to improve or disimprove relative to other countries. Neither does it tell us anything about how the income is distributed, in other words whether it results in widely shared development throughout society. For development is a dynamic process involving wealth creation but also wealth distribution and wealth retention. So, for example, if an economy is very productive and is showing high growth rates over a period of time, one cannot on this basis alone conclude that it is securely on the path to development. If a significant percentage of the wealth created leaves the national economy and if the wealth retained benefits the lives of only a section of the population, then economic growth may in fact be distorting the development of that society rather than putting it on a path to development. To obtain a fuller picture of Ireland's level of development therefore we need to pay attention not only to its growth rate but also to such indicators as its high rate of unemployment, particularly long-term unemployment, the percentage of GDP which is extracted from the national economy, and the legacy of a tradition of large-scale emigration.

This chapter takes this more comprehensive view in order to elaborate a clearer understanding of the nature of Irish development. It describes some central elements of Irish development and analyses what seem to be some key contradictions between high economic growth and entrenched social problems. In particular it examines how this situation has arisen and whether it may now be changing in a fundamental way. The chapter concludes by interrogating the concept of development itself in order to throw light on the extent to which we can call Ireland developed. This should be read in conjunction with the following chapter which examines some of the principal explanations offered for Ireland's problematic development, placing these in the context of development theory as elaborated in Part I. These two chapters therefore serve to place the Irish development experience in a wider theoretical context informed by development theory in the belief that this can help to deepen our understanding of the nature of that experience and focus attention on the developmental challenges still facing Irish society.

Relative decline?

Ireland's economic growth rates since 1988 have been very high by comparison to those of our EU partners, meriting the title "Celtic Tiger" for what is widely being regarded as something of an economic miracle. Yet, as recently as the late 1980s, studies were showing a very different picture, one of long-term economic decline relative to the rest of the developed world. These compared Ireland's development record in the 20th century to that of a range of other countries and concluded, in Joseph Lee's words, that "Irish economic performance has been the least impressive in western Europe, perhaps in all Europe, in the twentieth century".[5] Kennedy compares Ireland's gross national product (GNP) and per capita GNP to those of 28 other countries at two dates, 1913 and 1985. At the earlier date, Ireland's per capita income ranked 14th and was higher than that of Norway, Finland and Italy and only a little behind that of France. Sixty years later, however, the Republic of Ireland had fallen to 22nd place and had been overtaken by all western European countries (except Greece and Portugal), Japan, Czechoslovakia, Hungary and the Soviet Union.[6] A number of other studies have also highlighted Ireland's long-term decline. In his study of Europe's development, Dieter Senghaas concludes that "the history of Irish development is a prime example of emerging peripheralization"[7] while De Long groups Ireland with four other countries – Spain, Portugal, Argentina and Chile – "that one would in 1870 have thought capable of equally sharing this [post second World War] prosperity [and] have not done so".[8]

The exceptional performance since 1988, at a time when growth rates in much of the developed world were sluggish, has transformed perception of Ireland's performance, however. Following Ó Gráda and O'Rourke, we can compare average annual GDP growth rates for four periods between 1950 and 1994. In the first decade of this period, Europe was still recovering from the economic dislocation of the second World War and grew at an average annual rate of 3.7 per cent; Ireland's relative performance was however "disastrous"[9] at 2.2 per cent, worse than that of Britain at 2.3 per cent. The second period they take is the "Golden Age" of 1960-73 when Europe had an average annual growth rate of 4.2 per cent. By comparison, Ireland's annual rate was 3.7 per cent, worse than that of Europe but better than Britain's which was 2.6 per cent. As Ó Gráda and O'Rourke point out: "In relative terms, then, the 1960s were not such a success story for Ireland as some might suggest."[10] The third period begins with the first oil crisis of 1973 and thus is one of economic crisis and a downturn in growth rates. It lasts until 1988. In this period, European average annual growth rates declined to 1.9 per cent while Irish rates at 2.1 per cent were relatively good. Finally, it is in the period from 1988-94 that Ireland has outshone Europe with an average annual rate of 4.7 per cent compared to a European rate of 1.0 per cent.

Table 5.1: Average annual growth rates, GDP per capita, 1950-94

Period	Ireland	UK	Europe
1950-60	2.2	2.3	3.7
1960-73	3.7	2.6	4.2
1973-88	2.1	1.9	1.9
1988-94	4.7	0.4	1.0
1950-94	2.9	2.0	2.9

Source: Derived from OECD National Accounts (unpublished worksheets kindly supplied by Angus Maddison).
Taken from: Cormac Ó Gráda and Kevin O'Rourke: "Economic growth: performance and explanations" in J.W. O'Hagan, ed., *The Economy of Ireland*, Gill and Macmillan, 1995, p.212.

In looking at the period overall, Ó Gráda and O'Rourke show that the Irish and the European average annual rates end up as being the same – 2.9 per cent, with the bulk of the Irish growth coming in the final six years. Yet, they highlight a number of factors which show just how poor the Irish performance was for much of that period. For example, Greece, Portugal and Spain, other peripheral and relatively underdeveloped countries to which Ireland is often compared, grew at an annual rate of 3.8 per cent over the 44-year period, overtaking Ireland in terms of GDP per capita between 1950 and 1973. Only in the recent period did Ireland overtake them again. Furthermore, when the difference between Irish GDP and GNP is taken into account, the country's actual performance in terms of real living standards would be worse.[11]

Ireland's recent success has therefore transformed its relative position and given the lie to the view that its relative decline is somehow inexorable. But placing this success in a longer timeframe does raises questions about its sustainability. For it is the success which has been exceptional and it still remains to be seen whether it is "more than a transient phenomenon".[12] Can

Poverty Amid Plenty

we now feel more secure that, after a long period of relative decline, we are on an upward development path? The question is one that exercises Irish policymakers and politicians. For example, a major report by the semi-state agency Forfás for the government in May 1996 set out a strategy to halve the rate of unemployment, reduce the number of long-term unemployed to 50,000 and increase living standards to the EU average, all by 2010.[13] The previous month, the Department of Enterprise and Employment had published a strategy paper enunciating a goal of full employment and of greater equity in the labour market.[14] The aspiration for development is ambitious therefore, but are the goals realistic?

Before examining some of the more central problems of Irish development which will make these goals difficult to achieve, two comments need to be entered to allow for a more realistic assessment of Ireland's present impressive growth rates. The first relates to the impact of EU structural funds and the fact that the continuation of these beyond 1999 cannot be guaranteed; the second relates to some doubts raised about the growth figures themselves.

The period of high Irish growth rates coincides with a large increase in EU structural funds. With the effective doubling of structural funds for the 1993-99 period, Ireland has been in receipt of transfers worth around 10 per cent of its GNP. Alan Matthews has put this level of aid in a world context: "This is an extraordinarily high figure even by the standards of Third World aid. Only in poverty-stricken sub-Saharan Africa does one find official overseas transfers making up such a large proportion of a country's national income."[15] Such a level of receipts is therefore one reason for the high growth rates since the late 1980s; Matthews estimated that they would result in the annual rate of GNP growth being 0.5 to 0.6 of a percentage point higher than it would otherwise be and that Irish GNP might be around 5 per cent higher in 2000 as a result of these funds than it would be without them.[16] With the enlargement of the European Union to take in poorer countries in eastern and southern Europe (Cyprus, Malta, Poland, Hungary and the Czech Republic are in line for membership by around the year 2000), it is very unlikely that Ireland will be in receipt of such a high injection of aid following this round of structural funds. The big question raised by this scenario is therefore what impact a substantial reduction will have on Irish growth rates. Matthews poses the question starkly: "[W]ould Ireland stand strengthened to meet the rigours of competition in the twenty-first century or would it have become so dependent on these Funds that it would be unable to withstand the shock?"[17]

In practice, what is likely to happen is that the level of structural funds that Ireland will receive after 1999 will be much reduced and that such a reduction will have the effect of reducing Irish growth rates. Forfás calculates the GNP growth rates required by Ireland up to 2010 if it is to fulfill the target of increasing living standards to the EU average. With zero growth rates in the EU, Ireland would need a 2.9 per cent rate; with 2 per cent growth rates in the EU, Ireland would need a 4.9 rate; and with a 4 per cent EU rate, Ireland would need close to a 7 per cent rate.[18] Given that Ireland has achieved a 4.4 per cent growth rate over the 1992-95 period with an EU growth rate of 1.5 per cent, the Forfás projections seem based on maintaining a similar growth rate well into the next decade. This may prove overly optimistic.

A second and more serious question that has been raised about Irish growth rates concerns their reliability. Some economists believe figures for economic growth and labour productivity are severely distorted due to the practice of transfer pricing engaged in by multinational companies, declaring in the low-tax Irish economy profits which have been made elsewhere. As one economist, Antoin E. Murphy, put it: "The dominance of the foreign owned MNCs in the generation of manufacturing output and exports, combining with the belief that a great part of this growth is just transfer pricing, implies that a great part of Ireland's so called economic growth is illusory being derived from the accountants' pens rather than the effort of Irish workers."[19] This leads him to conclude that the government's performance in regard to such items as public sector expenditure, taxation, the Exchequer borrowing requirement and the public sector borrowing requirement may not in fact be as healthy as it seems.[20]

Despite doubts raised about the reliability of Irish economic indicators, it is clear that by the 1990s Ireland had entered a period of strong economic growth. Even if this slows a little, it seems reasonable to predict that the economy will not return to the situation of relative decline in which it seemed locked for too long. Yet, for the development theorist, economic growth may be a necessary condition for development[21] but it is by no means a sufficient condition. For example, the term "Celtic Tiger" implies that Ireland's performance emulates that of the East Asian "Tigers" of South Korea, Taiwan, Singapore and Hong Kong (see Chapter 3), the group of countries which have perhaps most successfully made the transition from underdevelopment to development since the second World War. But the success of this group was based on far more than healthy growth rates; it related very much to the structure of the economy and how this was nurtured by the state to develop indigenous high-tech industries capable of competing successfully on the international market. This leads us to examine the structure of the Irish economy and its adequacy to face the challenge of development in a globalised world economy.

A Celtic Tiger?

The challenges of developing a modern industrial economy in Ireland cannot be fully appreciated unless the structure of the economy inherited at independence and the various attempts to overcome this legacy are briefly dealt with. This then forms the backdrop for a critical discussion of more recent industrial policy. Two main trends dominated the development of the Irish economy in the 19th century. One of these was the growing dependence of agriculture on pasture, particularly in the post-Famine period, as the raising of cattle mostly for export became the dominant activity. By the time most of the island achieved independence in 1921, Irish agriculture approximated to a typical "Third World" mono-crop type. In 1929, 85.99 per cent of exports by value were agricultural and the export of live animals, mostly cattle, to Britain made up 42.08 per cent of all exports.

Meanwhile, most Irish industry was in decline, unable to compete in a free trade zone with technologically superior British industry. The one exception was the Belfast region which became a zone of industrial development within the British economy. Andy Bielenberg's pioneering study of industry in the Cork region concludes that "the industrial base of the Cork city region was narrower in 1900 than it had been in 1800 ... It is clear that most of the industries of the region were unable to respond to the changes brought about by the integration of the region into the more industrial British economy"[22]. This conclusion can be generalised for the rest of Ireland outside the north-east. By the early 20th century therefore, excluding food and drink, "the south was virtually without industries"[23] and the employment profile of the Free State economy had a typical "Third World" character with 36 per cent employed in agriculture, 24 per cent in industry and 41 per cent in services.[24]

For the first decade of independence, the Cumann na

nGaedheal government made little effort to change this situation and its export and economic policy was primarily based upon promoting the cattle trade with Britain. When Fianna Fáil came to power in 1932, policy changed completely as the new government made a determined attempt to develop native industry with active state involvement within a domestic economy protected by high tariff barriers. This policy approximated closely to the policy of import substitution industrialisation (ISI) followed by many underdeveloped countries at the time, most especially in Latin America (see Chapter 2). This policy succeeded in fostering the development of an indigenous Irish industrial base (predominantly though not exclusively Irish-owned) supplying domestic goods for the protected home market. By the early 1950s it had reached the limits of its expansion when timid industrial policy coupled with conservative fiscal management led to a severe crisis in the Irish economy. This led to a complete about-turn in policy with the adoption of an outward-looking industrial strategy following the *Programme for Economic Expansion* in 1958.

The liberalisation of the economy initiated the second major attempt to overcome the situation of underdevelopment inherited from the 19th century. Foreign investment in the form of multinational companies setting up plants throughout the Republic led to a second wave of industrialisation. On this occasion, however, it was oriented to export markets rather than to domestic needs and the requirements of the multinational sector gradually came to dominate state policy. Industrial employment and living standards grew, resulting in a reversal of the population decline through emigration which had reached alarming proportions in the 1950s. Native industry proved less than resilient in the newly competitive environment, however. Much of the indigenous industry built up behind tariff barriers found it hard to survive as became very evident in the 1980s which was a time of major downturn for the Irish economy. This saw sluggish growth rates and a severe contraction of employment which hit indigenous industry particularly hard as shown in Table 5:2. Thus the apparently modern industrial structure which was built up in Ireland from the 1960s to the 1990s hid a more typically dualistic "Third World" industrial structure. As O'Sullivan summed it up: "A modern sector with a high level of productivity which is for the most part foreign-owned coexists with a traditional indigenous sector characterised by low productivity that has been in decline since the 1970s."[25]

Table 5.2: Changes in industrial[a] employment[b], 1973-94

	Irish	Non-Irish	Total
Total employment 1973	145,815	69,388	215,203
Total employment 1994	114,613	90,099	204,712
Net change in employment 1973-94	– 31,202	20,711	– 10,491
Total job gain 1973-94	231,999	161,866	393,885
Total job loss 1973-94	263,201	141,175	404,376

Source: IDA Employment Survey files.

[a] Includes mining, quarrying and turf production

[b] Data in this table are those collected in the IDA Employment Surveys taken on 1 January 1973 and 1 November 1994.

Taken from: Mary O'Sullivan: "Manufacturing and Global Competition" in J.W. O'Hagan, ed: *The Economy of Ireland*, Gill and Macmillan, 1995, p.369.

It is the nature of the Irish indigenous sector which provides the greatest contrast with the East Asian "Tigers". In contrast to the innovative, high-tech indigenous sector built up through active government intervention in those countries, Irish indigenous industry is characterised by its low level of technological sophistication, being largely concentrated "in low-value-added activities often in sheltered sectors of the economy".[26] Even the few successful indigenous companies that have built up large reserves of cash have tended to re-invest it in expanding low-skilled, sheltered activities.[27] O'Sullivan sums up Irish industrial activity as being the very opposite of that in the East Asian "Tiger" countries: "Irish-based industrial activity seems to be caught in a vicious circle. It neither relies on highly-sophisticated technological nor marketing capabilities nor does it provide a basis on which such sophisticated capabilities can be developed. In the indigenous sector investments to develop such capabilities have never been made on a significant scale."[28] Charles Sabel, however, in his OECD study on local partnerships and social innovation in Ireland, found that a great deal is changing in Irish industry, both foreign plants and indigenous industry, in terms of new productive and organisational processes and systems though he does admit that the impact of these changes on the competitiveness of individual firms or of the economy as a whole "is difficult to gauge".[29]

Turning to the multinational industrial sector in Ireland, O'Sullivan points out that despite the move towards more high-tech industries such as electronics and chemicals in the late 1970s and the 1980s, only low levels of skill are demanded of most of the Irish workforce in these plants. The proportion of skilled workers in these plants compares unfavourably with more developed countries, she writes, and adds that most training for Irish workers is "designed to improve dexterity in routine operations rather than to develop multiple, flexible skills that could serve as a basis for innovative activities".[30] Because Irish policy has been oriented to attracting such industries to Ireland, the state here has made little effort to ensure either a strong level of linkages with domestic industry or access to their high-tech skills which could be put to use in other sectors of the Irish economy. This contrasts strongly with the practice of other relatively underdeveloped countries, particularly the East Asian "Tigers".

The dualistic nature of the Irish economy and the need to build strong, high-tech competitive indigenous industry has been recommended in numerous authoritative reports from Telesis (1982) to Culliton (1992). Yet, as O'Sullivan puts it, government response has been conservative and hesitant. Referring to the need recognised by the East Asian "Tigers" that sophisticated technological capabilities must be strategically created somewhere in the economy through active government intervention, O'Sullivan characterises Irish industrial policy by contrast as being based "on the hope that given the right financial incentives such capabilities would simply emerge, a hope that reflects a lack of understanding of the complexity of the social process underlying the process of development".[31] The high-level of government intervention in the economy has been directed more to ensuring that jobs are created through grants and other inducements rather than to ensuring that the necessary capabilities are built up in the economy, as happened in East Asia, she writes. Enormous effort and cost have been put into job creation in the two decades from 1973-94; this created a massive 393,885 jobs in that period but 404,376 jobs were lost in the same period.

Irish industrial policy therefore is running simply to keep up with itself. Ireland has been very successful in attracting foreign investment but reliance on such a motor force for development is at best precarious. More attention is now being given to indigenous industry but the scale of the challenges as outlined by O'Sullivan and the level of government market-friendly intervention required may neither be fully appreciated nor has the state showed the requisite capability to carry out such a role. In this crucial aspect then, Ireland is far from being a "Celtic

Tiger" and is, in fact, closer to the profile of a Third World country. As Barry has stated: "Notwithstanding the fact that Ireland has been regarded internationally as a successful example of the application of the outward-oriented strategy, the dual nature of its economy is very marked, and it might usefully be thought of as a high-income developing country rather than a low-income industrialized country."[32] Another formulation which seems to describe the Irish economy more accurately than does the term "Celtic Tiger" is that used by Dieter Senghaas who distinguishes between an export economy and an integrated national economy.[33] In the former, the wealth generated by a healthy export sector flows only partially through the national economy, being either concentrated in "enclaves" within the national economy or else flowing out in the forms of profit repatriation.[34] In addition to maintaining healthy growth rates, therefore, the Irish economy has still a long way to go if it is to develop the capabilities to generate the sort of self-sustaining, innovative indigenous enterprises that will provide a more firm foundation for all-around national development. Yet the quality of Irish entrepreneurship, so necessary for such a task, may also prove a problem.

Indigenous entrepreneurship

Attention has been drawn to the quality of Irish entrepreneurship by a series of scandals in major Irish companies in the early 1990s. In a study entitled *Culture and Capitalism in Contemporary Ireland*, Paul Keating and Derry Desmond examine the nature of Irish entrepreneurship as evidenced by low standards in high places. They identify four categories of disturbing behaviour.

The first relates to the "new class of politically-dependent capitalists"[35] which emerged in the 1960s with close links to senior figures in Fianna Fáil. But instead of their dynamism and political connections being used to develop the productive resources of the Irish economy, they were used almost exclusively to make large amounts of money quickly from speculation on property, much of it underwritten by the state. The second category relates to the Irish industrial establishment which the authors conclude has exhibited "complacency and 'short-termism'" in the face of the huge developmental challenges of the Irish economy.[36] Examples they give relate to the low level of investment in research and development and to widespread "moral laxity and easy-going attitudes to work and to business".[37] Thirdly, they examine attitudes in Irish agriculture and find "short-term greed, combined with a tolerance for a situation which discloses high levels of inefficiency, waste and slovenliness"[38] as evidenced by the state's poor record on the eradication of bovine TB, the failure to eradicate mastitis, the dependence on EU intervention schemes and on the Common Agricultural Policy and the starving of agriculture co-ops of long-term funds by farmers more interested in getting as high a price as possible for their milk. Keating and Desmond entitle their fourth category "failures, fraud and frolics".[39] Under this heading, they detail such practices as widespread tax evasion by companies and individuals, the failure to maintain high standards of quality in Irish products and what they call the "Phoenix syndrome" under which proprietors of limited liability companies run up debts, liquidate their companies to avoid payment and then establish new companies unhindered by liabilities.

The conclusions of Keating and Desmond seem important enough to quote at some length since they touch directly on the implications of these widespread practices for Irish development. One does not have to believe that entrepreneurship alone will solve all our developmental problems for us to agree that it is a necessary requirement for their solution. The authors write: "It is perfectly possible to specify the kind of entrepreneurial action which Ireland needs if it is to achieve the levels of economic development to which its people seem to aspire; given the small size of its home market its entrepreneurs need to become involved in the internationally-traded goods and services sectors; given Ireland's natural resource base – principally its agricultural potential – they need to raise productivity and add value to the natural products that are available; they need to develop new products for new markets, and, given the nature of the competition and the standards demanded by consumers, they need to attend to quality, to enhance reliability and to eschew those activities which can alienate customers and thus destroy opportunities for themselves and for others operating in their economy. When it is measured against these specifications, the behaviour of Irish entrepreneurs does not, in the main, seem to be the sort of behaviour that conduces to the achievement of economic development; they have not attacked opportunities lying in the internationally-traded goods and services sectors; they have not increased the value-added to the natural products of their country, being mainly content to continue in the traditional patterns of low value-added commodity trading; they

Poverty Amid Plenty

have not developed new products for new markets, but have been happy with a nice, neat little profit derived from operating on their traditional home markets; they have clearly also failed to service existing markets effectively through cultivating appropriate standards of quality and reliability; they have shown a capacity for unethical and imprudent dealing which has damaged their own reputations, the commercial reputation of the country, hindered the operation of other units operating in their economy, and, through tax evasion, damaged the Irish state. On the whole, therefore, the spirit of Irish entrepreneurship seems to rest in an easy-going, complacent attitude to economic activity which amounts to a 'sheer torpor' and which is too-often combined with unscrupulous and unethical dealing. Either way the result is the same: the cause of Irish economic development is not advanced, indeed, it is often frustrated and hindered."[40]

Entrenched poverty, inequality

The dualistic nature of the Irish economy and the outflow of profits alert us to another crucial issue for development. For growth rates and even a successful high-tech industrial sector alone cannot be said to constitute development if their benefits do not flow widely throughout society, helping to improve the living standards and opportunities of the vast majority of the population. An entrenched problem of poverty and particularly of social exclusion poses serious question marks therefore for development and requires examination in the Irish case.

A paper given by Séamus Ó Cinnéide[41] to a poverty conference organised by the Catholic bishops' Council for Social Welfare in 1971 is often referred to as the "rediscovery of poverty" in Ireland.[42] Since then, extensive quantitative research has deepened our knowledge of the extent of poverty. While the findings have been challenged,[43] there is widespread agreement among researchers, policymakers and social activists for the conclusions of Nolan and Callan that between the years 1973-87 "the proportion of people in poverty in Ireland is consistently seen to have risen, across a range of poverty lines and equivalence scales".[44] For the research on which this conclusion is based which was carried out in 1987, Nolan and Callan use poverty lines set at 40 per cent, 50 per cent and 60 per cent of average income. This shows that in 1973 between 15 and 18 per cent of the population lived on half the average income. By 1987 this had increased to 20-23 per cent.

There are many reasons why such a high proportion of the population should have been in poverty in the mid 1980s. Added to the poor performance of the economy from the beginning of the 1980s to 1987 was a very high economic dependency ratio throughout the same period, with high unemployment and a large child population. Since then, however, the situation has markedly improved.[45] Especially welcome was evidence from the 1995 labour force survey showing a substantial increase in numbers at work, from 1.176 million in 1994 to 1.231 million in 1995. These figures, coupled with a declining dependency ratio as the numbers at work grow and those dependent on them (especially children) fall, presents a far more favourable prospect for alleviating poverty in the years ahead. It is therefore to be expected that when the results of the 1994 ESRI poverty survey are published, they will show a decline in rates of poverty for the first time since figures began to be compiled in the early 1970s.

A number of indicators, however, give cause for concern that the crisis of the 1980s has left us with a structured problem of semi-permanent exclusion of a substantial minority from Irish society that may prove far from easy to eradicate, even if the will is there to do so. The first indicator is that at a time of sustained high growth rates, the rate of unemployment has remained stubbornly high. This the labour force survey put at 192,000 in April 1995 but a discrepancy between this figure and the numbers signing on for welfare assistance every month which totalled 276,000 in April 1995 has never been adequately explained. While the government likes to use the former figure, the discrepancy may indicate what Kieran Kennedy has called "a relatively high incidence of discouraged workers" in the Irish situation.[46] This relates to the fact that some groups, like housewives working solely in the home, will curb a desire to return to the labour force at times of poor economic growth but might begin to take initial steps into the workforce when growth picks up. It is therefore more likely that the real figure of those who want to find work in the Irish economy but fail to do so is closer to the higher figure than to that of the labour force survey.

A more worrying indicator of the extent of social exclusion in Irish society is the growth in the numbers of those out of work for a year or longer, the so-called long-term unemployed. A 1995 government report estimated that the rate of long-term unemployment rose from 35,000 or 2.8 per cent of the workforce in 1980 to 135,000 or 10 per cent of the workforce in 1993. Some 50 per cent of all those unemployed fall into this category. The report highlighted the distinctive nature of this

136   *Poverty Amid Plenty*

problem compared to the unemployment problem in other countries with which Ireland is normally grouped: "In fact, Irish long-term unemployment is higher than the overall unemployment rate in most OECD countries. This is despite the fact that our rate of short-term unemployment is broadly similar to those found elsewhere in the OECD."[47] Over half the long-term unemployed have been without work for over three years and two-fifths for more than five years, the report added.[48] Furthermore, as a May 1996 document of the National Economic and Social Forum pointed out, despite extensive government programmes to try to ensure that those who are long-term unemployed can benefit from new job opportunities, only one in every 16 job vacancies filled in 1995 went to a person who had been long-term unemployed.[49]

A third indicator of the depth of social exclusion is studies which show that the cost of economic restructuring has been borne by the unskilled manual working class[50] and that the state's taxation and welfare system operates in such as way that it fails to redistribute income from the beneficiaries of the economic system to its victims. As O'Connell and Rottman have written, the welfare system has resulted in "intervention spread thin, in the form of minimal social rights, rather than deep, in the form of programmes targeted to those most in need." As a result, it has not been "sufficient to overturn privilege".[51] Paradoxically, therefore, the welfare system in Ireland has tended to reinforce the inequalities generated by market forces. As Breen et al. grimly conclude, the only option for the state "is simply to maintain the most disadvantaged sections of the economically active population in their marginality. And if there are children, that marginality will be perpetuated in the next generation".[52]

A final indicator relates to growing inequality in income distribution and in life chances. In a situation in which a significant minority of the population depend on social welfare payments for an income, economic growth paradoxically tends to exacerbate inequality since wage rises tend to be greater than rises in social welfare. For example, between 1986 and 1993 average social welfare recipients saw their income increase by 28.9 per cent whereas the average industrial wage increased by 35.2 per cent, the wage of a clerical assistant in the civil service by 40.3 per cent, the wages of heads of department in large private-sector companies by 58.2 per cent and the wages of the secretaries of government departments by 72.4 per cent.[53] Even among those in employment, figures show the earnings of those in the expanding multinational sector rising substantially faster than those in low-tech indigenous sectors. Thus provisional Central Statistics Office figures for December 1995 showed that the average weekly earnings in manufacturing rose by slightly less than 2 per cent; in the office and data processing sector weekly pay rose from £251 to £289 between September 1994 and September 1995 but in clothing firms it rose by only 80p to £148, due to some extent to a slight fall in hours worked.[54] This may be no more than is expected but it does underline a steady rise in inequality. Unfortunately, little research has been done on trends in income distribution; in analysing the Household Budget Surveys' data from 1973, 1980 and 1987, Callan and Nolan found the distribution of gross income to have widened but of disposable income (after taxation and social welfare transfers) to have narrowed. They also point, however, to a major change in the composition of those on low income over that period, from elderly people to the unemployed. One of the results of this is a dramatic increase over the period in the numbers of children living in poverty, from 16 per cent to 26 per cent.[55] Again these findings are consistent with a problem of entrenched social exclusion. Finally, even less is known about trends in wealth distribution in Ireland which one would expect to be more unequal than income distribution.

Compounding this inequality are trends in class mobility. Research here also points to a problem of entrenched social exclusion. Breen and Whelan find a substantial improvement in the mobility chances of those from petit bourgeois and farming origins but an extremely low level of upward mobility from the working class, particularly the unskilled manual class. This latter figure marks out Ireland as being distinctive, they say.[56] Referring to the implications of these findings, they conclude: "A society with restricted opportunities for upward mobility automatically denies many the opportunity of sharing in important socially created goods while guaranteeing the privileged positions of certain groups. More recently concern has grown that those who are denied the opportunity for upward mobility are not simply trapped at the bottom of the class hierarchy but are, in an important sense, forced outside the class system and come to constitute an 'underclass'."[57]

Despite growing prosperity and higher living standards for many sectors of Irish society, therefore, a significant minority of the population has been left further and further behind. As the Taoiseach, John Bruton, put it, Irish society is "ever more polarised ... between the well-educated, securely employed and affluent majority, on the one hand, and the poorly educated, unemployed and/or intermittently employed poor" on the other.[58] Referring to two suburbs of Dublin, west Tallaght and north Clondalkin with a population of some 25,000 each and an unemployment rate of between 65 per cent and 75 per cent, a source close to junior minister Pat Rabbitte was quoted as saying that "they are almost totally unplugged from the economy. Capitalism does not exist there".[59] Statistics, however, fail to communicate the impact of such deprivation on the lives of people living in this situation; this is best understood from accounts written by these people.[60]

Emigration and demographics

The persistence of relatively high unemployment at a time of high economic growth alerts us to another feature of Ireland's development profile. For its high rate of emigration has acted as a safety valve whereby those who could not find work in the Irish economy went elsewhere to find it. At times of economic growth and improved opportunity at home, some of these return to take up the new jobs that become available. More importantly in terms of Ireland's longer term development, it has allowed Irish living standards rise in a situation of severe structural underdevelopment. As Kevin O'Rourke has put it, emigration has been "one of the key driving forces in the Irish economy" allowing rising living standards go hand in hand with deindustrialisation.[61]

The continuous decline of Ireland's population from the 1850s to the 1970s is unique. As the Norwegian social scientist, Lars Mjøset writes: "There is simply no similar demographic experience anywhere in the modern world, so far."[62] Mainstream academic consideration of the topic has been dominated by what Mac Laughlin calls the "narrow logic of cost-benefit analysis"[63] which weighs the pros and cons of emigration and concludes that it has had its benefits as well as its drawbacks for the national economy. Some establishment sectors have taken an even more upbeat view, expressed most memorably by the former Tánaiste, Brian Lenihan, when he said that "we can't all live on a small island" and that "we should be proud" of emigration.[64] This is an example of what Mac Laughlin regards as the redefinition of emigration since the modernisation of Irish society in the 1960s so that it is now presented as an example of the dynamic and enterprising spirit of young Irish people. This he regards as the "naturalisation and sanitation" of emigration.[65]

Emigration remains, however, both a symptom of the relative underdevelopment of the Irish economy and, for some scholars, a factor contributing to that underdevelopment. Mac Laughlin presents evidence showing that the difference between modern Irish emigrants and their predecessors has been greatly exaggerated. Most who leave Ireland do so at a young age, poorly qualified and out of economic and social necessity. Neither is emigration a path towards upward mobility for them as most end up in relatively low-level positions.[66] Persistent emigration is held by social scientists to have drained Irish society of its youthful dynamism, with the result that far less pressure has been applied for radical change at home than might otherwise have been the case. This, for example, is offered by some political scientists as a reason for the dominance of conservative politics within the Irish party system. The impact on rural communities has also been widely mentioned. For example, the much publicised report of the group Developing the West Together, entitled *A Crusade for Survival* and published in February 1994, spoke of "the disintegration of society caused by emigration".[67] In his study of Irish underdevelopment, Mjøset identified emigration as undermining the development of indigenous industry: "Cumulative processes involving emigration and a contracting domestic demand may be crucial factors in explaining the dismal development of indigenous Irish manufacturing industry."[68]

Emigration is therefore a complex phenomenon intimately linked to Ireland's development. It has given Ireland a unique demographic profile but, as argued in the previous section, key aspects of this profile such as its dependency ratio are now moving towards the EU norm. Indeed, with a growing workforce and small numbers of dependants, Ireland looks set to have a more favourable demographic profile for the early decades of the next century than most of our EU neighbours whose populations are fast ageing. This will certainly help us in the task of raising living standards and increasing employment. Yet, emigration remains an uncertain factor. On the one hand a booming economy at home tends to attract emigrants home, thus adding to the difficulty of drawing excluded sectors into the workforce. On the other hand, an upturn in the British and EU economy is expected to lead to a further outflow from the labour force at home thus improving the prospects for those who remain.[69] However, will such an outflow reduce the pressure required if we are to face the challenges of tackling the structural weaknesses of Irish industry and of the Irish social structure as outlined above? This remains a crucial question for Ireland's development prospects.

Interrogating development

In conclusion, we return to the question posed in the title to this chapter: in the light of our description of Irish society and the Irish economy, should we call Ireland developed or underdeveloped? Our dominant understandings of what constitutes development have been heavily influenced by modernisation theory (see Chapter 2). Thus, a state in which industry and services contribute more to GDP than does agriculture, in which most of the population lives in urban centres, and which has relatively high levels of literacy and life expectancy is seen as being well on the way to development. If this understanding of development is accepted, there is then no question but that Ireland is a developed country.

However, this chapter has highlighted some aspects of the Irish situation which pose serious questions about our level of development. While recent economic growth is a welcome phenomenon which opens prospects for development, it does not itself constitute development. Indeed, many underdeveloped countries have periods of substantial economic growth.[70] It is very important therefore to look further than growth rates and to ask deeper questions about a country's economic and social structure to determine its development prospects. The best time to ask such hard questions is at a time of growth when the real potential of an economy to generate sustainable social development can be most clearly seen.

Development theory draws a distinction between economic growth and social development. The former may be a necessary condition for the latter but theorists have also reminded us that growth can lead to a distorted development, improving the living standards of some sections of the population but leaving others ever further behind. Furthermore, questions need to be asked about the foundations of such growth. This concerns obvious questions such as whether it is based on a high level of foreign borrowing, a situation many countries fell into in the 1970s (including Ireland) and the costs of which they dearly paid in the 1980s (again including Ireland). But less attention has been paid to other questions about sustainability, namely whether the process of economic growth is accumulating the skills and innovative capacities in an economy which lay a firm foundation for maintaining a competitive edge in the future. The knock-on effects generated by these processes are neatly captured by Mjøset's typologies of vicious circles and virtuous circles.[71] While some of the elements constituting the vicious circles identified by

Mjøset may no longer apply, it is less sure that Ireland has entered a virtuous circle of development given the issues relating to the nature of Irish industrialisation and to social exclusion outlined in this chapter.

The issue of social exclusion reminds us that the links between economy and society can never be taken for granted. Indeed, the way the economy is embedded in society can be crucial to questions of distributing the benefits of economic growth. This process happens not just through the state's taxation and social welfare policies, creaming off a surplus and redistributing it, but through the very way the economy is structured. Thus, for example, an industrialisation process that develops through adding value in an ever more sophisticated manner to the raw materials of a country (such as Denmark where the processing of agricultural produce laid the basis not just for a food processing industry but also for engineering, mechanical and more recently high-tech manufacturing and is a good example for Ireland) is far more embedded in that country's social structure than an industrialisation process largely dependent on multinational companies setting up plants. Usually such plants and what they manufacture are not well related either to the raw materials of the region in which they set up nor to the skills of the local population. Similarly, state policies of education and training can be closely interlinked with the needs of industry or they can take a rather hit-and-miss approach, presuming that if enough people with needed technical skills are produced they will benefit the national economy. But, as the Irish experience shows, such people can often end up having to emigrate (thus constituting what Wickham has called "a free gift from Ireland to the richer economies of the US and Europe"[72]) and, perhaps more seriously still, the potential of such an educational and training policy for generating greater equality is greatly weakened. As the East Asian "Tigers" or the social democratic countries of Europe (particularly Scandinavia) show us, growth does not have to lead to inequality if the marginalised sectors of a country's society are linked in a firm way into the process of growth. These, then, are some of the issues to which development theory alerts us when considering a country's level of development. Based on them it is difficult to conclude that Ireland is at the developed end of the spectrum. Instead, the dualistic structure of its industrial sector and its problem of social exclusion are more typical of an underdeveloped country.

Is it accurate, then, to describe Ireland as occupying a semi-peripheral position in the world economic system, as was mentioned in Chapter 2? It seems to be where Wallerstein would

Poverty Amid Plenty

place Ireland as, in a listing of semi-peripheral states, he mentions "the whole outer rim of Europe"[73] and another study done from the same theoretical perspective found Ireland to occupy a semi-peripheral category with Cuba, former East Germany, Hungary, Cyprus, Bulgaria, Romania, USSR, Kenya, Iran, Turkey, Iraq, Lebanon, Jordan and Israel.[74] For our purposes, however, a more recent analysis by Michel Peillon is more useful. This compared Ireland with the other 11 countries of the European Union (before enlargement to 15 in 1995) under five headings – the pattern of economic development, the central place of the state, the growth of the state, a weak civil society and social inequalities. Only under the first heading does Peillon find Ireland to belong to the semi-peripheral grouping of Spain, Portugal and Greece. Under the other headings, Ireland is closer to the core countries. Thus, he concludes that Ireland "provides a striking illustration of the disjunction which emerges between a process of capitalist development and the institutional development in these countries."[75] Peillon's study is unsatisfactory, however, in that it gives the five headings used equal significance. It fails therefore to distinguish between what might be regarded as the causal mechanism of a country's position in the international economy (its dependent model of development with a large reliance on multinational industry as the motor of development) and some of the institutional consequences of that form of development. Thus the differences in the nature and role of the state in the Irish case are not necessarily sufficient to conclude that Ireland belongs to the core countries. Interestingly, Wallerstein himself offers a completely different set of criteria for identifying semi-peripheral countries than the ones Peillon uses – "a larger external and a weaker internal property-owning bourgeoisie; a better-paid professional sector and a more poorly paid sector of fully proletarianized workers, but a far larger (and probably worse off) sector of semiproletarianized workers".[76] It would be interesting to construct ways to measure where Ireland might stand on this set of criteria (in which Ireland's serious problem of social exclusion would find adequate recognition). This attempt to categorise Ireland's developmental status must therefore remain inconclusive. However, in one very crucial and probably decisive way, namely its dependent pattern of development, Ireland still clearly is a semi-peripheral country.

Finally, in discussing Ireland's developmental status it is important to make a distinction between the legacy of long-term underdevelopment and the effects of the current economic restructuring through which almost all the world's countries are passing under the impact of technological development and of the globalisation of production and finance. Most developed countries are exhibiting high levels of unemployment as traditional industries decline and new industries emerge. It is too early to say whether the developed world will, over the long term, have to come to live with relatively high levels of structural unemployment as is the case in Ireland. If so, then perhaps the conclusion will need to be drawn that they are underdeveloping. Meanwhile, it is clear that Ireland's development history and the problems highlighted in this chapter set it apart from most countries considered developed. For, as Mjøset points out, Ireland (excluding the north-east of the island) missed out on the "Golden Age" of economic and social development that western Europe experienced from the 1950s to the 1970s. He concludes therefore that Ireland's problems are more complex that theirs since it "must find a position in the restructuring race on the basis of having missed the opportunities of the Golden Age".[77] Kieran Kennedy draws attention to another challenge facing Ireland that is greater than that faced by most western European countries when he writes that "the employment challenge in Ireland is on an altogether higher relative scale than in the Community as a whole".[78] He finds it hard to believe that the high levels of disadvantage in the four periphery countries of the EU (Ireland, Spain, Portugal and Greece) "could be tackled effectively without substantial additional resources, going beyond the present level of CSF funding".[79]

There are many reasons for Ireland being in this position. There is the legacy of long-term underdevelopment inherited from the colonial period, a legacy which Ireland has never yet overcome with complete success. This has been exacerbated by the country's demographic profile in the 1980s when the dependency ratio placed great burdens on a relatively small workforce. Macro-economic management of the economy in the late 1970s and early 1980s also added a severe debt burden. On top of these problems, Ireland is having to cope with the same challenges as every other economy – technological innovation and economic globalisation. In this situation its performance since the late 1980s has been highly creditable. Yet, as this chapter has argued, deeper challenges remain. Until we face and overcome these, it is both inaccurate and unwise to regard Ireland as developed.

Footnotes

1 Kieran A. Kennedy, *Facing the Unemployment Crisis in Ireland*, Cork University Press, 1993, p.43

2 For an account by a former senior EU official which mentions this dual stand by the Irish government in late 1992 and early 1993, see Bernard Connolly, *The Rotten Heart of Europe*, Faber and Faber, 1995

3 See the World Bank's annual *World Development Report* published by Oxford University Press. In the 1995 report, Ireland was second from the bottom of the 24 "high-income economies" with a per capita GNP of $13,000, above New Zealand. In the 1994 report, Ireland was at the bottom of the 23 "high-income economies" listed, with a per capita income of $12,210 just below New Zealand. In 1993, Ireland was also at the bottom of this category.

4 Based on private consumption per capita using current purchasing power parities, from *OECD Economic Surveys 1995, Ireland*, OECD, 1995.

5 Joseph Lee, *Ireland Politics and Society, 1912-1985*, Cambridge, 1989, p.521

6 Kieran A. Kennedy, et al., *The Economic Development of Ireland in the Twentieth Century*, Routledge, 1988, p.14. See also D. M. W. N. Hitchens and J. E. Birnie, *The Competitiveness of Industry in Ireland*, Avebury, 1994.

7 Dieter Senghaas, *The European Experience: A Historical Critique of Development Theory*, Berg, 1985, p.129

8 J. Bradford De Long, "Productivity growth, convergence, and welfare: comment" in *The American Economic Review*, vol., 78, no., 5, 1988, p.1148

9 Cormac Ó Gráda and Kevin O'Rourke, "Economic growth: performance and explanations" in J. W. O'Hagan, ed., *The Economy of Ireland: Policy and Performance of a Small European Country*, Gill & Macmillan, 1995, p.213

10 ibid., p.213

11 For most countries, the difference between gross domestic product (GDP) and gross national product (GNP) is minimal. GDP measures the value of all the goods and services produced in the economy while GNP measures the value left in the economy after net flows of capital, factor payments and transfer payments are taken into account. The latter therefore is a better measure of income accruing to Irish people and is the relevant measure when we wish to assess the impact of economic growth on social development. In the Republic, the ratio of GNP to GDP has declined from almost 100 per cent in the early 1970s to 88 per cent in 1994.

12 Ó Gráda and O'Rourke, op. cit., p.226

13 *Shaping our Future: A Strategy for Enterprise in Ireland in the 21st Century*, Forfás, 1996, p.xxii

14 *Growing and Sharing our Employment: Strategy Paper on the Labour Market*, Department of Enterprise and Employment, 1996, p.16

15 Alan Matthews, *Managing the EU Structural Funds in Ireland*, Cork University Press, 1994, p.32

16 ibid., p.51

17 ibid., p.53

18 Forfás, op. cit., p.12

19 Antoin E. Murphy, *The Irish Economy: Celtic Tiger or Tortoise?*, Money Markets International, 1994, p.2

20 It has been pointed out, however, that even if export figures are exaggerated, this does not affect the balance of payments current account, since profit outflows are deductible under trading and investment income. See Dermot McAleese and Fiona Hayes, "European integration, the balance of payments and inflation" in J. W. O'Hagan, op. cit., p.269.

21 This comment is not meant to deny the position of some economists (as outlined in Chapter 4) that growth may itself have to be severely limited if development is to be sustainable. This position is not compatible with mainstream economics and development theory in the terms of which Ireland's performance is assessed in this chapter.

22 Andy Bielenberg, *Cork's Industrial Revolution 1780-1880: Development or Decline?*, Cork University Press, 1991, pp.116, 123

23 Cormac Ó Gráda, *Ireland, A New Economic History 1780-1939*, Clarendon Press, 1994, p.313

24 Richard Breen, Damian F. Hannan, David B. Rottman, Christopher T. Whelan, *Understanding Contemporary Ireland: State, Class and Development in the Republic of Ireland*, Gill & Macmillan, 1990, p.155

25 Mary O'Sullivan, "Manufacturing and global competition" in J. W. O'Hagan, op. cit., p.370

26 ibid., p.385
27 ibid., p.387
28 ibid., p.384
29 OECD, *Ireland: Local Partnerships and Social Innovation*, OECD, 1996, p.29. See also David Jacobson, "New forms of work organisation in Ireland: an annotated bibliography", DCU Business School, 1996 on which Sabel bases his conclusions.
30 ibid., p.388
31 ibid., p.391
32 Frank Barry, "Industrialization strategies for developing countries: lessons from the Irish experience" in *Development Policy Review*, vol. 9, 1991, p.86
33 See Lars Mjøset, "Comparative typologies of development patterns: the Menzel/Senghaas framework" in Lars Mjøset, ed, *Contributions to the Comparative Study of Development*, vol. 2, Institute for Social Research, Oslo, 1992, p.115.
34 Profit repatriation from Ireland continues to grow as a percentage of GNP from £128 million (2.5 per cent of GNP) in 1977, to £1,321 million (10 per cent) in 1985 to £4,001 million in 1994 (13 per cent). The significance of this outflow is disputed and some economists claim it is not a problem.
35 Paul Keating and Derry Desmond, *Culture and Capitalism in Contemporary Ireland*, Avebury, 1993, p.27
36 ibid., p.31
37 ibid., p.33
38 ibid., p.39
39 ibid., p.42
40 ibid., pp.48-9
41 Séamus Ó Cinnéide, "The extent of poverty in Ireland" in *Social Studies*, vol.1, no. 4, 1972, pp.381-400
42 Brian Nolan and Tim Callan, eds, *Poverty and Policy in Ireland*, Gill & Macmillan, 1994, p.22
43 Sean Barrett, "Measuring poverty in Ireland: an assessment of recent studies", *Economic and Social Review*, vol.20, no.4, 1989, pp.353-60
44 Nolan and Callan, eds, op. cit., p.313
45 The dependency ratio, defined as the number of dependants per member of the working population, has fallen from a high of 2.25 dependants per worker in the mid 1980s to 1.75 in 1995. The EU average is 1.4 dependants per worker and the trend in Ireland is moving in that direction.
46 Kieran A. Kennedy, "European unemployment and lessons for Ireland", in *Regional Studies*, vol.29, no.5, 1995, p.447
47 *Interim Report of the Task Force on Long-term Unemployment*, Office of the Tánaiste, 1995, p.75
48 ibid., p.76
49 *Long-term Unemployment Initiatives*, National Economic and Social Forum, Forum Opinion no.3, April 1996, p.12
50 Christopher T. Whelan, Richard Breen and Brendan J. Whelan, "Industrialisation, class formation and social mobility in Ireland" in J. H. Goldthorpe and C. T. Whelan, eds, *The Development of Industrial Society in Ireland*, Oxford University Press, 1992, pp.105-128
51 Philip J. O'Connell and David B. Rottman, "The Irish welfare state in comparative perspective" in J. H. Goldthorpe and C. T. Whelan, eds, op. cit., p.221
52 Richard Breen, et al, op. cit., p.100
53 Justice Commission of the Conference of Major Religious Superiors (CMRS, since renamed the Conference of Religious of Ireland, CORI), *Towards Full Citizenship for All*, n.d., p.20
54 Reported in *The Sunday Tribune*, 2 June 1996
55 Tim Callan and Brian Nolan: *Income Inequaliy and Poverty in Ireland in the 1970s and 1980s*, ESRI Working Paper 43, 1993. See also Brian Nolan, *The Wealth of Irish Households*, Combat Poverty Agency, 1991.

56 Richard Breen and Christopher T. Whelan, *Social Mobility and Social Class in Ireland*, Gill & Macmillan, 1996, p.171

57 ibid., p.169

58 Quoted in *The Irish Times*, 26 April 1995

59 Quoted in *The Sunday Tribune*, 24 September 1995. On unemployment figures in four West Tallaght estates, the 1994 CODAN report gave the following figures (population in brackets): Brookfield (3,015): 69.4 per cent; Fettercairn (2,992): 63.2 per cent; Jobstown (5,188): 66.8 per cent; Killinarden (7,043): 72 per cent.

60 For two such accounts, see *Pictures of Poverty: Twelve Accounts of Life on Low Income*, Combat Poverty Agency, 1989, and *One City, Two Tiers: A Theological Reflection on Life in a Divided Society*, Cherry Orchard Faith and Justice Group, 1996.

61 Kevin O'Rourke, "Emigration and living standards in Ireland since the Famine" in *Journal of Population Economics*, vol.8, part 4, p.420

62 Lars Mjøset, *The Irish Economy in a Comparative Institutional Perspective*, NESC, 1992, p.7

63 Jim Mac Laughlin, *Ireland: The Emigrant Nursery and the World Economy*, Cork University Press, 1994, p.1

64 "The new emigrants", *Newsweek*, 10 October 1987

65 Mac Laughlin, op. cit., p.1

66 ibid., pp.49-73

67 Developing the West Together, *A Crusade for Survival: Final Report of Study of the West of Ireland*, Euradvice Ltd., 1994, p.28

68 Mjøset, op. cit., p.67

69 Forfás in its report expects this to happen. Without such emigration, the labour force would be bigger by 140,000 in 2010, it predicts. See Forfás, op. cit., p. 84.

70 For example, between 1970-80 Brazilian GDP grew by an average of 8.1 per cent a year and Mexico grew by 6.3 per cent a year.

71 Lars Mjøset, op. cit., pp. 5-13

72 James Wickham, "'Industrialisation by invitation' crashes" in *The Irish Times*, 26 February 1993

73 Immanuel Wallerstein, *The Capitalist World Economy*, Cambridge, 1979, p.100. This does, however, place us among good bedfellows since Wallerstein mentions Norway and Finland as being semi-peripheral states.

74 David Snyder and Edward L. Kick, "Structural position in the world system and economic growth, 1955-1970: a multiple-network analysis of transnational interactions" in *American Journal of Sociology*, vol.84, no.5, 1979, p.1110

75 Michel Peillon, "Placing Ireland in a comparative perspective" in *The Economic and Social Review*, vol.25, no.2, 1994, p.193

76 Wallerstein, op. cit., p.103

77 Lars Mjøset, op. cit., p.18. Some economists however see this as a possible advantage as Ireland is not burdened with now often obsolete industrial sectors as are many western European countries.

78 Kieran A. Kennedy, "European unemployment and lessons for Ireland", op. cit., p.448

79 ibid., p.449. CSF refers to Community Support Framework, the framework drawn up for the spending of EU structural funds.

Chapter 6

Understanding Irish Development

"Irish culture in the twentieth century has displayed no shortage of creative energies, but as if bearing out the stereotype of the anti-intellectualism of the Celt, it has been less successful in generating its own criticism, or its intellectual terms of reference."

– Luke Gibbons[1]

By the mid 1990s Ireland's economic miracle was attracting attention well beyond its shores. A report by the Union Bank of Switzerland painted a glowing picture of Irish economic success which it saw as "the envy of Europe".[2] It was also reported that the EU was seeking to learn the lessons of what was being called "the Irish model" in order to revive the flagging economies of its member states.[3] On the other hand, evidence cited in Chapter 5 indicated that serious problems remain to be resolved, particularly in industrial policy and in social equity. Based on this, it was concluded that Ireland still displays significant elements of what are usually regarded as the characteristics of underdeveloped countries.

These differences in perception and in conclusion relate to differences in theoretical understanding. The objective reality is, of course, the same but the significance attached to different elements of that reality depends on the theoretical standpoint of the analyst. To understand the nature of Irish development/underdevelopment therefore, it is necessary to gain some understanding of the main theoretical approaches being used in analysing it. This is the purpose of this chapter. Apart from simply setting out some of the main positions of different theoretical approaches, however, this chapter questions how adequate these approaches are in diagnosing the causes of Ireland's development problems and in prescribing remedies for them.

The task of mapping out different theoretical approaches on development faces particular problems in the case of Ireland. Mac Laughlin has written of "the neglect of theoretical explanation"[4] in the extensive literature on Irish economics, politics and society. Until recently, there has been little theoretical debate on the nature of Irish development and little attempt to situate the Irish experience within wider development theory. O'Connell's comment that Irish political science "worries about its lack of data but blissfully ignores its theoretical shortcomings"[5] could also be applied to work on Irish development. To an extent this mirrors the easy assumptions of policymakers and politicians from the 1960s to the early 1980s that the inflow of foreign investment would solve Ireland's development problems. It is only since the 1980s that a stream of more critical works has begun to appear informed by theoretical perspectives that mirror those of development theory as mapped out in Part I. Many of these add new critical perspectives to our understanding of Ireland's longer-term development path.

The lack of attention to theoretical presuppositions also raises problems for defining a literature on Irish development since so few works explicitly address the problem of national development as such. This means drawing on historical studies and on works of neo-classical economics some of which show little acquaintance with development theory. But since such works have been far more influential in defining the dominant understanding of Irish development, they should not be neglected. The chapter begins therefore by looking at modernisation theory and then treats of neo-classical economics since both of these theoretical approaches are very pervasive in their influence. The chapter then goes on to outline some of the ideas of leading dependency theorists and of theorists whose work can be grouped under the heading of political economy. Attention is briefly paid to a Green view of Irish development before conclusions are drawn identifying some key issues requiring further attention. This division runs the risk of appearing to equate the impact of dependency theorists with that of neo-classical economists which is far from true. Despite this risk, it is important to place within the context of development theory the principal interpretations of Ireland's development path as it serves to undermine the pervasive view that Ireland is somehow a deviant case which defies classification.[6]

Modernisation: "The modern, young, progressive Ireland"

The influence of modernisation theory on explanations of Ireland's development has been pervasive, if little acknowledged in explicit terms. Indeed, as O'Dowd has written, both in Northern Ireland and in the Republic "development strategy remains identified with modernisation theories, i.e. with the view that the diffusion of entrepreneurial skills, technology and capital investment are the keys to economic growth".[7] And, as he put it elsewhere, "the strength of the modernisation theory may be gauged from the extent to which its assumptions are taken for granted as common sense by its adherents who frequently fail to realise or acknowledge that they are subscribing to a particular theory of social change."[8] This failure to acknowledge the dominant theoretical presuppositions informing much discussion of Irish development has meant that there is an almost complete absence of any assessment of the adequacy of modernisation theory to the Irish case. The following discussion pays particular attention therefore to authors who address this issue.

The dominance of modernisation theory as an interpretative paradigm can be seen in the way key issues have been defined in the dominant discourse of Irish society and the Irish media over the past three decades. For example, O'Connell finds that modernisation theory has had a pervasive influence on political research in Ireland based as it is on a contrast between traditional/rural and modern/urban values.[9] O'Dowd describes how categories drawn from modernisation theory proved unable to make sense of the sectarian divisions in Northern Ireland.[10] An example taken from a very different context concerns the categories used to interpret the struggles between developers and preservationists in Dublin in the 1960s and 1970s. Tovey examines how one influential journalist, Frank McDonald of *The Irish Times*, framed the issue as being one between urban and rural, "an Anglo-Irish civilised elite and a nation of 'peasants'".[11] In all these cases, the theoretical presupposition is that Ireland is a developed, industrialised society which is trying to shake off residues of a traditionalist past by opening itself to the outside world and especially to foreign investment and technology.

The work of Joseph Lee can be taken as an example of the application of modernisation theory to the Irish case. In his book entitled *The Modernisation of Irish Society 1848-1918*, he identifies four major elements through which this modernisation occurred – education, urbanisation, commercialisation and political participation. "Pre-famine Ireland," he writes, "though far from static, had been in many respects a tenaciously traditional society."[12] But, by 1918, "Southern Ireland [had] modernised probably as quickly as any other western European society during this period."[13] Thus Lee challenges those who see

Ireland's development as following a very particular path of its own and, instead, he characterises it as a quite typical case of the diffusion of "the administrative and cultural requirements of mass society".[14] His more recent work applies a similar theoretical approach to twentieth century Ireland. In particular, his distinction between the possessor and the performance ethic[15] is a direct application to Ireland of Talcott Parsons' evolutionary universals, one of which describes the move from a traditional to a modern society as involving the change from ascription to achievement (see Chapter 2).[16]

In discussing the adequacy of modernisation theory as an interpretative tool for the case of Ireland, Whelan acknowledges some of the difficulties involved. Thus, for example, key aspects of the Irish case (such as late industrialisation and the persistence of emigration) contradict essential tenets of modernisation theory which predict that industrial development and social advancement go hand in hand as an inevitable part of the modernisation process. He furthermore questions the validity of the transition from traditional to individualised values which modernisation theory predicts and its espousal of a view of economic advance which sees it as happening in well-defined stages. Yet, while denying its "social-evolutionary implications" he continues to hold to "the heuristic value of modernisation theory".[17] This discussion takes place in the context of an analysis of the results for the Republic of Ireland of the 1990 European Values Survey. The design of this survey was itself "mainly guided by broad ideas on the impact of modernisation", writes Whelan, which may account for his need to salvage some aspect of modernisation theory. Yet, the conclusion of his lengthy analysis serves to throw further doubt on the value of modernisation theory as an adequate tool to help interpret the Irish case.[18] Whelan writes: "While it may be helpful to describe individual values in terms of how 'backward' or 'advanced' they are, modernisation theory provides no infallible guide to where we are heading. The concept has value in guiding us through the maze, but in this and other areas we should not be surprised if the overall package reflects Ireland's own distinctive, angular variants of modern values rather than progressive movement towards a standard modern end-point."[19]

Ireland's development experience has also been found to contradict some other key assumptions of modernisation theory. Goldthorpe sees the Irish case as being a good one to test some of the key tenets of modernisation theory as it was "a kind of 'naturally occurring experiment' in which this theory was applied in the real world".[20] He examines the claims of the theory that progressive industrialisation leads to greater social mobility by weakening the ties between people's social origin, their educational attainment and therefore the level and kind of employment they attain. Instead of this happening in Ireland, however, Goldthorpe draws attention to the extent to which class inequalities have been found to persist, notwithstanding the rapidly changing structural and institutional context. Referring to the famous metaphor of Lemass that a rising tide will lift all boats, he concludes that with a free market strategy of facilitating economic growth in the expectation that it will then raise living standards throughout society "the most likely outcome must be that some boats will rise much higher than do others, and that some will indeed by left more or less deliberately stranded".[21] Breen and Whelan come to a similar conclusion in their study of social mobility in Ireland. They use evidence from the Irish experience to judge between the liberal tenets of modernisation theory and "the class analysis perspective which directs attention to the manner in which those who occupy positions of relative privilege can use their power and advantage to maintain their positions". The Irish experience of recent decades "provides substantial support for the latter perspective", they conclude.[22]

Neo-classical economics: liberating the market

Most discussion of Irish development takes place in the economics literature which, in Ireland, is predominantly neo-classical in its theoretical approach. Thus it is concerned primarily with efficiently allocating resources in a free market economy. This is regarded as the best way to ensure both the most productive and cost-effective use of resources and to ensure that the optimum human welfare is achieved throughout society from those resources. The principal means of achieving this is through allowing supply and demand establish prices for the various factors of production and for the goods produced; such prices ensure that the highest level of economic efficiency is attained. A number of consequences flow from these theoretical interests. Firstly, neo-classical economics tends to be interested in more immediate issues of allocating resources in an economy and in the behaviour of producers and consumers since this behaviour plays a crucial role in determining supply and demand. It devotes less attention to issues of long-term growth or to wider political or social structures. Secondly, it aspires to a high level of theoretical clarity and rigour; thus mathematical modelling of an economy is widely practised by neo-classical economists since this allows them to test the impact on the workings of the economy of particular policy changes or of shocks deriving from such things as major price rises of essential inputs. A third consequence relates to the role of the state. While this may be essential to regulate the conditions for the market to operate as efficiently as possible (by ensuring fair competition for example), state interference in setting prices or in distorting the free flow of economic resources from one use to another is regarded as "market imperfection". The consequence of this would be to lessen the efficiency of the economy and, by extension, to worsen the welfare of producers and consumers.

The dominance of such concerns in the Irish situation has meant that much of the literature on Irish economic development tends to deal with what one Irish economist has called "atemporal economic theory rather than ... the study of historical processes".[23] The result of this dominance of a neo-classical perspective has been, as Kieran A. Kennedy has pointed out, that "the many Irish economists who profess faith in the application of this paradigm have not sought to confront it with Ireland's long-term development experience". Concomitantly, he adds that none of the economists who have attempted to examine the reasons for Ireland's relative underdevelopment "has attempted to offer an explanation solely in terms of mainstream neo-classical economics. Presumably none of them was convinced that this framework was adequate".[24] While this is largely true it is not entirely so and neo-classical economists have addressed such issues as the causes of Ireland's unemployment, its industrial decline in the 19th century or the reasons for its relatively poor growth performance until recently.[25] A fuller though less scholarly account which makes a trenchant diagnosis of Ireland's development ills from a neo-classical perspective and which offers forceful prescriptions is *The Irish Disease and How to Cure It* by UCD economist, Cathal Guiomard. This work allows us engage with a neo-classical perspective on Irish development.

Guiomard is clear about where he lays the blame for Ireland's relative underdevelopment. Referring to the intervention of the state in the economy, he writes: "The grand scale of this redistributive and interventionist activity and the fact that it is at the expense both of productive activity and social equity, is at the heart of Irish economic underperformance."[26] His central concern then is to promote productive economic activity. Prices, profits and competition each act to make the economy productive, he writes, as prices reveal the productivity of a particular activity, profits reward that productivity and competition restrains through preventing overcharging of customers and suppliers.[27] In contrast to this picture of an efficient market economy, "at least half of the Irish economy is not a market economy and the behaviour of the remainder is heavily swayed by state regulations, taxes and subsidies," he writes.[28] The cure he recommends therefore is to radically restructure the state's role in the economy so that it is limited to achieving two gaols efficiently – correcting important market failures and promoting opportunity and social equity. Governments lack the capacity to be efficient producers, he says, and urges the liberalisation of the semi-state sector. Instead the state should concentrate on what it can do well – correct market failure through an efficient and active Competition Authority and through fostering decentralisation and competition in such areas as education, health care and the provision of infrastructure while ensuring maintenance of standards. The goal of fostering opportunity and social equity would require the state to redesign social programmes to ensure they met their targets of equity and, where necessary, to provide social safety nets for those unable to work and to boost the income of those on low-pay.

Turning to unemployment, Guiomard analyses it under three forms. Cyclical unemployment can be prevented through stable macroeconomic management of the economy; structural or long-term unemployment requires education and training programmes and special targeted measures; finally, productive job creation requires adequate economic incentives and well-functioning competitive markets, he writes. He warns again and again that it is counter-productive for the state to try to create jobs artificially and argues against those who believe technology or free trade are costing jobs. He urges raising productivity through businesses investing in plant and machinery, the state investing in infrastructure and workers investing in human capital.

A final aspect of Guiomard's prescription deals with the nature and role of institutions, normally not a major concern of neo-classical economists. Drawing on the work of the 1993 Nobel Prize winner in economics, Douglass North, he argues that a successful market economy requires a productive institutional framework.[29] This includes four elements: formal institutions like constitutions and parliaments that ensure an efficient regulatory regime; informal codes of conduct that uphold values such as honesty; a competent system of law enforcement; and "the sum of the attitudes and beliefs through which the public makes sense of the world around it". An example of this is a "muscular materialism" rather than "airy deValerean notions about frugality and spirituality",[30] he writes.

Guiomard's ideas are very close to the neo-liberal ideas being promoted by the World Bank in the Third World. Indeed many Third World governments have been implementing these very ideas which allows us to judge how they are operating when put into practice (see Chapter 3). But before turning to empirical evidence, it is important to engage theoretically with his ideas. It is to be acknowledged that Guiomard does accurately identify some major problems in the Irish situation. State involvement has led to inefficiency, it is widely acknowledged that the taxation system places too heavy a burden on income-earners, and there is much room for enhancing production and winning new markets for Irish products. But he takes his criticisms too far; thus he fails to acknowledge the success stories in the Irish semi-state sector and his claim that at least half the Irish economy is not a market economy seems greatly exaggerated. On many issues his prescriptions are excessively vague – his concern for increasing opportunity and social equity is very worthy but the means he offers for doing so sidesteps the enormous complexities of the issue.

A more serious theoretical disagreement relates to the role of the state and the belief that stimulating enterprise and productivity by the private sector in a free market is sufficient to address the huge job creation challenge facing the Irish economy. In this regard, the developmental successes of the East Asian countries, for which he expresses such admiration, are instructive to examine. For, as argued in Chapter 3, their success is built on following very different policies to the ones he proposes with a strong state involvement in building up technical capacity in indigenous industry. Mary O'Sullivan has drawn attention to this failure of neo-classical economics to acknowledge that "the 'perfect market' benchmark is the wrong one in the study of the process of industrial development".[31] This is because it fails to recognise the weak position of relatively underdeveloped economies like that of Ireland when it comes to open competition in the international marketplace. The lesson of the East Asian countries is that if industrial latecomers are to build up the technical sophistication and innovative capabilities to allow them compete successfully in high value-added sectors, then the government must play a central role in co-operation with the private sector in systematically developing these capabilities. Her criticism of the failure of neo-classical economics to appreciate this key point highlights the seriousness of what is at stake: "If conventional economic doctrine systematically ignores the social foundations of the development process, policies based upon it that attempt to foster economic development will systematically ignore them too. Indeed, in an attempt to remove 'imperfections', policies based on the theory of the market economy may undermine the very organisations and institutions that promote industrial development."[32]

Finally, it is worth taking a glance at the empirical evidence from Latin America to see if the application of the ideas advocated by Guiomard is leading to the economic and social success he predicts for them. We can look at it under the two headings he himself provides – the productive economy and the targeting of state social spending on the poorest. Carlos M. Vilas, a Mexican sociologist, sums up the impact of neo-liberal policies on Latin America a decade after their implementation: "The increase in productivity and economic output have [sic] not generated corresponding increases in employment levels and better working conditions. Employment, when it expands, does not keep pace with population growth. Real wages remain depressed as well. The biggest surge in employment is taking place in the informal sector, which offers work that is precarious and low-paying. Of the 15.7 million jobs created in all of Latin America over the last five years, 13.6 million of those came from the informal sector."[33] Reform of the social services throughout Latin America has followed the lines advocated by Guiomard for Ireland: services have been decentralised, competition by the private sector encouraged, user fees introduced and spending targeted on providing a social net for the poorest. While this has helped reduce the number of absolute poor in parts of Latin America, it has changed the whole nature of social policy, argues Vilas: "Rather than improving the working and living conditions of low-income groups, social policy tries to assist the many victims of structural adjustment, and to prevent further deterioration in the living standards of the population already below the poverty line. Neoliberal social policy doesn't help these people get out of the hole of poverty; it simply tries to prevent them from sinking further into it."[34]

Dependency: "chasing progress"

Where neo-classical theory focuses almost entirely on the internal microeconomic workings of the economy, dependency theory devotes most attention to the ways in which the economies of underdeveloped countries are structurally dependent on those of the core or developed countries, to the detriment of the former and the benefit of the latter. It is thus a far more pessimistic view than that of neo-classical economics and is based on a wider worldview which presupposes that political struggle (whether between rich and poor within individual countries or between rich and poor countries at a world level) is a central determinant of progress.

Not surprisingly, therefore, dependency theorists paint a less positive picture than do neo-classical theorists, characterising Ireland as a case of "uneven development",[35] of "emerging peripheralisation"[36] or of "dependent industrialisation".[37] These situate Ireland within a global capitalist economy divided into core and periphery regions (with, for world-systems theorists, semi-periphery regions displaying features of both core and periphery[38]), devote particular attention to the highly dependent form of reliance upon multinational industry through which Ireland has chosen to develop itself in recent times, and analyse the consequences of this dependency both for Irish society and for its longer term development prospects. The group of scholars who take this approach to Irish development can be divided into three overlapping but distinct categories – dependency theorists, world-systems theorists and the theory of capitalist colonial undevelopment elaborated by Raymond Crotty.

a) Dependent development: Orridge, Wickham, O'Hearn, Jacobsen

Up to the liberalisation of the economy in the late 1950s, Ireland displayed many of the features which dependency theorists such as André Gunder Frank identify as the classic marks of dependence, writes Wickham.[39] These include the dependence on one unprocessed raw material, live cattle, for the bulk of exports; the dependence on one country, Britain, as the main export market, and the dependence of the national economy on agriculture to generate most of the national income in a social structure marked by the dominance of small family enterprises in agriculture, services and even industry. Orridge applies some of the main tenets of dependency theory in a systematic way to the

Ireland of the early 1930s, particularly to its internal political divisions, and concludes that dependency theory is useful in the interpretation of "the shape of the satellite economy and the implications this has for social and political divisions in the peripheral society".[40] He argues that Fianna Fáil's attempt to promote indigenous industrialisation in the 1930s as a way out of Ireland's dependence was met by resistance from "pro-metropolitan" political forces within the state (mostly grouped around Cumann na nGaedheal), something to be expected according to dependency theory as such forces have a vested interest in maintaining the structure of dependence from which they benefit. But he goes on to add that dependency theory is less helpful in indicating the possibilities of capitalist industrialisation in a dependent economy.

The success of Ireland's industrialisation drive in the 1960s and 1970s seemed to give the lie to the predictions of dependency theory that development was not possible without delinking from the world capitalist economy (see Chapter 2). The features of classic dependence have been eroded with the growth in Irish industrial exports, the diversification of export markets and the decline in agriculture as a sector of the national economy. However, Wickham argues that Ireland's experience justifies the description of "dependent industrialisation" taken from the work of the dependency theorist, Fernando Henrique Cardoso, while Jacobsen argues that the Irish case fits the definition of "dependent development" as elaborated by Peter Evans.[41]

The nature and deficiencies of this form of development have been analysed in the work of Denis O'Hearn. He compares Ireland's "open, foreign-dominated, free-enterprise regime" which he judges "an abject failure" in development terms[42] to the success of the East Asian "gang of four" which are characterised by "strong state intervention in business, widespread use of selective protection and import-substitution, and a definite preference for domestic industry".[43] He argues that the level of foreign penetration of the Irish economy is exceptional both because of the high proportion of foreign firms within new industry and because of the decline of domestic industry. This model of dependent industrialisation chosen by the Irish state has had a number of severely adverse consequences for Irish development. The first is decapitalisation as transnational corporations (TNCs) drain capital out of the host country. The reality of decapitalisation by TNCs in Ireland "strongly supports dependency", argues O'Hearn[44] and he adds that "the situation for Ireland is bad and getting worse".[45] The second adverse consequence is linkages as the structure of TNC production in Ireland creates relatively few knock-on effects in stimulating local industry. The extent of such linkages is "extremely low" in Ireland compared to other dependent countries such as Mexico and Brazil since so much TNC production in Ireland is for export. The result of this is that "the contribution of new TNCs to growth is practically restricted to the activities of the TNCs themselves. Foreign investment creates few multipliers that lead to the growth of domestic investment".[46] Another set of consequences of this model of dependent industrialisation identified by O'Hearn relate to income distribution within Ireland. This model involves "the large-scale movement of incomes from wages to profits, and within profits from domestic industry to the TNCs," he writes.[47] Thus it has "unquestionably caused higher inequality of direct incomes".[48] Writing more recently, O'Hearn draws attention to the fact that a disjunction between economic growth and employment growth "has been true of the whole dependent period of Irish development".[49]

John Kurt Jacobsen in his study places the focus on the elites within Ireland who have chosen this highly dependent model of development and on the ways they have legitimised this option. He argues that a crucial factor affecting the development chances of late developers such as Ireland is how the opportunities and constraints of the international situation are mediated by local elites and emerge as policy options. Irish elites have chosen to rely on multinational capital not because this path has been shown to be inherently better nor because of the lack of alternatives (these have been proposed in Ireland by the left, by trade unions and, rather more timidly, research bodies such as the National Economic and Social Council) but, he contends, because of their power to dominate discourse and allow little space for a serious consideration of alternatives. Facilitating this, Jacobsen identifies "a high degree of deference ... a high propensity by non-elites to defer to policy prescriptions".[50]

b) Putting Ireland in a global context: O'Hearn, Mac Laughlin

While world-systems theorists situate themselves broadly within a dependency perspective, they place greater emphasis on the nature of the world capitalist system and its hierarchical division into core, semi-peripheral and peripheral regions. Arguing from this standpoint, O'Hearn is therefore critical of those who seek to explain Irish underdevelopment by concentrating on internal factors and actors. Instead, he argues that it cannot be understood "without a clear analysis of the structure and dynamics of global uneven development".[51]

For world-systems theorists there is a single world system which, over the last five centuries, has expanded and incorporated more and more of the world within itself as core powers have imposed control over peripheral regions for their own benefit. This is a dynamic process, however, as the system is ever changing: it has already gone through three periods, first under Dutch control, then under Britain and, more recently, under the US. The transition from one to the other involves opportunities for peripheral regions as control by the core is weakened; when a new power assumes hegemony, however, the periphery is re-incorporated around the needs of the new power. O'Hearn identifies two periods during which Ireland attempted to de-link from the British core of the world-system and take charge of its own development, both of them during crises within the world system – in 1783-1801 and again in 1932-1945. Both of them failed as Ireland was re-incorporated as a dependent element into the world system – firstly by an ascendant Britain in the 19th century and more recently by the US. O'Hearn argues that the opening of the Irish economy in the late 1950s "was more a matter of adopting as policy what was already a *fait accompli* [sic], rather than real autonomous policymaking in any sense". Much of the pressure was exerted through the conditions attached to Marshall Aid after the second World War, he writes, and Ireland found itself forced to engage in export-led industrialisation and European integration "on the pain of becoming an outcast from Europe and the global system if it did not do so".[52]

Mac Laughlin uses a world-systems perspective to interpret the persistence of emigration from Ireland. He rejects dominant explanations based on the mobility or aspirations of young Irish adults in favour of an explanation rooted in Ireland's peripheralisation within the international economy. "The global division of labour in the second half of the nineteenth century ... suited the core areas of industrial capitalism and converted Ireland into a global emigrant nursery which supplied Great Britain and North America with cheap labour," he writes.[53] Furthermore, he argues that emigration reflected "the structural dependence of post-independence Ireland on overseas labour markets throughout the twentieth century"[54] with the only change being that new destinations for Irish emigrants emerged as countries such as Japan emerged to core status within the world system.

c) Capitalist colonial undevelopment: Crotty

Although Raymond Crotty's analysis has been described as being "similar to Frank's early dependency analysis",[55] his work is in fact highly idiosyncratic. For example, he argues that capitalism began 5,000 years ago in central western Europe with the beginnings of settled agriculture.[56] His analysis of the causes of Irish underdevelopment, however, bears some resemblance to that of dependency theorists as he likens Ireland to what he calls the "undeveloping Third World"[57] and he agrees that "capitalist colonialism expedited Irish peripheralisation".[58] But Crotty very precisely locates the cause of underdevelopment as being the forceful superimposition of "an alien, individualistic, capitalist culture ... on an indigenous, collectivist, non-capitalist society of food producers".[59] He outlines a number of consequences that have resulted from this imposition in Ireland such as the "squeezing" of the indigenous agricultural population and its virtual extermination, the expropriation of land and the emergence of a ruling class distinct in race and religion from the majority. However, Crotty identifies the introduction of property in land as being the key to the process of Irish undevelopment, as he calls it. Profits made from this land, he argues, were used to replace people by livestock which produced less but made more profit, or were exported to England to help the financing of factory capitalism which was playing havoc with Irish cottage and craft industries.

For Crotty, this historical experience leaves as a legacy an "inefficient and inequitable social order":[60] "The low cost of holding land, the low cost of borrowing capital, and the high cost of employing labour in all the former capitalist colonies are major elements of the capitalist colonial heritage. Everywhere this heritage results in inefficient land use, the waste of capital and the unemployment of labour. Production in all the former colonies is depressed by this incorrect pricing of the factors of production."[61] The way to undo this heritage therefore and to stimulate development is through rectifying this system so that "the prices of factors of production are made to reflect the economic realities of the former capitalist colonies rather than the privileges created there by capitalist colonialism; and then securing the benefits of this correction equally for all members of society".[62]

He thus proposes taxing land so as to force its more productive use and taxing bank deposits to force the banks to direct funds to those able to make the best use of them. He furthermore proposes reducing government expenditure through repudiating the national debt and argues that public sector capital formation should be scrapped since all it has done is lead to a bloated public sector without creating any additional jobs in the economy. Finally, he argues for scrapping taxes on income. He summarises what he believes the effects of such measures would be: "The changes proposed are, first, the establishment by appropriate fiscal means of factor prices that reflect economic realities and social priorities. Factor prices now preserve individualistic interests that are part of the capitalist colonial heritage and that are socially destructive. The establishment of economically correct factor prices will cause resources to be used efficiently. It is proposed to distribute the social surplus that will accrue from efficient resource use as a national dividend, paid equally to everyone on the voters' register and resident in Ireland. These measures would effectively undo the Conquest. They would replace an inefficient and inequitable social order with an efficient and equitable one and they would secure a livelihood for all the people of Ireland in Ireland."[63]

The main contribution of dependency theory to our understanding of underdevelopment is that it focuses attention on the structural inequalities that are a central part of the world economic system. In the literature on Irish development, this redresses a major weakness of neo-classical analysis which tends to ignore such structural factors. But a major problem with dependency analysis is that it emphasises the external structural constraints on a country's development to such an extent that it appears to leave little room for internal actors to influence the course of development. Thus O'Hearn's analysis concentrates on negative factors such as decapitalisation, weak linkages and worsening income distribution while paying little attention to some of the more positive achievements of recent decades – rising living standards, modernisation of the social structure, greater opportunities for many and, more recently, very positive growth rates.

A certain theoretical imprecision attaches to the category of dependency as applied in these writings to the Irish situation. As a descriptive term about the form Irish industrialisation has taken, it is accurate. For example, Liam Kennedy (who is not a dependency theorist) can write that the dependence of industry in the Republic on multinationals and the dependence of the

North's economy on subventions from the British Exchequer mean that both economies "exhibit substantial and increasing vulnerability to supra-local forces".[64] But dependency theorists elevate this into a cause of underdevelopment while failing to reveal adequately the mechanisms which make it so. For O'Hearn, one of these mechanisms is decapitalisation as multinationals drain capital from the national economy. This, however, is hotly contested by many economists and O'Hearn's examination of the issue (in his 1989 article) offers comprehensive figures only up to 1982.

A final weakness follows from the above and relates to the policy prescriptions of dependency theorists. O'Hearn admits that he is sceptical whether "successful democratic development strategies can be implemented by single semiperipheral countries such as Ireland within the capitalist world-system."[65] He puts his hope in networks of local movements as "realistic building blocks for dependency reversal and democratic development".[66] Thus any hope of development is relegated to some vague and far-distant future.

Raymond Crotty's work raises problems over and above those of dependency theorists. While his attention to the impact of colonialism on Irish development is valuable, identifying the introduction of property in land as the main cause of Irish underdevelopment gives far too much prominence to one factor. His proposed solution of taxing land so as to make it more productive follows from this. However, this solution is extended to include repudiating the national debt and scrapping public sector capital formation, extreme moves that are both highly unrealistic and more than likely to have catastrophic consequences for the economy and living standards.

Political economy: institutions and innovation

Modernisation theory and neo-classical economics on the one hand and dependency theory on the other offer diametrically opposed readings of Irish development. Yet, as we have emphasised, each holds important insights into the nature of underdevelopment and how to address it even if such insights are at times taken too far. This leads us to another group of recent studies reflecting· new approaches within development theory, building on some. of the insights of the theoretical approaches already outlined but paying particular attention to institutions and innovation. The principal scholars adopting these approaches will be dealt with separately, except in the case of two works which treat of the Irish state.

a) The challenge for the latecomer: O'Malley

Countries like Ireland with a weak industrial base face daunting challenges in today's world economy as they try to industrialise, according to O'Malley. Such latecomers, as he calls them, need to develop industries which can compete in the international marketplace but they are at a severe disadvantage in doing so due to the head start gained by a wide range of industries, most of them based in the advanced industrial countries. Elements such as advanced technology, large capital requirements, highly skilled labour and the economies of scale associated with large industries all constitute "barriers to entry" for the latecomer, writes O'Malley.[67] In this context, following conventional free trade and free market strategies will have the result that countries with a weak industrial base will never succeed in developing industries strong enough to compete internationally and will be confined to a limited range of fairly simple processing activities, particularly for the domestic market. O'Malley concludes that Ireland's experience bears out this contention: its industrialisation has relied heavily on multinational industries setting up in the country while indigenous industry has, if anything, grown weaker as a result of following a conventional strategy.

The reliance on multinationals "can ultimately prove to be a temporary phenomenon – a phase which eventually passes", writes O'Malley which led him to conclude when writing in 1988 that "the country's present economic situation is particularly precarious".[68] As an alternative to the conventional, free-market strategy, O'Malley looks at the success of Japan, South Korea and Taiwan which have used selective and active state guidance to nurture indigenous industries so that they overcome the barriers to entry facing the latecomers. He recommends a similar strategy for Ireland. In a later work,[69] he examines the ways in which a more active state policy since the mid 1980s to develop indigenous industry has resulted in a marked growth of exports from that sector and an increase in the proportion of its output going to export markets since 1986. He urges, however, that this approach should be taken further through a greater degree of state initiative and participation and not be limited by what Ireland's relatively small private firms can be encouraged or persuaded to do.

b) An extensive but weak state: Breen et al., Girvin

Works by Breen et al. and Girvin have devoted attention to the Irish state and the ways in which crucial decisions made by the state in the late 1950s and 1960s have led to the problems of the 1990s. Breen et al. examine a number of these decisions and their effects. The decision to rely on multinational firms as the motor force of industrialisation has entailed high costs to the exchequer both because of the high level of incentives needed to attract these firms and because of the capital lost in permitting the free repatriation of profits.[70] Secondly this decision has placed severe limitations on the autonomy of the state since the only option open to it is to offer ever higher incentives to attract overseas firms.

A second decision by the Irish state relates to the attempts to accommodate conflicting social interests. This took on increasing importance as the development model chosen by the state "led to an increasing bifurcation of the class structure"[71] between those who benefited from it such as the urban middle class and the upper working class and better off farmers and those who were further marginalised by it such as the unskilled working class and small farmers. An expanding economy up to the mid 1970s allowed the development of a welfare state but its maintenance in an era of economic downturn forced the state to resort to increased borrowing which itself became a major problem by the mid 1980s and further diminished the state's development options. A taxation regime designed to attract foreign firms led the state to impose ever higher taxes on wage earners whom it then compensated by a welfare system which in key areas such as education expenditure was greatly to their benefit. Furthermore, an attempt to satisfy all social interests has helped sustain vested interest groups "which encouraged divisiveness rather than coherence", write Breen et al.[72] This study concludes that "the major factor dictating policy is political expediency".[73] "Bluntly, the State has tended to give in rather than develop an overall strategy of development."[74]

Girvin's study examines economic policymaking from the foundation of the state until 1961. He argues that the crisis of the 1950s was not a crisis of the model of native industrialisation but a crisis of agriculture, "the result of the failure of a traditional society to move beyond the limits imposed by this".[75] Again he argues that decisions taken during the 1960s constrained policymakers thereafter but adds that there were alternatives open to the Irish state during the second half of the 1960s. Among these he lists the possibility of deepening the planning process and of further state intervention to direct the economy. Instead, the state opted for a seemingly painless strategy that "could be introduced with few changes to the traditional political structure, to society or its culture".[76] The result was that "Ireland became dependent on others to provide for its welfare without developing a society that could provide for itself."[77] Girvin concludes that Ireland remains a developing rather than a developed society and that it requires "a strong state to direct the economy and to provide for the welfare of the society".[78]

c) Systems of national innovation: Mjøset

The study of the Irish economy in a comparative institutional perspective by the Norwegian social scientist, Lars Mjøset breaks substantial new ground in the literature on Irish development. Firstly, it compares Ireland to a number of small European states which, unlike Ireland, have been developmental success cases – Sweden, Finland, Denmark, Austria and Switzerland. Secondly, it draws in an explicit way on development theory, something not done by other scholars except for O'Malley's work on theories of industrialisation. Thus Mjøset draws distinctions which are very useful for understanding the Irish experience, particularly that between autocentric development (growth with development under national direction) and peripheral or dependent development (growth without development where the benefits flow out of the national economy). He situates Ireland's development experience somewhere between these two categories. Thirdly, he takes a long-term historical perspective to understand the deep-rooted causes of Ireland's malaise.

Mjøset refuses to identify one primary cause of Irish underdevelopment, preferring instead to speak of clusters of causal factors all re-enforcing each other and leading to a vicious circle from which Ireland has yet to escape. Thus he identifies the weak development of indigenous industry, the existence of "a social structure which had emigration as a condition of its continuance"[79] and the fact that Ireland has missed opportunities for autocentric development in the past (for example, in the period immediately after the second World War), to highlight the enormous challenges which face the country. The key to successful development he regards as being a system of national innovation which he defines as "the institutions and economic structures which affect the rate and direction of innovative activities in the economy".[80] Instead of developing a system of national innovation, Ireland has tried to import a foreign system of innovation, he argues. As a result, it now faces problems even more complex than any of his contrast countries which have developed their own systems of national innovation. Developing such a system will entail working on such issues as identifying the national advantages which Ireland possesses, a tax system to stimulate development, institutions to encourage indigenous industry, decentralisation and, perhaps the most difficult, "institutional innovations aimed at stemming a migratory outflow which is considered too large".[81] Mjøset strongly implies that Ireland must stop trying to copy other countries and his emphasis on a system of national innovation, which he makes clear relies on "national economic structures, values, cultures, institutions, and histories",[82] puts the focus on ourselves and our own cultural and institutional capacities.

d) Performance and potential: Kennedy

The work of economist Kieran A. Kennedy has persistently interrogated the record of Irish economic development and found it wanting. The economic history of Ireland in the twentieth century which he co-authored reviews specific aspects of Irish economic performance such as capital resources and investment, foreign trade, agriculture and manufacturing and finds that "it has to be conceded that this performance often fell well short of potential – even making due allowance for the constraints".[83] The authors identify three weaknesses operative in all major areas of policy throughout the period – failure to grasp the implications of the small size of the country, absence of long-term perspective and neglect of human resource dimensions.

In other works, Kennedy acknowledges that these weaknesses "are clearly symptoms of something deeper, the more fundamental explanation of which may lie in the culture, political framework, distribution of power and resources"[84] or other forces. The current unemployment crisis, he writes, "is not so much a new problem, as a new manifestation of a deeper problem that has been endemic in Irish history", in large part "a long-standing problem of underdevelopment".[85] He identifies four long-term strategic options facing Ireland in this situation. The first he calls the Korean model which would require GNP growth of 6 to 7 per cent sustained over the next 10 to 15 years. Yet, he recognises that this would demand "a sea change in our whole philosophy and organisation of economic and social life of a kind that is difficult even to visualise".[86] The second option is the American model which would involve creating conditions in

Poverty Amid Plenty

which low-wage services employment could flourish. The consequence of this in Ireland might be to force people to emigrate rather than to enter into such employment, he acknowledges. The third option is the Scandinavian model, involving high taxes and pro-active manpower policies in order to prioritise employment. Growing harmonisation within the EU makes such an option less and less possible, he writes, even if the political and social will existed in Irish society for it. The fourth option is an enhanced traditional Irish model, meaning the active encouragement of emigration as a way of finding employment for surplus Irish labour. This would have the counter-productive effect of encouraging the export of our most skilled labour, he adds. However, Kennedy wonders whether Irish society is ready to accept the kinds of changes needed to address the unemployment crisis, to bring performance into line with potential.

The very diverse nature of the works included under this section have in common that they eschew grand theoretical frameworks in favour of drawing selectively on theory to elucidate particular problems. Thus O'Malley focuses on such problems as barriers to entry and draws on industrial theory to clarify ways in which latecomers to industrialisation can overcome such barriers. Mjøset eclectically draws on different theoretical traditions to help him understand the problems of Irish underdevelopment. These works are not without their problems. For example, the theories of state used by Breen et al. and by Girvin are less than adequate to the Irish experience, a point further developed in Chapter 8 below. Mjøset's national system of innovation remains a very vague concept in his work despite the fact that he makes it his most important recommendation for policymakers if Ireland is to graduate to a virtuous circle of development. But these studies do emphasise the room for manoeuvre that exists for state and society in Ireland to influence the country's future development direction while being aware of the real constraints, internal and external, on achieving the advance they seek.

New paradigms: the growth illusion

Chapter 4 outlined the "Green alternative" as it has emerged within development theory and practice worldwide. Many of the values informing this alternative motivate groups in Ireland, especially in the community and environmental sector.[87] The survey of some of the principal theories of Irish development in this chapter would not be complete, therefore, without mention of an environmental or anti-growth perspective, though little theoretical elaboration of such a perspective has yet been done in the Irish context.

The Growth Illusion is a lengthy work by economist and former Green Party candidate for the European Parliament, Richard Douthwaite, the sub-title of which explains its argument: "How economic growth has enriched the few, impoverished the many, and endangered the planet."[88] While most of this work concerns itself with Britain, in one chapter on Ireland entitled "De Valera's Dream", Douthwaite applies his analysis to the Irish situation. Referring to T. K. Whitaker, the architect of the opening of the Irish economy in the late 1950s, he writes that "Whitaker's system has made Ireland too poor to employ its own people to do the jobs it needs done".[89] This, he argues, is because the level of employment must be kept down in order to keep the value of the currency up. This is the only option available to the government under conventional wisdom, writes Douthwaite.

Instead, he urges, Ireland faces "a straight choice between a higher standard of living and a higher quality of life" and argues that the economy does not need to grow any more – it can satisfy the needs of all its people better by redistributing its existing resources rather than by trying to generate higher incomes, what he calls "a non-wasteful system".[90] Taxes on fossil fuels imposed in response to the threat of global warming would make small Irish farmers much more competitive again, stem the flight from the land and help conserve the countryside through the retention of traditional farming methods. Such taxes could also be used to cut employees' social welfare contributions thus making it cheaper to employ workers. This would help reduce unemployment, stem emigration and increase the national income, argues Douthwaite. He concludes: "My hope, certainly, is that restrictions on burning fossil fuel will enable Ireland to turn its back on policies which have made the country as helpless economically as it became after the Act of Union, and give it instead a basis from which it can work towards a society based on a vision, towards the modern equivalent of de Valera's dream."[91]

Douthwaite's espousal of a higher quality of life over a higher standard of living may be very worthwhile (though for those on low incomes the latter may be a necessary condition for the former) but it remains a highly challenging option for which to win widespread political support. To say this, of course, is not to invalidate it. His one practical suggestion, and one on which he places great hopes for improving the quality of life throughout Irish society, is a tax on fossil fuels. The positive impact he hopes for from such a tax is far from certain, however, and other economists have argued that it could increase costs, make farming less competitive and therefore result in either lower wages or higher emigration.

Conclusion

The first conclusion that seems warranted from this examination of some of the principal theories of Irish development is that no one theory has the full answer. Important insights can be gained from many different perspectives. In this regard, what the economist John Sheahan wrote of Latin America can also be applied here: "In a sense, structuralism and neo-classical economics need each other: the former brings out the problems that neo-classical economics obscures, and the latter directs attention to crucial questions that structuralism leaves out."[92]

This opens the way for two other conclusions. The first concerns a widespread consensus in the literature, namely that the answer to our development problems will have to come from ourselves and that Irish society urgently needs to find what Kennedy calls "a sense of purpose and direction"[93] in facing its developmental challenges. The second conclusion relates to the emphasis in many studies on the means to address these challenges, namely the capacity of the Irish state on the one hand and of Irish civil society on the other. The many prescriptions for Ireland's development ills presuppose in one way or another some combination of both of these, the first more cultural, the second more institutional and political. Yet, the literature has taken them for granted rather than addressed them as deficiencies to be remedied. The final two chapters of this work look at ways of addressing these two issues.

Footnotes
1 Luke Gibbons, *Transformations in Irish Culture*, Cork University Press, 1996, p.xi
2 See "Celtic Tiger" in *The Sunday Business Post*, 12 May 1996
3 See "EU plots the path to EMU on Irish economic model" in *The Irish Times*, 24 May 1996

4 Jim Mac Laughlin, *Ireland: The Emigrant Nursery and the World Economy*, Cork University Press, 1994, p.45

5 Declan O'Connell, "Sociological theory and Irish political research" in Mary Kelly et al., eds, *Power, Conflict and Inequality*, Turoe Press, 1982, p.186

6 Michel Peillon, *Contemporary Irish Society: An Introduction*, Gill & Macmillan, 1982, p.1

7 Liam O'Dowd, "Beyond industrial society" in Patrick Clancy et al, eds, *Ireland: A Sociological Profile*, IPA, 1986, p.200

8 Liam O'Dowd, "Development or dependency? State, economy and society in Northern Ireland" in Patrick Clancy et al., eds, *Irish Society: Sociological Perspectives*, IPA, 1995, p.168

9 O'Connell, op. cit., p.187. For an example of political analysis based on this paradigm see Tom Garvin, "Change and the political system" in Frank Litton, ed: *Unequal Achievement: The Irish Experience 1957-1982*, IPA, 1982, pp.21-40.

10 Liam O'Dowd, "New Introduction" in Albert Memmi, *The Colonizer and the Colonized*, Earthscan, 1990. O'Dowd writes: "To many intellectuals – conservative, liberal and socialist – Northern Ireland was simply a backward province of Britain. If the conflict raised fundamental questions for them, it was not the 'anachronistic' ones of colonizer versus colonized, or Protestant 'settler' versus Catholic 'native'. The marginal role of moderates and intellectuals encouraged them instead to claim the high moral ground 'above' the conflict, often from a sense of deep personal commitment and concern. Here the Northern Ireland problem was posed as a series of choices: archaic religious passions versus secular humanism, terrorism versus the rule of law, benighted nationalism versus pluralism" (pp.37-38).

11 Hilary Tovey, "Environmentalism in Ireland: modernisation and identity" in Patrick Clancy et al, eds, *Ireland and Poland: Comparative Perspectives*, Department of Sociology, University College Dublin, 1992, p.280. In a classic statement of a modernisation perspective, Tovey concludes: "Official environmentalism posits Irish 'backwardness' and 'traditionalism' against British and international 'modernity'", p.278.

12 Joseph Lee, *The Modernisation of Irish Society 1848-1918*, Gill & Macmillan, 1973, p.163

13 ibid., p.168

14 ibid., p. 140

15 Joseph Lee, *Ireland 1912-1985: Politics and Society*, Cambridge University Press, 1989, p.390

16 This view of Lee's work is based largely on Terry Mulhall, *The State and Agrarian Reform: The Case of Ireland 1800-1940*, unpublished PhD thesis, University of London, 1992, pp.89-93

17 Christopher T. Whelan, *Values and Social Change in Ireland*, Gill & Macmillan, 1994, p.4

18 ibid., p.2

19 ibid., p.215. For a more developed view of this critique of modernisation theory, see Peadar Kirby, "Valuing social change in Ireland" in *Doctrine & Life*, vol. 44, September 1994, pp.418-25

20 John H. Goldthorpe, "The theory of industrialism and the Irish case" in J. H. Goldthorpe and C. T. Whelan, eds, *The Development of Industrial Society in Ireland*, Oxford University Press, 1992, p.420

21 ibid., p.427

22 Richard Breen and Christopher T. Whelan, *Social Mobility and Social Class in Ireland*, Gill & Macmillan, 1996, p.174

23 Frank Barry: "Review Symposium" in *The Economic and Social Review*, vol. 21, no. 2, January 1990, p.235

24 Kieran A. Kennedy, "The context of economic development" in J. H. Goldthorpe and C. T. Whelan, eds, *The Development of Industrial Society in Ireland*, Oxford University Press, 1992, p.19

25 See, for example, Frank Barry and John Bradley, *On the Causes of Ireland's*

Unemployment, Centre for Economic Research, UCD, Working Paper WP 91/1, 1991; Cormac Ó Gráda: *Ireland: A New Economic History 1780-1939*, Clarendon Press, Oxford, 1994; and Cormac Ó Gráda and Kevin O'Rourke, "Economic growth: performance and explanations" in J. W. O'Hagan, ed., *The Economy of Ireland: Policy and Performance of a Small European Country*, Gill & Macmillan, 1995, pp 198-227. To the development theorist, however, these discussions are quite inconclusive.

26 Cathal Guiomard, *The Irish Disease and How to Cure It: Common-Sense Economics for a Competitive World*, Oak Tree Press, 1995, p.34

27 ibid., p.62

28 ibid., p.239

29 North, a public choice theorist, has worked to incorporate his concern with institutions into neo-classical analysis.

30 Guiomard, op. cit., p.38

31 Mary O'Sullivan, "Manufacturing and global competition" in J. W. O'Hagan, op. cit., p.374. She gives the following reasons why this is invalid: "It is wrong because the theory of the market economy contains no theory of the development and utilisation of productive resources. The theory of the market economy posits that the free working of the market mechanism results in the superior utilisation of productive resources. But the theory of the market economy takes the productive capability of these resources and the alternative uses to which they can be allocated as given, and makes no attempt to analyse the development of superior products and processes. In the absence of this development, productivity is increased through the more complete utilisation of resources, but industrial development does not occur. It is for this reason that neoclassical growth theory has long treated much of productivity growth as an unexplained residual."

32 ibid., p.379

33 Carlos M. Vilas, "Neoliberal social policy" in *Nacla*, vol.29, no.6, 1996, p.25

34 ibid., p.18

35 Peter Shirlow, "Introduction" in Peter Shirlow, ed., *Development Ireland: Contemporary Issues*, Pluto, 1995, p.3

36 Dieter Senghaas, *The European Experience*, Berg, 1985, p.129

37 James Wickham, "Dependence and state structure: foreign firms and industrial policy in the Republic of Ireland" in Otmar Höll, ed., *Small States in Europe and Dependence*, Austrian Institute for International Affairs, 1983, p.167

38 O'Hearn describes the differences as follows: "Core regions specialise in capital-intensive products, using skilled and relatively high-wage labour. Peripheral regions specialise in labour-intensive products, using unskilled and low-wage labour. Semi-peripheral regions mix both types of production. This is associated with a hierarchy of incomes between rich, moderately poor, and poor regions. A few countries move between zones, giving the appearance of mobility, but the hierarchy remains." See Denis O'Hearn, *Putting Ireland in a Global Context*, Department of Sociology, University College, Cork, n.d., pp.7,8

39 James Wickham, op. cit., p.165

40 Andrew W. Orridge, "The Blueshirts and the 'Economic War': A study of Ireland in the context of dependency theory" in *Political Studies*, vol.31, 1983, p.366

41 John Kurt Jacobsen, *Chasing Progress in the Irish Republic*, Cambridge University Press, 1994, p.20

42 Denis O'Hearn, "The Irish case of dependency: an exception to the exceptions?" in *American Sociological Review*, vol.54, 1989, p.579

43 ibid., p.581

44 ibid., p.582

45 ibid., p.583

46 ibid., p.586

47 ibid., p.591

48 ibid., p.590
49 Denis O'Hearn, "Global restructuring and the Irish political economy" in Patrick Clancy et al, eds, *Irish Society: Sociological Perspectives*, IPA, 1995, p.102
50 John Kurt Jacobsen, op. cit., p.95
51 Denis O'Hearn, *Putting Ireland in a Global Context*, Department of Sociology, University College Cork, n.d., p.4
52 ibid., p.23
53 Jim Mac Laughlin, "Emigration and the peripheralization of Ireland in the global economy" in *Review*, vol.17, no.2, Spring 1994, p.257
54 ibid., p.258
55 Denis O'Hearn, "Global restructuring and the Irish political economy" in Patrick Clancy et al., eds, *Irish Society: Sociological Perspectives*, IPA, 1995, p.92
56 Raymond Crotty, *Ireland in Crisis: A Study in Capitalist Colonial Undevelopment*, Brandon, 1989, pp.184-9
57 ibid., p.16
58 Raymond Crotty, "Capitalist colonialism and peripheralisation: the Irish case" in Dudley Seers et al, eds, *Underdeveloped Europe: Studies in Core-Periphery Relations*, Harvester Press, 1979, p.229
59 Crotty, *Ireland in Crisis*, op. cit., p.16
60 ibid., p.112
61 ibid., p.115
62 ibid., p.117
63 ibid., pp.129-30
64 Liam Kennedy, *The Modern Industrialisation of Ireland 1940-1988*, The Economic and Social History Society of Ireland, 1989, p.50
65 Denis O'Hearn, "Global restructuring and the Irish political economy", op.cit., p.126
66 ibid., p.126
67 Eoin O'Malley, *Industry and Economic Development: The Challenge for the Latecomer*, Gill & Macmillan, 1989, p.259
68 ibid., pp.265, 266
69 Eoin O'Malley, "Problems of industrialisation in Ireland" in J.H.Goldthorpe and C.T. Whelan, eds, *The Development of Industrial Society in Ireland*, Oxford University Press, 1992, pp.31-52
70 Richard Breen et al, *Understanding Contemporary Ireland: State, Class and Development in the Republic of Ireland*, Gill & Macmillan, 1990, p.210
71 ibid., p.212
72 ibid., p.214
73 ibid., p.216
74 ibid., p.218
75 Brian Girvin, *Between Two Worlds: Politics and Economy in Independent Ireland*, Gill & Macmillan, 1989, p 202
76 ibid., p.207
77 ibid., p.207
78 ibid., p. 211
79 Lars Mjøset, *The Irish Economy in a Comparative Institutional Perspective*, NESC, 1992, p.17
80 ibid., p.45. He takes the definition from Charles Edquist and Bengt-Åke Lundvall, "Comparing small Nordic systems of innovation" in Richard R. Nelson, ed., *National Innovation Systems*, Oxford, 1992
81 ibid., p.23
82 ibid., p.47
83 Kieran A. Kennedy et al., *The Economic Development of Ireland in the Twentieth Century*, Routledge, 1988, p.257
84 Kieran A. Kennedy, "The context of economic development" in J. H. Goldthorpe and C. T. Whelan, op. cit., p.21
85 Kieran A. Kennedy, *Facing the Unemployment Crisis in Ireland*, Undercurrents, Cork University Press, 1993, pp.4, 43

86 ibid., p.30
87 See Hilary Tovey, "Environmentalism in Ireland: two versions of development and modernity" in *International Sociology*, vol.8, no.4, 1993, pp.413-430
88 Richard Douthwaite, *The Growth Illusion: How Economic Growth has Enriched the Few, Impoverished the Many, and Endangered the Planet*, The Lilliput Press, 1992
89 ibid., p.279
90 ibid., pp.280, 281
91 ibid., p.283
92 John Sheahan, *Patterns of Development in Latin America: Poverty, Repression, and Economic Strategy*, Princeton University Press, 1987, p.13
93 Kennedy et al., op. cit., p.262

Chapter 7

Resources for Development I: A Sense of Nationhood

"We need a spirit of self-reliance – a determination to take charge of our future – to build an economy of real strength and permanence which will give jobs and wealth sufficient to our needs."

– A Time for Change, Culliton Report, 1992[1]

The developmental successes of Japan, South Korea, Taiwan and Singapore have prompted much examination of what enabled these relatively backward countries to surge forward in the decades since the second World War. Among the elements most commonly referred to are the nature and role of the state in leading the drive to development, the selective use of protectionism to build up indigenous industries until they are strong enough to win markets overseas and the fact that greater social equality allowed the benefits of growth to spread widely throughout society (see Chapter 3 above). Some analysts have gone further, pointing to the strong sense of national identity and purpose which motivates the various policies used and which provides the motivation for the drive to develop. Fallows sums up the secret of the East Asian success as follows: "It can best be thought of as a useful kind of 'nationalism'. East Asia's economic catch-up over the past century has fundamentally had a political, rather than a purely economic, root. First Japan, then the other countries in succession, have struggled for ways to apply technology and develop industries so as to avoid weakness relative to other nations – not 'markets', not 'companies' – in the world."[2]

This draws attention to an element of the East Asian development model which is surprising, even shocking, to Western ears since it seems to contradict both the tenets of the dominant neo-classical economics and the widespread view that nationalism is an anachronism in the era of global capitalism. To Irish ears, it draws attention to a political outlook on life which,

as the *Irish Times* columnist, Mary Holland, has written "has
come to be regarded almost as an embarrassment, something we
have to live with but must try to keep decently hidden".[3] The
association with Irish nationalism of the armed campaign of
Northern Ireland paramilitaries over a quarter century is one very
understandable reason for the "marked reluctance of politicians
and intellectuals in this State to engage in any serious discussion
of what nationalism means", as Holland put it. But it also mirrors
a wider failure among scholars in the developed English-speaking
world to examine the phenomenon more rigorously with the
result that the resurgence of nationalism in the Western world in
the 1980s caused surprise and puzzlement. To some extent this
was due to the association of nationalism with German fascism
with the result that nationalism "gained a reputation from which
it has not recovered".[4]

An a priori hostility towards nationalism has characterised the
work of a number of leading Irish historians and social scientists
usually referred to as "revisionists". In their work, the Irish
nationalist tradition is treated "as purveying a racist and thereby
an exclusivist concept of Irishness".[5] This treatment has helped
shape public attitudes, nowhere more so than in the writings of
Conor Cruise O'Brien. He has described Irish nationalism as "an
ideology that is warlike and anti-democratic, and calls
increasingly for further human sacrifice".[6] This is indeed
sweeping, paying no attention to what Boyce calls "the rich
variety of the nationalist tradition in Ireland"[7], choosing to
overlook what Garvin calls "the ideological shapelessness of the
separatist tradition"[8] and dismissing what Larkin calls the
"essentially democratic and representative nature of the Irish
nationalist tradition".[9] As one of the leading contemporary
scholars of nationalism in the English-speaking world, Ernest
Gellner, has pointed out, the problem here is that there is "a
touch of intellectual autism in O'Brien's thought"[10] and he goes
on to list the leading scholars of nationalism all of whom are
ignored by O'Brien.

If some scholars of the developmental successes in East Asia
regard nationalism as a central element of that success and if the
recent denigration of nationalism in Ireland is based on a lack of
acquaintance with the lively debates taking place elsewhere on
the subject, then the time seems ripe for a re-evaluation of the
Irish nationalist tradition and for asking what it may have to
contribute to the challenges of development. This is what Jim
Mac Laughlin seems to have in mind when he refers to the
devaluation of Irish nationalism as a philosophy informing social

and economic policy. "This reluctance to examine the contemporary significance of nationalism, has meant that we are more concerned about attracting high-tech industry and tourists to Ireland than thinking about ways of blocking the haemorrhage of young adults from the country," he writes.[11] This chapter therefore interrogates nationalism in the light of the challenges of development. It starts by looking at the more nuanced understanding of nationalism emerging from the scholarly debates now raging on the subject. It then goes on to examine more closely the link between nationalism and development in East Asia and in Latin America. Finally, it focuses on the nature of Irish nationalism, identifying some positive contributions it may have to make to the task of development.

Re-evaluating nationalism

Though nationalism may have a bad reputation because of its association with some of the principal villains of the 20th century (and the Bosnian Serb leader, Dr Radovan Karadzic, has done little to retrieve its reputation in the popular mind), recent scholarship is helping rescue nationalism from its exclusive identification with ethnicity and therefore with xenophobia. According to the typology of John A. Hall, this ethnic or integral nationalism, in which the nation is defined on the basis of racial purity, dates largely from the period after the first World War and is seen as a reaction to the Versailles treaty.[12] Even though that treaty was an attempt to satisfy nationalist aspirations and legitimised the establishment of a patchwork of new nation states, particularly in eastern Europe, it also frustrated the aspirations of groups who found themselves trapped as ethnic minorities in states in which they felt themselves strangers. This, for example, provided the first justification for Nazi expansionism and, in the shape of the Bosnian conflict, has come to haunt Europe at the close of the 20th century.

But scholars are largely agreed that nationalism is a far wider and more variegated tradition than this highly illiberal variant. Following Hall's typology, some of the principal forms of nationalism can be identified. Though nationalism as a political force of mass appeal is linked in the work of Ernst Gellner to the logic of industry, some theorists date the emergence of nationalism from before the industrial revolution. First to be identified is the official "top down" nationalism of states like Britain and the Netherlands in which ruling elites from the early modern era successfully unified diverse cultural and economic units into strong, well-integrated and prosperous states (though, of course, in the case of Britain, Ireland constituted a problem which is still being grappled with today). Secondly, there is what is sometimes called the constitutional nationalism of the US and French revolutions at the end of the 18th century, defining membership of the nation not on ethnic or cultural grounds but on grounds of citizenship. This was very influential in the emergence of Irish nationalism and has remained a major strain within it. Hall identifies in Japan and Prussia a third form of nationalism in which elite ruling classes were forced to reform society and extend citizenship for the sake of the very survival of their societies. Fourthly, comes the case of Latin America in which "liberal" elites took power and established their own republics in order to preserve their privileges and strenuously avoid the mobilisation of the people which is such a feature of nationalist politics. To this form of nationalism and the unfinished business it has left as a legacy we will return below.

Hall's fifth category of nationalism deserves more attention as it exemplifies what has become the dominant strain in Irish nationalism. This is what he calls "risorgimento nationalism" or cultural nationalism, a highly potent force which originates not from elites but from civil society and appeals primarily to the excluded masses. This typically goes through three stages and, in this regard, the Irish case is typical. It begins through the collection of folklore and the rediscovery of the cultural heritage of the past. In this first stage it remains a purely cultural endeavour. But it then moves into a second stage in which this discovery of the past is used to develop a new understanding of nationhood, the creation of a national culture with mass appeal through song and dance, games, etc. The third stage comes when this cultural movement begins to make demands for political statehood. In some cases this final stage may not arrive at all, or may remain very weak. Wales is a good example of strong cultural nationalism side by side with weak political nationalism. But in most cases the transition is made due, Hall speculates, to blocked social mobility as the leading sectors in this newly defined national community see social, political and economic advancement blocked while they remain part of the dynastic/imperial state. Again, this is exactly what happened in the Irish case as the work of Tom Garvin makes clear.[13] Finally, a few important points need to be made about this form of nationalism which have been obscured in recent treatment of Irish nationalism. As Hall puts it, this type of nationalism

180   *Poverty Amid Plenty*

"deserves to be considered liberal – that is, it stressed civic loyalty within a democratic regime rather than ethnicity". Furthermore, the hope of this essentially 19th century movement "was that the setting free of oppressed peoples would usher in a reign of peace". But, as Hall so wisely adds, "there is a blissful innocence about their particular dreams".[14] This blissful innocence has left its mark on the dreams of Irish nationalism right down to the present day.

Among the generalisations that can be drawn from recent scholarship on nationalism is the link with modernity, namely that nationalism emerges out of the transition from a closed, traditional society to an open and modern society and is a key element in that transition.[15] As Hall notes about many of the nationalist leaders of the 20th century: "They are modernizers consciously aware of how to create industrial society. Such modernizers seek to break down the segments of the traditional order so as to create a common culture capable of integrating all citizens."[16] This task of creating a common integrative culture at the service of economic and political modernisation is central to most forms of nationalism. There is, however, less agreement on identifying the key aspects of modernity that stimulate the emergence of nationalism. Gellner identifies industrialisation[17] while Anderson rests content with capitalism[18] as the forces which stimulate the emergence of a common culture and of new, local elites seeking political power. What is clear is the fact that nationalism emerges as part of the process of development and plays a crucial role in at least awakening among the masses the aspiration to be beneficiaries rather than victims of that process.

Two studies which involve consideration of the Irish case serve to clarify the crucial role that nationalism plays in this context. Hechter's internal colonialism thesis argues that Irish nationalism developed as a reaction to a particular core-periphery relationship in which the English core developed at the expense of the Celtic periphery. The fact that Ireland, outside the industrialised north-east, emerged in the second half of the 19th century as a region depending on the export of capital-intensive agricultural produce to Britain stimulated the emergence of nationalism as a form of "high political consciousness on the part of groups seeking to alter the cultural division of labour," he writes.[19] Hutchinson, in his examination of cultural nationalism, sees it as emerging out of a reaction against attempts to assimilate the colony as an integral economic, political and cultural region of the metropolitan power. The cultural nationalist reaction, Hutchinson clarifies, is not traditionalist but seeks to combine elements of modernity and of tradition in its "search for alternative external political models capable of realizing the developmental potential of the indigenous community".[20]

In summary, therefore, cultural nationalism of the Irish kind can be seen as the means through which elites in economically peripheral regions seek to define their own responses to the challenges of modernisation and insertion into a global capitalist order. Central to this response is mobilisation around a distinctive cultural identity, the development of mass politics and the attempt to ensure that the insertion into the international economy happens in ways that are beneficial to the peripheral and underdeveloped region.[21] It is important to clarify, however, that nationalism is an impulse as much as a coherent ideology; within a particular nationalist movement there may be competing ideologies, as is clearly the case in Irish nationalism with socially radical sectors, including a socialist current, in competition with socially and culturally conservative sectors.

Before moving on, a final point needs to be made about the current re-evaluation of nationalism. This concerns the status of the nation – is it, as nationalists like to claim, a pre-ordained entity awaiting its chance to be recognised or is it an "imagined community", in Anderson's term? In other words, are nations invented? This is an important point as it is sometimes used to dismiss the validity of nationalism. In this regard, Anderson's rebuke to Gellner is instructive as he reminds him that accepting the nation as an imagined community is not the same as stating that it is a fabrication. Rather, Anderson likens it to an act of creation.[22] Whatever one's view on this point, Anthony Smith argues that "nations and some kinds of nationalism are necessary, functional and continuous with older forms of collective cultural identity and community. It is not possible today, or for the foreseeable future, to envisage a realistic social and political basis for humanity in either incipient or advanced industrial societies without a cultural and political division into ethnic communities and national states. Nor can we seriously propose an alternative to the myth and ideal of nationalism as a cement and vision for large groupings of human beings, one which is both ideologically acceptable and sociologically feasible."[23]

Nationalism and development

While recent theoretical work on the nature of nationalism clearly establishes its link with the impulse to development, we need to turn now to examine concrete cases to draw out its necessary contribution in practice. In the case of East Asia, we have already seen that nationalism is regarded as a key ingredient of successful development. This section identifies in more detail the specific contribution it has made. Secondly, the less successful development of Latin America is examined where nationalism remains an unfulfilled impulse but one which is still seen as a necessary element for future development strategies.

a) East Asia

In his study of the rise of the new East Asian economic and political system, James Fallows identifies four elements that distinguish "the Asian model" from the prevailing Western model. The purpose of economic life is not to increase the individual buying power of consumers but rather to increase the collective national strength, he writes. For this purpose, elaborate systems have been developed to seek to ensure that power will be used for the long-term national good. This sense of the long-term national good causes the Asian model to deeply distrust markets, he writes; these may be a useful tool for keeping companies on their toes but they are not the way to resolve questions about how a society should be run or its economy unfold. Finally, Fallows identifies in the Asian model what he calls a "view of national borders and an us-versus-them concept of the world": "People everywhere are xenophobic and exclusive, but in the Anglo-American model this is defined as a lamentable, surmountable failing. The Asian-style model assumes it is a more natural and permanent condition. The world consists of 'us' and 'them', and no one will look out for 'us' if we don't look out for ourselves."[24] For a country like Ireland, which has for over 30 years depended on multinational companies to develop its economy for it and where they are often viewed in the popular mind as equivalent to charitable organisations, the contrast could not be more stark.

The theoretical basis for these essentially nationalist views Fallows traces to the work of the early 19th century German economist, Friedrich List. In his book, *The Natural System of Political Economy*, List challenged the dominant laissez faire economic theories of his time, arguing instead that successful development for the latecomer would require a deliberate state-led mobilisation of forces to enhance productive capacities and to ensure that development benefited the whole community of the nation and not just elites within it. International trade he likened to war in which countries have to struggle for competitive advantage. Interestingly, among Irish nationalist leaders, Arthur Griffith was devoted to the views of List and actively promoted them through the various papers he edited. However, as Mary Daly has written, these theories were quickly dismissed by Ireland's first independent government and had no followers among the economic establishment of the time.[25]

In reflecting on the role culture has played in the success of the East Asians and the relative failure of the Latin Americans, Ronald Dore makes some observations pertinent to the case of Ireland. The first of them concerns the ability to learn, an ability which Joseph Lee has identified as being singularly lacking in Ireland.[26] Dore finds among the East Asians what he calls "the inability to tolerate black boxes without wanting to take them apart" and he draws on this to describe the process of technology transfer as it happens in East Asia: "Technology transfer is not a simple all-or-nothing process. When a new plant is bought, and the embodied technological knowledge with it, it is one thing to learn to run the plant efficiently in normal operation. It is a significantly different thing to be able fully to repair and maintain the plant with one's own indigenous resources. It is yet another thing to understand enough about the plant, and about the scientific principles again to be able to reproduce it with significant modifications derived from the experience of running it. All that learning takes place faster in societies with a higher density of people who suffer from the 'intolerance of black boxes' syndrome. My impression from descriptive literature and businessman talk – perhaps there are survey data but I do not know of them – is that that density is rather higher among the products of East Asian universities than among the products of the more status-preoccupied higher education systems of Latin America – or of Europe, for that matter."[27]

While there is no necessary link between this creative urge to learn and a strong sense of national interest, it can be expected that the latter might stimulate the former, especially where there is an emphasis in the national culture on developing strong indigenous industries to compete successfully abroad. The strong East Asian "sense of nationhood"[28] would also serve to stimulate this learning capacity. Dore argues that it was paradoxically the very sense of backwardness, "shared by the intellectuals and political leaders of the late-developing country, which provided a charter for state action to mobilize resources and to take initiatives and risks."[29] But, for the East Asians, the bond of nationhood proved much stronger than for the Latin Americans

Poverty Amid Plenty

whose elites felt much closer to the elites of North America and Europe than to the masses of their own peoples. So the drive to catch up, the motivation of national pride, proved much stronger for the East Asians.

b) Latin America

If the average Japanese economist or doctor felt more in common with a Japanese farmer than with a US economist or doctor, it was the opposite for Latin Americans, Dore says. This draws attention to the weakness of Latin American nationalism in which a rhetoric of national community has been used to exclude most of the people from the benefits of nationhood or, as Etienne Balibar has put it, "the contradiction between the pretension of the modern state to constitute a 'community' and the reality of different forms of exclusion".[30] Nationalism or nation-building in Latin America is therefore unfinished business, says Castañeda, and he defines a key task of development as being to "give back the nation to the people" or more accurately "to give the millions of excluded citizens of the hemisphere the nation they never had".[31]

In this reading, the existence of gross social inequality in Latin America serves both as a huge challenge to development but also greatly weakens the very sense of nationhood that for the East Asians is one of the preconditions for their success. This is a major warning signal for Ireland where, as evidenced in Chapter 5, a significant problem of social exclusion is emerging. While the extent of social exclusion in Ireland may not be as great as in Latin America, it does constitute a similar sociological reality. In Latin America, this reality results in "a brittle national consciousness",[32] says Castañeda; the evidence of low ethical standards in high places in Irish business presented in Chapter 5 may indicate the emergence of a similar brittle national consciousness in Irish society. Castañeda's comments on the need for a new nationalism in this era of "social apartheid"[33] and the "denationalisation of elites"[34] are therefore pertinent to Ireland.

The goal of this "new nationalism", as he calls it, is building an inclusive national community. To this end, it needs to defend national sovereignty against the sorts of glib disregard often exhibited by the United States (the invasion of Panama being one example he mentions). With regard to economic matters, however, Castañeda recognises that regional integration among countries at a similar level of development is the only way to avoid "their subordinate inclusion in wealthy nations' economic spheres of influence": "Conserving the nation state as the prime area of economic activity appears impossible; joining one of the three large economic spheres of influence [the US, the EU and the Japanese] at a time of great flux and under conditions of gaping disparities and overwhelming weakness cannot be a desirable option, even if some resignedly accept it. Regional economic integration is a halfway house that possesses intrinsic merits and is preferable to existing alternatives. It can be either a lasting solution or a stepping-stone to a better world, when it comes."[35] As examples of this kind of regional integration, Castañeda mentions Mercosur (which joins Brazil, Argentina, Uruguay and Paraguay), the Central American Common Market, and the integration process underway between Colombia and Venezuela. Industrial policy along the lines of East Asia and mechanisms for social transfers like those of the European Union should be developed as part of this process of integration, he says.

Castañeda calls the nationalism he espouses vertical since its proponents will often find more in common with groups in other countries than with elite groups in their own. He instances, for example, the support the Sandinistas were able to find among sectors of US society who actively opposed the policies of the Reagan administration in regard to Nicaragua.[36] But he also alludes to the important North-South dimensions of such a vertical nationalism in that it provides the basis for social sectors in all underdeveloped countries to find common cause in seeking models of development which might favour the weaker players on the world stage. Paradoxically, such a nationalism offers a far more secure basis for a stable internationalism than does the neo-liberalism which results in the dependent insertion of underdeveloped countries into the global market place and further deepens the divide between the world's rich and poor.

Irish nationalism: seeking a national model of progress

What unites the examples of contemporary nationalism in East Asia and Latin America is the promotion of a national development project, one that seeks to ensure the economy is at the service of building a strong and inclusive national community. While nationalism does not in itself provide policies

Poverty Amid Plenty

to achieve this end, it does act as a guiding inspiration and impulse for appropriate policies. It offers at least two key elements to guide the elaboration of development policy: firstly, the aspiration towards a form of development that is balanced and that seeks to integrate excluded social sectors and, secondly, the national self-confidence that is a necessary precondition for the ability to learn creatively from others and to build alliances internationally that serve one's national interest.

It is paradoxical therefore that, instead of drawing on its strongest indigenous political tradition for the task of national development, Ireland has over the past three decades turned its back on nationalism. As a result, its path of development has resulted in a greatly weakened national community – the Irish economy has been inserted into the international economy in a highly dependent way and the state has made little effort to define and strategically promote a national development project that might maximise the benefits of such insertion to the national economy. As Shirlow has written, the reintegration of the Republic's economy within the global economy "was achieved through the abandonment of economic nationalism in favour of a pseudo-cosmopolitanism and almost total subservience to international capital".[37] One of the results is that "present development policies throughout Ireland are nothing more than aspirational: they continually assume that the protracted support of economic growth structures will somehow automatically produce widespread socio-economic benefits".[38] Furthermore, he identifies "one of the central limitations of economic development policies" as being "the failure of both states to challenge the extent of inequality within social conditions".[39]

One of the reasons why this dependent model of development is not more in contention has been its success in creating a sense of identity which serves to obscure and even legitimate the growing inequality in Irish society.[40] The new enlarged secular intelligentsia, writes O'Dowd, which has in many cases such a vested interest in this model of development "has proved capable of manufacturing national consensus even in the face of growing economic crisis and social inequalities".[41] Thus, as Mac Laughlin has pointed out, emigration is transformed from being a symptom of persistent underdevelopment to being a sign of the dynamism of our well-educated youth[42] while Kennedy again and again draws attention to the lack of disposition to tackle our high levels of unemployment.[43] This draws attention to the central role played by identity in the development process. "Politics ... is basically about identities, and human identities are never merely given, they are always 'under construction'. I believe that the current crisis deeply challenges the definitions of identity which have been an essential ingredient of the 'modernisation project' of the last three decades in Ireland," writes Maguire.[44] It follows therefore that an essential element if we are ever as a society to find the energies and resources to tackle our serious developmental problems is the refashioning of a sense of identity adequate to the task. Such a sense of identity seems a necessary precondition to rediscovering that spirit of self-reliance, that determination to take charge of our future, as called for in the Culliton report on industrial policy quoted at the beginning of this chapter. Professor Sabel's report on Irish partnerships and social innovation for the OECD draws attention to other dimensions of a renewed sense of national identity which are crucial to the challenge of combating social exclusion – a vibrant sense of solidarity with the excluded and a will to learn the lessons of successful inclusion so as to generalise them throughout society and thereby "reduce the chances that citizens anywhere would be victimised by the economic ignorance or self-interest of local elites".[45]

As a contribution to fashioning a new sense of identity, we could usefully return to the lively period of the 1890s. The decades prior to independence were marked by a cultural nationalism which focused in very practical ways on issues of development. Hutchinson describes the ideological themes of the period as promoted by Griffith and Moran in the pages of the newspapers they edited: "Hand in hand with their promotion of Irish culture went a campaign not for the defence of the Gaeltacht but for a projected ascetic, sober and industrious urban middle-class nation, educated for Ireland's economic and social development rather than for the British civil service. Support for technical education, for Plunkett's agricultural co-operative movement, for Irish industrial regeneration, for the temperance crusade and the battle against 'immoral' English popular culture were all grafted on to the Irish cultural renaissance."[46] The founding of the Gaelic League in 1892 was also motivated by a concern for the fashioning of a more independent identity that could creatively confront the developmental challenges of the country. As the League's newspaper, *An Claidheamh Solais* put it: "The decay of the native language is everywhere accompanied by industrial and general decadence ... The language, the industries and the very existence of a people are all interdependent, and whoever has a living care for the one cannot be unmindful of the other."[47]

Poverty Amid Plenty

This link between cultural identity and development is, for Hutchinson, a central element of cultural nationalism. Such nationalism is a recurring force, he argues, "regularly crystallizing at times of crisis generated by the modernisation process with the goal of providing 'authentic' national models of progress".[48] The present conjuncture in Ireland, which can be defined as "a crisis generated by the modernization process" provides the conditions, therefore, for the re-emergence of cultural nationalism. Central to these conditions is the presence of a sizeable excluded sector aspiring to upward mobility and a share in the benefits of development. Yet for these, present developmental policies offer little hope for inclusion and for advancement. Furthermore, the dominant ideological perspective offers a choice between an assimilationist option of integrating ourselves more and more in a dependent way into multinational capitalism and a traditionalist option of turning our backs on modernity. This creates the ideological conditions for cultural nationalism with its search for a new option combining the insights of modernity with those of tradition to find an authentically national model of development.[49] Tucker further clarifies what cultural nationalism might have to offer: "Central to any authentic development project is the right of peoples to have a say in shaping their own destiny, in naming the world as they see it."[50] This returns us to the argument earlier in this chapter that nationalism is a force arising in peripheral regions which defines its own responses to the challenges of modernisation and insertion into a global capitalist order so as to ensure a form of insertion as beneficial as possible to the balanced and equitable development of the peripheral region. A return to these central concerns in the elaboration of Irish development policy and the mobilisation of excluded sectors around these concerns is an urgent imperative for Irish society.

Yet the revaluing of nationalism raises a number of difficult questions. The most difficult in the Irish case concerns the fact that nationalism has been a political force that both united and divided Irish people. A strong sense of inclusive community was defined, of necessity, against the unionist community. Yet it must also be remembered that the anti-nationalism of southern elites over the past three decades has contributed little to overcoming the nationalist-unionist divide. Indeed, it is possible to argue that the failure to develop a sense of the vital contribution nationalism could make in terms of development has allowed a traditionalist Catholic nationalism hold sway. A renewed developmental nationalism could instead act as a force to unite around the common challenges of overcoming persistent challenges now more common to Northern Ireland[51] and the Republic than ever before.

A second difficulty to be faced relates to the fact that cultural nationalism did not historically provide a sound basis for policies of economic development. As Daly argues, the Irish state inherited "a confused baggage of ideals" in the elaboration and application of which "no account was taken of the dictates of the market economy".[52] The Fianna Fáil policies of economic nationalism in the 1930s are also held now to have been inadequate to the challenges of development. Yet the relative failure of development policies over the past 30 years draws attention to the fact that failure ascribed to the nationalist basis of policy may in fact have been due more to persistent instititutional and cultural deficiences. In other words, a far more nuanced and sympathetic interpretation of past efforts is needed in order to learn from their inadequacies rather than dismiss them completely.

As has been mentioned on a number of occasions in this chapter, nationalism is an impulse rather than an ideology. As such, it can be wedded to different ideologies, of left or right. However, in Anthony Smith's view quoted above, it remains a cement and vision for large groupings of human beings that is ideologically acceptable and sociologically feasible. And, as the countries of East Asia have shown, this cement and vision have been the impulse for the one group of underdeveloped countries that has successfully "made it" in development terms in the post-War period. As such, nationalism seems a prerequisite for a sense of national self-confidence and for a robust sense of an inclusive national community which remain the inspiration and goals of all development.

Footnotes

1 Report of the Industrial Policy Review Group, *A Time for Change: Industrial Policy for the 1990s*, The Stationery Office, 1992, p.7
2 James Fallows, *Looking at the Sun: The Rise of the New East Asian Economic and Political System*, Pantheon, 1994, p.367
3 Mary Holland, "A reluctance to examine what nationalism really means to us", *The Irish Times*, 26 August 1993
4 John A. Hall, "Nationalisms, classified and explained" in Sukumar Periwal, *Notions of Nationalism*, Central European University Press, 1995, p.20
5 Brendan Bradshaw, "Nationalism and historical scholarship in modern Ireland" in Ciaran Brady, ed., *Interpreting Irish History: The Debate on Historical Revisionism*, Irish Academic Press, 1994 p.214
6 Conor Cruise O'Brien, "Ireland: The Shirt of Nessus", in Seamus Deane, ed., *The Field Day Anthology of Irish Writing*, vol. III, Derry, 1991, p.601

Poverty Amid Plenty

7 D. George Boyce, *Nationalism in Ireland*, Croom Helm, London, 1982, p.380

8 Tom Garvin, *Nationalist Revolutionaries in Ireland 1858-1928*, Clarendon Press, 1987, p.v

9 Emmet Larkin, "The Irish political tradition" in Thomas E. Hachey and Lawrence J. McCaffrey, eds., *Perspectives on Irish Nationalism*, The University Press of Kentucky, 1989, p.111

10 Ernest Gellner, *Encounters with Nationalism*, Blackwell, 1994, p.61. Autism is defined in the Oxford Dictionary as the condition of "having a form of mental illness that causes a person to withdraw into a private world of fantasy and be unable to communicate with others or respond to his real environment."

11 ibid., p.33

12 John A. Hall, op. cit., pp.8-33

13 Tom Garvin, op. cit.

14 John A. Hall, op. cit., p.16

15 John Breuilly, "Reflections on nationalism" in *Philosophy and Social Science*, vol. 15, 1985, pp.74-5

16 John A. Hall, op. cit., p.11

17 Ernest Gellner, *Nations and Nationalism*, Blackwell, 1983

18 Benedict Anderson, *Imagined Communities*, Verso, 1992

19 Michael Hechter, *Internal Colonialism: The Celtic Fringe in British National Development 1536-1966*, Routledge and Kegan Paul, 1975, p.340

20 John Hutchinson: *The Dynamics of Cultural Nationalism: The Gaelic Revival and the Creation of the Irish Nation State*, Allen and Unwin, 1987, p.312

21 In *The Break-up of Britain* (New Left Books, 1977), Tom Nairn describes in more detail this process: "Unable to literally 'copy' the advanced lands (which would have entailed repeating the stages of slow growth that had led to the breakthrough), the backward regions were forced to take what they wanted and cobble it on to their own native inheritance of social forms. In the annals of this kind of theorizing the procedure is called 'uneven and combined development'. To defend themselves, the peripheral countries were compelled to try and advance 'in their own way', to 'do it for themselves'. Their rulers – or at least the newly awakened elites who now came to power – had to mobilize their societies for this historical shortcut. This meant the conscious formation of a militant, underclass community rendered strongly (if mythically) aware of its own separate identity vis-à-vis the outside forces of domination. There was no other way of doing it" (pp.339-340). While regarding nationalism as inevitable, however, Nairn characterises it as "the pathology of modern developmental history, as inescapable as 'neurosis' in the individual, with much the same essential ambiguity attaching to it" (p. 359). This misunderstands nationalism and fails to appreciate its essential but not sufficient contribution to development; for nationalism is not a coherent ideology in its own right but rather an impulse motivating excluded sectors to seek forms of development from which they can benefit.

22 "Gellner is so anxious to show that nationalism masquerades under false pretences that he assimilates 'invention' to 'fabrication' and 'falsity', rather than to 'imagining' and 'creation'. In this way he implies that 'true' communities exist which can be advantageously juxtaposed to nations. In fact, all communities larger than primordial villages of face-to-face contact (and perhaps even these) are imagined. Communities are to be distinguished, not by their falsity/genuineness, but by the style in which they are imagined." Benedict Anderson, op. cit., p 6.

23 Anthony Smith, "Ties that bind" in *LSE Magazine*, Spring 1993, p.8

24 James Fallows, *Looking at the Sun: The Rise of the New East Asian Economic and Political System*, Pantheon, 1994, pp.208-9

25 Mary Daly, *Irish Industrial Development and Cultural Identity*, Gill & Macmillan, 1992, pp. 177, 178.

26 Joseph Lee, *Ireland: Politics and Society, 1912-1985*, Cambridge, 1989, pp.627-43

27 Ronald Dore, "Reflections on culture and social change" in Gary Gereffi and Donald L. Wyman, eds, *Manufacturing Miracles: Paths of Industrialization in Latin America and East Asia*, Princeton University Press, 1990, p.365

28 ibid., p.360

29 ibid., p.359

30 Quoted in Jorge G. Castañeda, *Utopia Unarmed: The Latin American Left after the Cold War*, Vintage Books, 1993, p.283

31 ibid., p.325

32 ibid., p.286

33 ibid., p.303

34 ibid., p.304

35 ibid., p.313

36 For a first hand account of such support, see Peadar Kirby, *Dialann ó Nicearagua*, An Clóchomhar, 1990.

37 Peter Shirlow, "Introduction" in Peter Shirlow, ed., *Development Ireland: Contemporary Issues*, Pluto Press, 1995, p.5

38 ibid., p.11

39 ibid., p.1. These conclusions may, however, need to be revised in the light of the OECD report by Professor Charles Sabel entitled *Ireland: Local Partnerships and Social Innovation* (OECD, 1996). Sabel's analysis is outlined in Chapter 8 below.

40 John Maguire, "The case for a new social order" in Miriam Hederman, ed., *The Clash of Ideas*, Gill & Macmillan, 1988, p.80

41 Liam O'Dowd, "State legitimacy and nationalism in Ireland" in Patrick Clancy et al, eds, *Ireland and Poland: Comparative Perspectives*, Department of Sociology, UCD, 1992, p.37

42 Jim Mac Laughlin, *Ireland: The Emigrant Nursery and the World Economy*, Cork University Press, 1994, pp.30-49

43 See, for example, a report in *The Irish Times*, 29 June 1994 entitled "ESRI director calls for sharper focus on jobless" which quotes Professor Kennedy as saying of unemployment: "It remains for too many only a verbal crisis, analogous to Republicanism of former times."

44 Maguire, op. cit., p.62

45 OECD, op. cit., p.97

46 Hutchinson, op. cit., pp.168-9

47 Quoted in Kevin B. Nowlan, "The Gaelic League and other national movements" in Seán Ó Tuama, ed., *The Gaelic League Idea*, Mercier, 2nd edition, 1993, pp.46-7

48 Hutchinson, op. cit., p.9

49 Charles Sabel's analysis of the international significance of Ireland's innovative efforts at local partnerships between the state, the social partners and the community sector in addressing unemployment and social exclusion is a very good example of such a new option. See OECD, op. cit.

50 Vincent Tucker, *The Myth of Development*, Department of Sociology, UCC, 1992, p.34

51 For evidence on the state of the Northern Ireland economy, see Ronnie Munck, *The Irish Economy: Results and Prospects*, Pluto Press, 1993, chapter 3, and for an earlier though still relevant analysis see Bob Rowthorn, "Northern Ireland: an economy in crisis" in Paul Teague, ed., *Beyond the Rhetoric: Politics, the Economy and Social Policy in Northern Ireland*, Lawrence & Wishart, 1987

52 Daly, op. cit., p.11

Chapter 8

Resources for Development II: State and Society

"The key issue for late-late developers is not whether to have state intervention or not. The key issue is effective versus ineffective state intervention."

– Nicos Mouzelis[1]

All mainstream proposals to stimulate Irish development presuppose an able state. Even those, such as Guiomard or Crotty, who in their different ways advocate the drastic slimming down of the state presuppose its fine tuning so that it can efficiently play the role allocated to it (see Chapter 6). Most scholars of Irish development, however, advocate a more active role for the state particularly in fostering a more competitive and stronger indigenous industrial sector. Ireland "continues to require a strong state to direct the economy and to provide for the welfare of the society," concludes Girvin.[2] Here the question of ability looms large yet little attention has been devoted to whether the Irish state is able to play the role expected of it, the reasons for its deficiencies and the ways it could be transformed into a more efficient agent for development. Such ability is simply presupposed. This is a major weakness as the most detailed and finely honed proposals will be quickly blunted unless accompanied by a state that can set developmental goals and help society implement them effectively.

Extensive attention has been paid recently to the nature and role of the state in development. A growing literature has identified the state as one of the crucial determinants of the development success of countries like Japan, South Korea and Taiwan (see Chapter 3). In a recent work, Nicos Mouzelis observes that "certain states are better than others at drawing up and implementing development strategies" and goes as far as to say that "it is in fact the actual structure of the state that is the most crucial aspect for understanding why late developers with comparable starting points and resources have performed so unevenly within the world economy".[3] We do not have to go as far as this to agree that the nature and role of the state in a late developer like Ireland requires more active attention. This is the aim of this chapter.

The chapter has three parts. The first part looks at how the Irish state has been understood and identifies some key elements that make it what it is. The second part draws on various theories of the state to flesh out an understanding of a state that might more adequately serve development. This brings civil society into the forefront of the discussion. The final part looks at recent developments in civil society in Ireland and the potential for Ireland's development of a new partnership between the community sector, the social partners and the state.

The Irish state: illusory capacity

In their study of state, class and development in the Republic of Ireland, Breen et al. undertake a rare examination of the nature of the Irish state. They identify a number of themes which have been widely noted. Among these is that the Irish state has been more prone to "coaxing and facilitating rather than directing economic growth",[4] that the civil service inherited from colonial times acted to ensure stability rather than to promote change, and that the voting system (based on proportional representation with a single transferable vote) reinforced a political system based on two catch-all parties seeking cross-class support which greatly constrained the possibility for more decisive state action. What this study added to these observations was an attempt to draw conclusions about the sort of state that exists in Ireland. Thus they conclude that the Irish state until recently "retained substantial autonomy but exercised only a limited capacity".[5] The greatly expanded role of the state since the 1960s "did not translate into the necessary institutional arrangements for problem solving or analysis. The state's capacity – so formidable on paper – on closer examination proves to be illusory," they conclude.[6]

This may be true as far as it goes but it leaves the most important questions unasked. If autonomy refers to the ability of a state to formulate and pursue its own goals, why did the Irish state remain "active but essentially directionless"?[7] The authors define capacity as the state's ability to implement the policies suggested by its goals and they say that the Irish state's capacity proved illusory. Yet, they go on to say that "the state has a considerable potential for purposeful intervention" but in practice "it does not exercise that potential".[8] The reason for this goes back to the lack of "a core that could provide direction".[9] This vague and in part contradictory presentation fails to throw light on some of the key factors that have moulded and constrained the Irish state; because of this, it also fails to recognise fundamental changes which hold at least the potential to help transform that state.

Breen et al. claim that the main constraints on the autonomy of the Irish state were external rather than internal, referring presumably to the constraints on all late developers on the semi-periphery of the world economic system and their limited room for manoeuvre. They add that, in the post-War years, political instability altered the autonomy once enjoyed by the Irish state since frequent elections fought on economic issues constrained the state's economic policy. Yet this account essentially conceives of the state as an autonomous entity facing some restrictions to its autonomy from outside itself. It fails to take into account that all states are embedded in particular societies which mould and constrain them in particular ways.[10] In this regard, Girvin's formulation gets far closer to an accurate description of the constraints on state power: "There may be objective circumstances to which every state has to react: energy prices, inflation, or competition, but the reaction depends on the decisions taken by the nation state. These in turn are dependent on the relationships between the different social groups making up the society. The options available to a government and its flexibility in the face of change are in the end structured by the political culture."[11]

If it is in the domain of civil society and its political culture that we look for some of the key elements which make the state what it is, then an examination of what constrained state action at three moments in the history of the Irish state which were decisive for its socio-economic development will help identify some of the elements that have made the Irish state what it is. The first moment happened during the Economic War from 1932-35 when an attempt was made for the first time by the new Fianna Fáil government to develop native industry and to decisively re-orient the economy away from dependence on the export of live cattle to Britain. Orridge identifies the main political opposition to this aggressive economic nationalism as coming from a pro-metropolitan interest linked to Fine Gael. The opposition of this sector, however, was not decisive in defeating the attempt to fundamentally re-structure the nature of the Irish economy; rather, he argues that it was the very structure of the dependency relationship on the British market that led to the defeat as there was no success in finding alternative markets for Irish agricultural products. The 1938 Anglo-Irish Agreements therefore restored Ireland's position as an agricultural supplier to the British market.[12]

Yet the policy of native industrialisation remained in place and immediately after the second World War Sean Lemass, the main architect of this policy, proposed a series of radical measures to deepen the industrialisation drive, improve its efficiency and win export markets. He also urged a change in Fianna Fáil agricultural policy of keeping small producers on the land in favour of increasing output and efficiency in agriculture. The means proposed by Lemass involved greater state planning and intervention in building up large-scale industry and overcoming the financial and technological obstacles in the way of this.[13] This was the second key moment in the socio-economic development of the Irish state. Yet this was defeated by entrenched vested interests both within the highest echelons of Fianna Fáil[14] and in Irish society: Lemass "knew what he wanted, but was not always clear on how to obtain this. He opted for what he knew best, state intervention, but in doing so he confronted all the main vested interests in the economy".[15] Against this, Lemass' support base was relatively narrow and "he could not generate a large constituency for such policies".[16]

The third key moment in the Irish state's development history was the change over from the policy of protectionism to a liberal, open economy in the late 1950s. On the surface, this seemed a paradoxical move as a class of Irish industrialists had come into being due to the policy of protectionism and their existence depended in many cases on its continuation. Yet, whenever Irish bureaucrats tried to stimulate further industrial expansion these native industrialists resisted any moves towards what they regarded as state encroachment.[17] Referring to those bureaucrats who sought expansion in the Irish economy ("the expansionary coalition"), O'Hearn concludes: "The only remaining option for the expansionary coalition was to introduce incentives for new export-oriented investment – to enter into a coalition with a *new* (primarily foreign) section of capital."[18] The second element which led to the liberalisation of the economy was pressure from the US after Ireland accepted Marshall Aid, according to O'Hearn.

Examination of these three key moments in Ireland's

development history contradicts many of the principal conclusions of Breen et al. Firstly, the state's autonomy was greatly circumscribed both from within and from without. Secondly, the problem was not a lack of direction by the state as competing directions both within the state bureaucracy and in civil society. Thirdly, the state's capacity was not as illusory as suggested by Breen et al. as it did display a relative capacity[19] in pursuing the developmental direction that constraints permitted. The main conclusion that can be drawn therefore is that the problem lay principally not in the capacity of the Irish state per se but rather in the developmental direction it took, a direction directly responsive to conservative forces in Irish society and their inclination to choose the soft option instead of seeking a more robust national project of development. As both Breen et al and Girvin acknowledge, many of the major problems faced by the Irish economy and Irish society today stem from the decisions made in the late 1950s and early 1960s to opt for a highly dependent and relatively powerless insertion into the international economy. To have done otherwise would have demanded a greater mobilisation of resources and energies for which neither the state nor most of civil society had any stomach.

State constraints: emigration, populism and the post-colonial state

A brief examination of some major constraints on the Irish state following a more determined development path will close this section. The first is suggested by Girvin's comment on Lemass having a weak support base. The reference here is to the weakness in civil society of those elements that might be expected to espouse a more radical development option. What marks Irish society out from other post-colonial semi-peripheral states is the fact that in every generation since the 1840s it has exported the victims of its development failures. As Hirschman puts it so graphically: "People who chose emigration were obviously dissatisfied in some way with the country and society but they were leaving. With exit available as an outlet for the disaffected, they were less likely to resort to protest: the ships carrying the migrants contained many actual or potential anarchists and socialists, reformers and revolutionaries."[20] This, then, was why the support base for a more forceful developmental effort was so weak; among those who left, of course, were some who espoused more radical politics than did

Lemass; the overall impact of their presence would have been to tilt the balance in favour of more forceful state action.

With such a weak base for a decisive developmental drive it is not surprising that political life has, since 1932, been dominated by populist politics. As is familiar to students of Latin American development, this is the predominant form that progressive politics takes in late developing countries which lack both a strong working class and a strong bourgeoisie from which substantial class-based parties could emerge. In order to challenge the stranglehold of pro-metropolitan interests on national development, therefore, a form of politics emerges that mobilises marginalised urban and rural sectors as well as middle class sectors such as the intelligentsia and the native industrialists behind a drive for national development. The party which can maintain this cross-class support base does so through the strong appeal of a charismatic leader and through clientelistic ties of dependence to its supporters. Its policy orientation, however, remains fluid and ill-defined and the populist party depends a lot on rhetoric to strengthen its appeal.[21] Fianna Fáil is a classic populist party in this understanding of the term; as Curran puts it: "The success of Fianna Fáil populism resided in its representation of the problems of development, and the postulation of solutions which appealed to the small manufacturers, the rural poor and the working class. In posing the problem of development in populist terms, Fianna Fáil was able to gain popular support for the project of industrialisation."[22] While this form of politics does result in a state-led development drive, it also serves to blunt that drive when it runs into opposition from vested interests. This happens in two principal ways. Firstly, the cross-class nature of populist politics predisposes the use of state resources for the short-term satisfaction of different constituencies rather than for a long-term development drive. This has characterised not only Fianna Fáil's governance of the Irish state but also that of its opponents who have sought to emulate Fianna Fáil's electoral appeal. Secondly, the clientelistic nature of populist politics tends to incorporate organisations of civil society in a vertical way, weakening their autonomy and limiting their understanding of politics to the struggle to gain benefits from the state.[23] This may account for the "high propensity by non-elites to defer to policy prescriptions" which Jacobsen identifies in the Irish case.[24] This weakness of populism has been well summed up by the Mexican political scientist, Jorge G. Castañeda who speaks of "a compromise between limited political will to impose reform from

Poverty Amid Plenty

above, and limited capacity to fight for reform from below".[25] The dominance of populist politics can therefore be identified as a major element constraining the Irish state.

The final feature worthy of brief mention is the nature of the post-colonial state. The colonial state, as Carter has pointed out, sought to maximise the extraction of wealth from the colony.[26] Thus, it differed from a national state which sought to enhance the productive capacity of the ruling class in the national society and was the forum which competing class interests fought to control in order to advance their own developmental project. It is recognised that a key developmental moment in most western states was when the political and economic dominance of the class of large landowners was broken through the pressure of the middle class. In Ireland this happened in a very decisive way through the virtual abolition of the large landowning class in the last decades of the 19th century. Yet, as Mulhall has shown, this happened not as a result of the pressure of the middle class but as a result of the actions of the colonial state, seeking to resolve what it regarded as a growing security problem.[27] This example draws our attention to the weak relationship between state and civil society inherited from colonial times. This may help account for the Irish state's tendency to manage society rather than to innovate as evidenced by its failure to develop institutional arrangements for problem solving or analysis and by its pervasive culture of secrecy and of competent bureaucratic conservatism.

Based on the above, we can apply to each national state White's comment on each national form of democracy that it "takes on its particular character in response to the specific character of the society in which it is embedded and the specific historical conditions under which it emerges".[28] Do we have to go further, however, and conclude that the Irish state is destined to remain a victim of the constraints on its ability to be a vigorous and effective agent for development? To answer this, we need to look more closely at the nature of the developmental state.

"Bringing the state back in"

The Irish state emerges from the examination above as one that is, if not quite anti-developmental, inadequate to respond with vigour, creativity and effectiveness to the challenges of equitable social and economic development. Yet recent development theory argues that states have a vital role to play in stimulating and leading development and the term "developmental state" has come into wide use to describe the state that fulfills this function with success. What constitutes this developmental state and what is the crucial role it plays?

Following decades of relative neglect, the state has again become the focus of extensive theoretical work since the 1970s. The neglect of the state had been due to a large extent to the rather crude perspectives of marxist theory which had relegated it to a very secondary role as the expression of the interests of the ruling class. This began to be challenged by marxist scholars who argued that the state has to be understood as a power structure in its own right, exercising a major impact on all social classes. This re-evaluation of the state resulted in growing attention being paid to civil society and the ways in which social struggles set limits to the state's freedom of action. Thus the state could no longer be dismissed as simply facilitating exploitation by the bourgeoisie and coercing the rest of society to acquiesce in this exploitation. The work of Nicos Poulantzas and Claus Offe is widely seen as marking the move from marxist to post-marxist theory on the state. As Chandhoke summarises their contribution: "Ultimately as the capitalist state is forced to respond to the various social movements, its project either of reproducing capitalism, or seeking legitimacy is moderated. The state then can be seen as situated in a field of political contestation. This perspective rather than treating the state as autonomous, focused on the limits which social movements impose upon the state."[29] The state now became a far more interesting entity – adaptable, multi-dimensional and open to re-shaping from below.

If we can characterise this as a bottom-up view of the state, alongside it has emerged a top-down view, emphasising the autonomy of the state and its ability to "formulate and pursue goals that are not simply reflective of the demands or interests of social groups, classes, or society".[30] This approach has emerged from studies of the state's role in development, both in the developed and in the underdeveloped world. Studies of Japan, South Korea and Taiwan in particular have led to the identification of a type of state which is to be distinguished from the command states of the former communist countries of eastern Europe and from the regulatory social democratic states of western Europe. This is what has come to be known as the developmental state. In his survey which includes Botswana, Singapore, China, Indonesia, Thailand and Malaysia as well as the three East Asian countries mentioned above, Adrian Leftwich identifies six major components which define the developmental

Poverty Amid Plenty

state model.[31] These are: i) a determined developmental elite, "a small cadre of developmentally-determined senior politicians and bureaucrats";[32] ii) relative autonomy "from the demanding clamour of vested interests (whether class, regional or sectoral)";[33] iii) a powerful, competent and insulated economic bureaucracy; iv) a weak and subordinated civil society; v) the effective management of non-state economic interests, for example "setting terms which have attracted foreign capital while making it serve the state's domestic economic developmental priorities",[34] and, vi) repression, legitimacy and performance, namely "the combination of their sometimes brutal suppression of civil rights, their apparently wide measure of legitimacy and their generally sustained performance in delivering developmental goods".[35] Leftwich concludes: "Few societies in the modern world will make speedy transitions from poverty without states which approximate this model of a developmental state (ideally, but not necessarily, the democratic kind). Without such states, transitions may be slow but the human cost immense."[36]

This identification of a form of state capable of leading a determined developmental drive seems persuasive until we ask about the relationship of these states to their civil societies. How does a determined developmental elite emerge, how does it achieve autonomy from competing vested interests, how does the state maintain legitimacy with repression and, if a weak civil society is a pre-condition for the developmental state, how will it maintain itself as civil society becomes stronger and more sophisticated? As Chandhoke sums up: "The statists give us states without constituencies or contexts. In effect, the statists give us states without societies, without either origins, or conditions of reception. Their state exists in a social vacuum."[37] Do we have to conclude therefore that a developmental state is only achievable in very exceptional circumstances such as those which pertained in Japan and South Korea after the virtual collapse of those societies at the end of the second World War or in Taiwan after its effective takeover by the Kuomintang in 1949? Is the developmental state necessarily authoritarian and repressive?

Returning to the discussion of the Irish case earlier in this chapter may help find a route out of this dilemma. The conclusions included the point that a key developmental weakness of the Irish state lay not so much in lack of capacity as in lack of an appropriate direction. That the Irish state had the capacity to follow a direction laid out for it can be concluded from its relative success in attracting multinational industry once that route to development was chosen. Furthermore, the Industrial Development Authority (IDA), the semi-state body which carried the main responsibility for implementing this development strategy, bears some of the hallmarks of the powerful, competent and insulated economic bureaucracy of the developmental state. While there is undoubted need for a strengthening of state capacity in certain areas and for a greater coherence between different organs of the state, the central problem in the Irish case seems to lie not primarily in the capacity of the state as in its developmental direction. Thus the principal prospect for the emergence of a more developmental and interventionist state in the Irish case seems to depend on the "social struggle to gain the power to define the developmental project"[38] rather than on the administrative capacity of state officials and organs. This returns us to the terrain of civil society and its potential for setting a different developmental direction for the Irish state.

A counter-hegemonic project: towards a developmental state

For Chandhoke "civil society provides the terrain where a counter-hegemonic project can be launched ... since it provides the site, the institutions, the values and the processes through which the state can be challenged". Since she argues that "the state is defined by the kind of civil society that exists",[39] a challenge from civil society has the potential to re-define the state in developmental terms. However, this challenge faces immense difficulties. First of all, civil society is by no means homogeneous and is constituted by many sectors some of which (business, large farmers, the bureaucracy) actively support and promote the state's project. Secondly, civil society is constantly subject to the ability of the state to divide and conquer, to co-opt or, if necessary, to repress. Thirdly, even if significant sectors of civil society can coalesce around a political project which seeks to challenge that of the state, they can be less than effective in promoting that project.

The Irish state has since its foundation faced sectors of civil society which espoused a counter-hegemonic project. The most significant of these were republicans but, since Fianna Fáil entered electoral politics in 1927, these have never posed more than a minor irritant at times to the state. The left, either the moderate left constituted by the Labour Party and sectors of the trade union movement or the more hard left of socialist and communist groups, remained divided and outflanked by Fianna Fáil's vigorous espousal of socio-economic development, industrialisation and a welfare state. In the context of massive emigration, however, the support base for such sectors was bound to remain weak; instead, "the project of the bourgeoisie, focused on economic growth, has become the major aim of Irish society as a whole, backed up not only by the state but also by the farmers and the trade unions".[40] In this situation, the main pressure on the state has been for resources as competing interest groups sought to maximise their share of the cake. Any challenge to the developmental direction of the state has been extremely weak.

This has changed dramatically in the last 20 years as growing unemployment and inequality have generated within Ireland for the first time since the Great Famine a significant sector of society marginalised in a semi-permanent sense from power or wealth. For over a century, emigration had ensured that such an outcome of Ireland's relative underdevelopment was avoided. From this marginalised sector have emerged significant local movements of protest and self-help, espousing a more inclusive development strategy than that of the state.[41] With the deepening of the socio-economic crisis in the 1980s, this "community sector" came "to be constituted as a significant actor in its own right in policy discourse if not in the development process itself".[42] Yet, as a sector, it is rooted among those who are the victims of the Irish development model and so it struggles to move beyond piecemeal and fragmented policies of poverty alleviation (often supported by the state) to "developing a more just and equitable society through collective means ... based on principles of participation and empowerment".[43] It is this aspiration that marks the community sector out as providing the terrain from which to launch a counter-hegemonic project. Such a project would involve challenging the state to transform itself into a more effective agent for national development.

Different tendencies are identified in the relationship of the community sector to the state. Curtin and Varley distinguish between an "oppositional tendency" which sees the state as an obstacle to the kind of development it seeks and therefore works to oppose or pressure the state, and an "integrationist tendency" which works in partnership with the state to resolve development problems.[44] Tucker lists three trends – one which be called a status quo one, which seeks simply to alleviate distress; a reformist one which accepts the existing political and economic system but seeks to reform it and a radical approach calling for a fundamental overhaul of the existing system.[45] As acknowledged by Curtin and Varley, however, these distinctions may be overdrawn and what distinguishes the community sector is the ability to identify the needs of the excluded and to promote these through collective action. The willingness to work with the state has greatly increased as various state-funded schemes have been developed. This may entail the danger of co-option by the state but it has also expanded the opportunities for working in partnership to address the major developmental challenges facing Irish society – unemployment, deprivation and social exclusion.

This partnership now takes manifold forms, at local, at regional and at national level. At local level, for example, there is strong community sector involvement in the 38 area-based partnerships (ABPs) funded under the EU structural funds as there is in the EU LEADER programme for integrated rural development. At regional level, the community sector is involved in the County Enterprise Boards (CEBs) which are intended to harness local participation in addressing the challenge of economic development, and in the committees of the regional authorities monitoring EU funds. At national level, the community sector has representatives on the National Economic and Social Forum, is actively involved in the government's Anti-Poverty Strategy (APS) and has had representatives on the Task Force on Travellers and on the Commission on People with Disabilities. The organisational forms this partnership takes, however, fail to capture the innovative ways these forms bring representatives of statutory bodies, of the social partners (business, trade unions, farmers) and of the community sector together to address creatively problems of unemployment, deprivation and social exclusion at local level.

It is this aspect which has been highlighted by Professor Charles Sabel of Columbia Law School in a 1996 report for the Organisation for Economic Co-operation and Development (OECD) in which he holds up as an example for the countries of the OECD the Irish effort "to foster development and welfare through new forms of public and private local co-ordination ... in a way that blurs familiar distinctions between public and private, national and local, and representative and participative democracy".[46] What this report highlights in particular are the ways in which these forms of partnership bring together social and economic development, aspects which are usually treated separately in other countries. Secondly, they involve the local community in seeking innovative responses to their problems instead of designing such responses at central government for implementation locally. Thirdly, he discovers that approaches towards job creation in these partnerships are informed by some of the most advanced thinking internationally, "an ensemble of expectations about what the 'modern' firm should look like and the skills necessary to build and work in one".[47] Thus he concludes: "The Irish experience demonstrates that the principles guiding current economic restructuring contain the means for addressing some of the dislocations that restructuring itself causes, and especially for combining active, decentralised participation and the achievement of autonomy."[48]

While Sabel places emphasis on the backing given by the Department of the Taoiseach to this innovative approach, his emphasis on the values informing it such as participation, autonomy (from simply being implementing agencies for decisions taken elsewhere), innovation and solidarity make it clear that it reflects far more the ethos and organising style of the community sector.[49] He also makes clear that these new forms of partnership challenge the state to reform itself in fundamental ways so as to be more capable of responding to the challenges of a real bottom-up model of development.[50] This, of course, implies a real will on the part of the state to take these challenges seriously.

Other observers closer to the Irish experience are not, however, as positive in their evaluation of the potential of these new forms of partnership. Rafferty says the ABPs are seen "as mere conduits for EU money" and that the "marginalised remain powerless to determine the distribution of resources".[51] Varley and Ruddy write that "community groups have been granted but a token part in many of the area-based partnerships"[52] while Crickley is critical of the lack of opportunity afforded the community sector to influence national policy or even resource allocation.[53] While acknowledging the major constraints on the area partnerships due to the "national context of centralised and compartmentalised decision-making", Sarah Craig in her evaluation of the original 12 ABPs which had been set up on a pilot basis, concluded however that they "succeeded in starting a process of change" in that "individuals from the three sectors represented have begun to work together at local level in a new and constructive way."[54]

In highlighting the significance and novelty of these responses to social exclusion, Sabel also acknowledges that "these promising beginnings are little more than that, and many of the harshest tests ... surely lie ahead."[55] Among these tests, he lists vulnerability due to the novel character of these experiments and due to the fact that they do not fit into traditional administrative structures of democratic accountability. Secondly, he points to the fact that they are heavily dependent on EU funding which may not be available after the present round of structural funds runs out in 1999. Thirdly, he perceptively points to the potential tensions that exist between the values and ethos of community groups and those of business; these have largely been kept in check up to now due to the novelty of the partnerships. He writes, for example, of the "potentially paralysing conflicts between solidarity and self-interest that could develop within the partnerships".[56] Most important, however, is Sabel's warning that it is not clear what lessons are being drawn from these experiments either by the national offices of welfare and development agencies or by the social partners. His principal recommendations, therefore, relate to the importance of putting in place forms of evaluation that allow real policy learning to take place so as to be able to generalise the successes "through some combination of national reform and local adaptation".[57]

Attaching such international significance to the new forms of partnerships between state and civil society which have emerged piecemeal in Ireland over the last decade to address social exclusion is important. It at least alerts us to the fact "that 'Irish' surprises of improbable development may be lurking in many apparent backwaters, hidden by the mist of old expectations of stagnation".[58] But if it alerts us to the promise of these grassroots approaches towards building social inclusion, as Sabel puts it, it also alerts us to their great fragility. He acknowledges the major reform of state structures, ways of operating and learning abilities that will be required if the promise is not to be snuffed out. His comments invite the question: is the political will be there to continue this "democratic experimentalism", as he calls it, when hard decisions have to be made about the national exchequer making funding available after 1999?

These considerations place the onus back on civil society, and espousal of a counter-hegemonic project. For Sabel's report is weak in acknowledging that, as White puts it, "there is a potential conflict between a neo-liberal regulative strategy and a redistributive poverty-oriented strategy in terms of the power weightings behind each strategy".[59] The community sector may have succeeded in strengthening the power weighting behind a redistributive poverty-oriented strategy in the Irish case but it is still relatively weak and needs to be further strengthened if the developmental promise of the present is to be realised. What this means in the Irish case is that the challenge of inclusive development demands fundamental changes both in the nature and orientation of the state and in its developmental strategy. Key problems such as the need for a more active state involvement in building a strong, innovative indigenous industrial sector and the need for a welfare policy that redistributes wealth effectively towards the marginalised (see Chapter 5) will have to be addressed more forcefully than they ever have been. As Niall Crowley has stated, much work remains to be done "in examining existing models of development, exploring what integrated social and economic development analysis might be, and identifying new and more equitable and sustainable approaches to development."[60] With all our serious developmental problems, it is amazing how little of this work is being done.

This, then, places the focus on mobilising wider sectors of civil society in support of a counter-hegemonic project. As a critique of the dominant model of development is elaborated, so also is the potential to mobilise around it – environmental groups, NGOs, women, trade unions, religious. Thus the sector could take on that wider identity which it has achieved in parts of the Third World where civil society is now recognised as a "Third Sector" alongside the state and the market. As Siddhartha has written: "People need not feel powerless if there is a chance that the discussions and actions in their local groups, neighbourhood associations, NGOs, unions, etc. are actually leading to another kind of democratic practice where, directly or indirectly, the State and the Market are progressively made less alienating and more and more accountable to the interactions within civil society."[61] Thus is generated a more active sense of citizenship and a more participative democracy in which the emphasis is not on the traditional political aim of taking state power but rather on the diffusion of power more widely throughout society. Such a diffusion of power can put pressure on the state to restructure itself so as to serve more adequately the task of development.

Conclusion

Despite widespread acclaim for Ireland's so-called "economic miracle", a huge developmental challenge still faces Irish society. This is to generate from our own creativity and resources the dynamism to lay the foundations of a national economy, the benefits of which serve our society as equitably as possible. This book has shown how Ireland shares this challenge with most countries of the world and how it requires innovative approaches if we are to reverse the tendency towards entrenched social exclusion. It has also shown how civil society is emerging as an important actor in the struggle for such a form of development as the people who are often the victims of others' development begin to claim back their power and demand to be considered. This seems the only way of ensuring that values such as social justice, solidarity, equality, participation and accountability are not sacrificed in the drive for development. We are approaching the close of a century which has seen greater technological progress than ever before in human history. However, it also leaves us with a legacy of grim poverty and deprivation side by side with opulence and technical prowess that was completely unimaginable a century ago. Thus no easy optimism is possible. If technology will not suffice to develop us, perhaps we need to foster a "democratic experimentalism" which can engage human ingenuity and solidarity as fully as possible in the task of development.

Footnotes

1 Nicos Mouzelis, "The state in late development: historical and comparative perspectives" unpublished paper, p.194

2 Brian Girvin, *Between Two Worlds: Politics and Economy in Independent Ireland*, Gill & Macmillan, 1989, p.211

3 ibid., p.170

4 Richard Breen et al., *Understanding Contemporary Ireland: State, Class and Development in the Republic of Ireland*, Gill & Macmillan, 1990, p.40

5 ibid., p.20

6 ibid., p.213

7 ibid., p.43

8 ibid., p.47

9 ibid., p.47

10 Neera Chandhoke, *State and Civil Society: Explorations in Political Theory*, Sage, 1995, pp. 71-3

11 Brian Girvin, op. cit., p.203

12 Andrew W. Orridge, "The Blueshirts and the 'Economic War': A study of Ireland in the context of dependency theory" in *Political Studies*, 1983, vol.31, pp.358-66

13 For a discussion of Lemass' proposals see Brian Girvin, op. cit., chapter 5.

14 On this point, see Richard Dunphy, *The Making of Fianna Fáil Power in Ireland 1923-1948*, Clarendon Press Oxford, 1995, pp. 217, 229.

15 ibid., p.167

16 ibid., p.160

17 For an account of four cases of such resistance, see Denis O'Hearn, "The road from import-substituting to export-led industrialization in Ireland: who mixed the asphalt, who drove the machinery, and who kept making them change directions?" in *Politics and Society*, vol.18, no. 1, 1990, pp.14-17

18 ibid., p.17

19 On the concept of relative capacity, see D. Michael Shafer, *Winners and Losers: How Sectors Shape the Developmental Prospects of States,* Cornell University Press, 1994, pp.46-8.

20 Albert O. Hirschman, "Exit, voice, and the state" in *World Politics,* vol.31, no.1, 1978, p.102

21 For a discussion of Latin American populism see Michael L. Conniff, ed., *Latin American Populism in Comparative Perspective,* University of New Mexico Press, 1982; Torcuato S. Di Tella, *Latin American Politics: A Theoretical Framework,* University of Texas Press, 1990; Robert H. Dix, "Populism: authoritarian and democratic" in *Latin American Research Review,* vol.20, no.2, 1985, pp.29-52.

22 Catherine Curran, *The* Irish Press *and Populism in Ireland,* unpublished PhD thesis, Dublin City University, 1994, p.106

23 For a discussion of clientelism in the context of populist politics, see Nicos P. Mouzelis, *Politics in the Semi-Periphery: Early Parliamentarism and Late Industrialisation in the Balkans and Latin America,* Macmillan, 1986, pp.73-94.

24 John Kurt Jacobsen, *Chasing Progress in the Irish Republic: Ideology, Democracy and Dependent Development,* Cambridge University Press, 1994, p.95

25 Jorge G. Castañeda, *Utopia Unarmed: The Latin American Left after the Cold War,* Vantage Books, 1993, p.46

26 Alan Carter, "The nation-state and underdevelopment" in *Third World Quarterly,* vol.16, no.4, 1995, p.605

27 Terry Mulhall, *The State and Agrarian Reform: The Case of Ireland 1800-1940,* unpublished PhD thesis, University of London, 1992

28 Gordon White, "Towards a democratic developmental state" in *IDS Bulletin,* vol.26, no.2, 1995, p.32

29 Neera Chandhoke, op. cit., 1995, p.24

30 Theda Skocpol, "Bringing the state back in: strategies of analysis in current research" in Peter B. Evans, Dietrich Rueschemeyer and Theda Skocpol, eds., *Bringing the State Back In,* Cambridge University Press, 1985, p.9

31 Adrian Leftwich, "Bringing politics back in: towards a model of the developmental state" in *The Journal of Development Studies,* vol.31, no.3, 1995, pp.400-27

32 ibid., p.405

33 ibid., p.408

34 ibid., p.417

35 ibid., p.418

36 ibid., p.421

37 Neera Chandhoke, op. cit., p.56

38 Jacobsen, op. cit., p.102

39 Neera Chandhoke, op. cit., p.72

40 Michel Peillon, *Contemporary Irish Society: An Introduction,* Gill & Macmillan, 1982, p.59

41 For a brief history of some of the major grassroots movements which arose since the 1960s, see Patricia Kelleher and Mary Whelan, *Dublin Communities in Action,* Community Action Network and Combat Poverty Agency, 1992, pp 3-12. For an account of the Glencolumbcille rural development project and its implications for state/community relations, see Vincent Tucker, "State and community: a case study of Glencolumbcille" in Chris Curtin and Thomas M. Wilson, eds, *Ireland from Below: Social Change and Local Communities,* Galway University Press, 1990, pp. 283-300

42 Chris Curtin and Tony Varley, "Community action and the state" in Patrick Clancy et al.: *Irish Society: Sociological Perspectives,* IPA, 1995, p.382

43 Anastasia Crickley and Maurice Devlin, "Community work in the Eighties: an overview" in *Community Work in Ireland: Trends in the 80s, Options for the 90s,* Combat Poverty Agency, 1990, p.62

44 Curtin and Varley, op. cit., pp.379-80

45 Vincent Tucker, "Community work and social change" in *Community Work in Ireland*, op. cit., p.36

46 OECD, *Ireland: Local Partnerships and Social Innovation*, OECD, 1996, p.9

47 ibid., p.13

48 ibid., p.13

49 Niall Crowley outlines very clearly what these values are and how they are reflected in the fluid and responsive forms of organisation being evolved by the community sector. See Niall Crowley, "Frameworks for partnership: emerging models and responses" in *Partnership in Action: The Role of Community Development and Partnership in Ireland*, Community Workers' Co-operative, 1996, pp.155-68.

50 Sabel writes: "[T]o co-operate and learn from local activities the administrations [government departments and agencies such as Forbairt and FÁS] would have to decentralise authority internally themselves, a slow and difficult process under any circumstances, and given the many imponderables of the situation – in particular, the uncertain future of the partnerships – it is not surprising that they have not been eager to pursue this course. For example, the same office that is charting the bewildering complexity of local administration and devising plans for its simplification also admitted that co-ordination among regional-level officials within its own organisation was weak." OECD, op. cit., p.90

51 Mick Rafferty, "Between Scylla and Charybdis", in *Partnership in Action*, op. cit., p.60

52 Tony Varley and Mary Ruddy, "Partners worthy of the name?" in *Partnership in Action*, op. cit., p.81

53 Anastasia Crickley, "The role of community development: the development of partnerships" in *Partnership in Action*, op. cit., p.25

54 Sarah Craig, *Progress through Partnership*, Combat Poverty Agency, 1994, p.80

55 OECD, op. cit., p.10

56 ibid., p.82

57 ibid., p.11

58 ibid., p.80

59 Gordon White, op. cit., p.35, footnote 17

60 Niall Crowley, op. cit., p.167

61 Siddhartha, "Introduction: Asian reflections on civil society in Brazil" in Rubem César Fernandes, *Private but Public: The Third Sector in Latin America*, Civicus and Network Cultures – Asia, 1994, p.ix

Bibliography

The bibliography is divided into two parts, each corresponding to Parts I and II of the book.

Part I

Adams, Nassau A., *Worlds Apart: The North-South Divide and the International System*, Zed Books, 1993

Adams, W.M., *Green Development: Environment and Sustainability in the Third World*, Routledge, 1990

Amin, Samir, *Empire of Chaos*, Monthly Review Press, 1992

Amin, Samir, *Delinking*, Zed Books, 1990

Amin, Samir, *Maldevelopment: Anatomy of a Global Failure*, Zed Books, 1990

Amin, Samir, *Eurocentrism*, Monthly Review Press, 1989

Amin, Samir, *The Law of Value and Historical Materialism*, Monthly Review Press, 1978

Amin, Samir, *Unequal Development*, Monthly Review Press, 1976

Amin, Samir, *Accumulation on a World Scale*, Monthly Review Press, 1974

Arndt, H.W., *Economic Development: The History of an Idea*, University of Chicago Press, 1987

Arrighi, Giovanni, "World income inequalities and the future of socialism" in *New Left Review*, no.189, 1991, pp.39-66

Banck, Geert A., "Cultural dilemmas behind strategy: Brazilian neighbourhood movements and Catholic discourse" in *European Journal of Development Research*, vol.2, no.1, 1990, pp.65-88

Baran, Paul A., *The Political Economy of Growth*, Monthly Review Press, 1957

Barrat Brown, Michael, *Models in Political Economy*, Penguin, second edition, 1995

Bello, Walden, *Dark Victory: United States, Structural Adjustment and Global Poverty*, Pluto Press, 1994

Bernstein, H, "Breakdowns of modernisation" in *Journal of Development Studies*, vol.8, no.2, 1972, pp. 309-318

Berger, Mark T., "The end of the 'Third World'?" in *Third World Quarterly*, vol.15, no 2, 1994, pp. 257-75

Biersteker, Thomas J., "The 'triumph' of liberal economic ideas" in Barbara Stallings, ed., *Global Change, Regional Response: The New International Context of Development*, Cambridge University Press, 1995, pp.174-96

Booth, David, ed., *Rethinking Social Development: Theory, Research and Practice*, Longman, 1994

Booth, David, "Marxism and development sociology: interpreting the impasse" in *World Development*, vol.13, no.7, 1985, pp.761-87

Boserup, Esther, *Women's Role in Economic Development*, Allen & Unwin, 1970

Braidotti, Rosi et al., *Women, the Environment and Sustainable Development*, Zed Books, 1994

Brydon, Lynne and Sylvia Chant, *Women in the Third World: Gender Issues in Rural and Urban Areas*, Edward Elgar, 1989

Cardoso, Fernando H., "The originality of a copy: CEPAL and the ideas of development" in *Cepal Review*, no.2, 1977, pp.7-36

Cardoso, Fernando H. and E. Faletto, *Dependency and Development in Latin America*, University of California Press, 1971

Castañeda, Jorge G., *Utopia Unarmed: The Latin American Left after the Cold War*, Vantage Books, 1993

CEPAL, *Panorama Social de America Latina 1995*, CEPAL, 1995

Chambers, Robert, *Poverty and Livelihoods: Whose Reality Counts?*, UNDP, 1995

Chambers, Robert, "Sustainable rural livelihoods: a key strategy for people, environment and development" in C. Conroy and M. Litvinoff, eds, *The Greening of Aid: Sustainable Livelihoods in Practice*, Earthscan, 1988, pp. 1-17

Chandhoke, Neera, *State and Civil Society: Explorations in Political Theory*, Sage, 1995

Christian Aid, *Who Runs the World?* Christian Aid, 1994

Chu, Yun-Han, "The East Asian NICs: a state-led path to the developed world" in Barbara Stallings, ed., *Global Change, Regional Response*, Cambridge University Press, 1995, pp.199-237

Clark, John, "The state, popular participation, and the voluntary sector" in *World Development*, vol.23, no.4, 1995, pp.593-601

Colman, David and Frederick Nixson, "The concept and measurement of development" in Anna Farmer, ed., *The Developing World*, DESC, 1988, pp. 28-43

Craig, Gary and Marjorie. Mayo, eds, *Community Empowerment: A Reader in Participation and Development*, Zed Books, 1995

Dallmayr, Fred, "Modernization and postmodernization: whither India?" in *Alternatives*, vol.17, 1992, pp.421-52

Daly, Herman E., "Sustainable growth: an impossibility theorem" in *Development*, vol.3, no.4, 1990, pp.45-47

Daly, Herman, *Steady-state Economics: The Economics of Biophysical Equilibrium and Moral Growth*, W. H. Freeman, 1977

Dankelman, Irene and Joan Davidson, *Women and Environment in the Third World: Alliance for the Future*, Earthscan with IUCN, 1988

Department of Foreign Affairs, *Challenges and Opportunities Abroad: White Paper on Foreign Policy*, Department of Foreign Affairs, Dublin, 1996

Department of Foreign Affairs, *Irish Aid: Consolidation and Growth – A Strategy Plan*, Department of Foreign Affairs, Dublin, 1993

Edwards, Michael, "The irrelevance of development studies" in *Third World Quarterly*, vol.11, no.1, 1989, pp. 116-35

Eisenstadt, S.N., "Social change, differentiation and evolution" in *American Sociological Review*, vol. 29, no 3, 1964, pp. 375-386

Emmanuel, Arghiri, *Unequal Exchange*, New Left Books, 1972

Esteva, Gustavo, "Development" in Wolfgang Sachs, ed., *The Development Dictionary: A Guide to Knowledge as Power*, Zed Books, 1992, pp 6-25

Evans, Peter, "After dependency: recent studies of class, state, and industrialization" in *Latin American Research Review*, vol.20, no.2, 1985, pp.149-160

Evans, Peter B. and John D. Stephens, "Development and the world economy" in Neil Smelser, ed., *Handbook of Sociology*, Sage, 1988, pp.739-73

Fallows, James, *Looking at the Sun: The Rise of the New East Asian Economic and Political System*, Pantheon, 1994

Fishlow, Albert, et al., *Miracle or Design? Lessons from the East Asian Experience*, Overseas Development Council, 1994

Poverty Amid Plenty

Foster-Carter, Aidan, "From Rostow to Gunder Frank: conflicting paradigms in the analysis of underdevelopment" in *World Development,* vol.4, no.3, 1976, pp.167-80

Frank, André Gunder, "Latin American Development theories revisited" in *Latin American Perspectives,* issue 73, vol.19, no.2, 1992, pp.125-39

Frank, André Gunder, "The underdevelopment of development" in *Scandinavian Journal of Development Alternatives,* vol.X, no.3, 1991, pp.5-72

Frank, André Gunder, *Capitalism and Underdevelopment in Latin America: Historical Studies of Chile and Brazil,* Monthly Review Press, 1967

Friberg, Mats and Bjorn Hettne, "The greening of the world: towards a non-deterministic model of global processes" in Herb Addo et al., *Development as Social Transformation: Reflections on the Global Problematique,* Hodder and Stoughton, 1985, pp.204-70

Friedmann, John, *Empowerment: The Politics of Alternative Development,* Blackwell, 1992

Fuentes, Marta and A. G. Frank, "Ten thesis on social movements" in *World Development,* vol.17, no.2, 1989, pp.179-91

Galeano, Eduardo, *The Open Veins of Latin America,* Monthly Review Press, 1973

Garst, Daniel, "Wallerstein and his critics" in *Theory and Society,* vol,14, no.4, 1985, pp.469-95

George, Susan and Fabrizio Sabelli, *Faith and Credit: The World Bank's Secular Empire,* Penguin, 1994

Gereffi, Gary, "Global production systems and third world development" in Barbara Stallings, ed., *Global Change, Regional Response,* Cambridge University Press, 1995, pp.100-42

Ghai, Dharam, et al., *Globalization and Social Integration,* UNDP, 1995

Girvin, Brian, *Between Two Worlds: Politics and Economy in Independent Ireland,* Gill & Macmillan, 1989

Gorostiaga, Xavier, "Latin America in the 'New World Order'" in *TNIdeas,* November 1992, pp.10-19

Goulet, Denis, "Development: creator and destroyer of values" in *World Development,* vol.20, no.3, 1992, pp.467-75

Green, Duncan, *Silent Revolution: The Rise of Market Economics in Latin America,* LAB, 1995

Grindle, John, *Bread and Freedom: Basic Human Needs and Human Rights,* Trócaire and Gill & Macmillan, 1992

Halliday, Fred, *Islam and the Myth of Confrontation,* I. B. Tauris, 1996

Harris, Nigel, *The End of the Third World,* Pelican, 1987

Harrison, D, *The Sociology of Modernization and Development,* Unwin Hyman, 1988

Hettne, Björn, "Introduction: towards an international political economy of development" in *European Journal of Development Research,* vol.7, no.2, 1995, pp.223-32

Hiro, Dilip, *Iran under the Ayatollahs,* Routledge and Kegan Paul, 1987

Hirschman, Albert O., *Getting Ahead Collectively: Grassroots Experiences in Latin America,* Pergamon Press, 1984

Hobsbawm, Eric, *Age of Extremes: The Short Twentieth Century 1914-1992,* Michael Joseph, 1994

Hoogvelt, Ankie M. M., *The Third World in Global Development,* Macmillan, 1982

Hulme, D. and Mark M. Turner, *Sociology and Development,* Harvester Wheatsheaf, 1990

Hunt, Diana, *Economic Theories of Development: An analysis of competing paradigms*, Harvester Wheatsheaf, 1989

Huntington, Samuel, *Political Order in Changing Societies*, Yale, 1968

Jones, Charles A., *The North-South Dialogue: A Brief History*, Frances Pinter, 1983

Kabbani, Rana, *Women in Muslim Society*, Department of Sociology, UCC, 1992

Kay, Cristóbal, "For a renewal of development studies: Latin American theories and neoliberalism in the era of structural adjustment" in *Third World Quarterly*, vol.14, no.4, 1993, pp.691-702

Kay, Cristóbal, *Latin American Theories of Development and Underdevelopment*, Routledge, 1989

Kirby, Peadar, *Adjusting to Develop? The Impact of Neo-liberalism in Mexico*, Oxfam, 1994

Kitching, Gavin, *Development and Underdevelopment in Historical Perspective: Populism, Nationalism and Industrialization*, Routledge, 1989

Kuhn, Thomas, *The Structure of Scientific Revolutions*, University of Chicago Press, 1970

Laclau, Ernesto, "Feudalism and capitalism in Latin America" in *New Left Review*, no.67, 1971, pp.19-38

Larrain, Jorge, *Theories of Development*, Polity Press, 1989

Lee, Joseph, *Ireland: Politics and Society 1912-1985*, Cambridge University Press, 1989

Lehmann, David, *Democracy and Development in Latin America*, Polity Press, 1990

Leipziger, Danny M. and Vinod Thomas, *The Lessons of East Asia: An Overview of Country Experience*, World Bank, 1993

Lélé, Sharachchandra M., "Sustainable development: a critical review" in *World Development*, vol.19, no.6, 1991, pp.607-21

Lerner, David, *The Passing of Traditional Society*, The Free Press, 1964

Leys, Colin, "The crisis in 'development theory'" in *New Political Economy*, vol.1 no.1, 1996 pp.41-58

Leys, Colin, *The Rise and Fall of Development Theory*, Indiana University Press, 1996

Lovett, Brendan, *Life Before Death: Inculturating Hope*, Claretian Publications, 1986

Lustig, Nora, "From structuralism to neostructuralism: the search for a heterodox paradigm" in Patricio Meller, ed., *The Latin American Development Debate*, Westview Press, 1991, pp.27-42

Lyon, David, *Postmodernity*, Open University Press, 1994

Max-Neef, Manfred A, *From the Outside Looking In: Experiences in 'Barefoot Economics'*, Zed Books, 1992

Mainwaring, Scott, "Urban popular movements, identity, and democratization in Brazil" in *Comparative Political Studies*, vol.20, no.2, 1987, pp.131-59

McCarthy, Mary R. and Thomas G. McCarthy, *Third World Debt: Towards an Equitable Solution*, Trócaire and Gill & Macmillan, 1994

McClelland, David, *The Achieving Society*, Van Nostrand, 1961

Mehmet, Ozay, *Westernizing the Third World: The Eurocentricity of Economic Development Theories*, Routledge, 1995

Middleton, Neil et al., *Tears of the Crocodile: From Rio to Reality in the Developing World*, Pluto, 1993

Mies, Maria and Vandana Shiva, *Ecofeminism*, Fernwood Publications and Zed Books, 1993

Mjøset, Lars, *The Irish Economy in a Comparative Institutional Perspective*, NESC, 1992

Molyneux, Maxine and Deborah Lynn Steinberg, "Mies and Shiva's 'Ecofeminism': A New Testament?" in *Feminist Review,* no.49, Spring 1995, pp. 86-107

Moser, Caroline O. N, "Gender planning in the Third World: meeting practical and strategic gender needs" in *World Development,* vol.17, no.11, 1989, pp. 1799-1825

Mouzelis, Nicos, *Politics in the Semi-Periphery,* Macmillan, 1986

Mouzelis, Nicos P., "Sociology of development: reflections on the present crisis" in *Sociology,* vol.22, no.1, 1988, pp.23-44

O'Brien, Philip J., "A critique of Latin American theories of dependency" in Oxaal et al, eds, *Beyond the Sociology of Development,* Routledge and Kegan Paul, 1975, pp.7-27

Oxfam, *The Oxfam Poverty Report,* 1995

Oxfam Ireland, *The Failure of IMF/World Bank Policies in Africa,* Oxfam, 1994

Oxfam Ireland, *Multilateral Debt as an Obstacle to Recovery: The Case of Uganda,* Oxfam, 1994

Oxfam Ireland, *The Impact of Structural Adjustment Programmes on Women,* Oxfam, 1994

Oxfam Ireland, *Economic Reform and Inequality in Latin America,* Oxfam, 1994

Oxfam Ireland, *Embracing the Future,* Oxfam, 1994

Packenham, Robert A., *The Dependency Movement: Scholarship and Politics in Development Studies,* Harvard University Press, 1992

Parsons, Talcott, *The Social System,* The Free Press, 1951

Parsons, Talcott, "Evolutionary universals in society" in *American Sociological Review,* vol.29, no.3, June 1964, pp.339-57

Pomfret, Richard, *Diverse Paths of Economic Development,* Harvester Wheatsheaf, 1992

Portes, Alejandro, "Latin American class structures: the composition and change during the last decades" in *Latin American Research Review,* vol.20, no.3, 1985, pp.7-40

Redclift, Michael, *Sustainable Development: Exploring the Contradictions,* Methuen, 1987

Rostow, W. W., *The Stages of Economic Growth,* Cambridge University Press, 1960

Roxborough, Ian, *Theories of Underdevelopment,* Macmillan, 1979

Roxborough, Ian, "Dependency and development: Cardoso and Faletto: multiple paths" in Archetti, E. et al, eds., *Sociology of 'Developing Societies': Latin America,* Macmillan, 1978, pp.3-8

Sachs, Wolfgang, *On the Archaeology of the Development Idea,* Pennsylvania State University Science, Technology and Society Programme, 1989

Schuurman, Frans J., ed., *Beyond the Impasse: New Directions in Development Theory,* Zed Books, 1993

Schuurman, Frans J., "Urban social movements: between regressive utopia and socialist panacea" in Frans Schuurman and Ton van Naerssen, eds., *Urban Movements in the Third World,* Routledge, 1989, pp.9-26

Scott, Alan, *Ideology and the New Social Movements,* Routledge, 1990

Seers, Dudley, "Challenges to development theories and strategies" in *International Development,* 1969, pp.5-20.

Sen, Amartya, "Concepts of poverty" in Anna Farmar, ed., *The Developing World: An Introduction to Development Studies through Selected Readings,* DESC, 1988, pp.22-7

Sen, Gita and Caren Grown, *Development, Crises and Alternative Visions,* Earthscan, 1988

Shannon, Thomas R., *An Introduction to the World-System Perspective,* Westview Press, 1989

Shaw, Timothy M., "Globalisation, regionalisms and the South in the 1990s: towards a new political economy of development" in *European Journal of Development Research*, vol.7, no.2, 1995, pp.257-75

Sheahan, John, *Patterns of Development in Latin America: Poverty, Repression and Economic Strategy*, Princeton University Press, 1987

Skinner, Quentin, *The Return of Grand Theory in the Human Sciences*, Cambridge, 1990

Sklair, Leslie, *Sociology of the Global System*, Prentice Hall, 2nd edition, 1995

Sklair, Leslie, "Transcending the impasse: metatheory, theory and empirical research in the sociology of development and underdevelopment" in *World Development*, vol.16, no.6, 1988, pp.697-709

Stallings, Barbara, "Introduction" in Barbara Stallings, ed., *Global Change, Regional Response*, Cambridge University Press, 1995, pp.1-30

Stewart, Frances, *Planning to Meet Basic Needs*, Macmillan, 1985

Stokes, Susan C., "Politics and Latin America's urban poor: reflections from a Lima shantytown" in *Latin American Research Review*, vol.26, no.2, 1991, pp.75-101

Timberlake, Lloyd, *Africa in Crisis: The causes, the cures of environmental bankruptcy*, Earthscan, 1988

Todaro, Michael P., *Economic Development*, Longman, 5th edition, 1994

Toye, John, *Dilemmas of Development*, Basil Blackwell, 2nd edition, 1993

Trainer, Ted., *Developed to Death: Rethinking Third World Development*, Green Print, 1989

Tucker, Vincent, *The Myth of Development*, Department of Sociology, UCC, 1992

ul Haq, Mahbub, *New Imperatives of Human Security*, UNDP, 1995

UNDP, *Human Development Report 1990*, Oxford University Press, 1990

UNDP, *Human Development Report 1992*, Oxford University Press, 1992

UNDP, *Human Development Report 1993*, Oxford University Press, 1993

UNDP, *Human Development Report 1995*, Oxford University Press, 1995

van der Borgh, Chris, "A comparison of four development models in Latin America" in *European Journal of Development Research*, vol.7, no.2, 1995, pp.276-96

van Lieshout, Mary, ed., *A Woman's World: Beyond the Headlines*, Oxfam and Attic Press, 1996

van Nieuwenhuijze C.A.O., "Does development have anything to do with culture? in van Nieuwenhuijze, ed., *Development Regardless of Culture?*, E.J.Brill, 1984, pp.11-24

Verhelst, Thierry G., *No Life Without Roots: Culture and Development*, Zed Books, 1990

Wade, Robert, "Japan, the World Bank, and the art of paradigm maintenance" in *New Left Review*, no.217, 1996, pp.3-36

Wallerstein, Immanuel, *After Liberalism*, The New Press, 1995

Wallerstein, Immanuel, *Geopolitics and Geoculture: Essays on the Changing World-System*, Cambridge University Press, 1991

Wallerstein, Immanuel, *The Modern World System III: The Second Era of Great Expansion of the Capitalist World-Economy 1730s-1840s*, Academic Press, 1989

Wallerstein, Immanuel, *The Modern World System II: Mercantilism and the Consolidation of the European World-Economy 1600-1750*, Academic Press, 1980

Wallersetin, Immanuel, *The Capitalist World Economy*, Cambridge University Press, 1979

Wallerstein, Immanuel, *The Modern World System: Capitalist Agriculture and the Origins of the European World-Economy in the Sixteenth Century*, Academic Press, 1974

Wallerstein, Immanuel, "The rise and future demise of the world capitalist system: concepts for comparative analysis" in *Comparative Studies in Society and History*, vol.16, no.4, 1974, pp.387-415

Wandergeest, Peter and Frederick H. Buttel, "Marx, Weber, and development sociology: beyond the impasse" in *World Development*, vol.16, no.6, 1988, pp.683-95

Warren, Bill, *Imperialism: Pioneer of Capitalism*, Verso, 1980

Waylen, Georgina, "Women's movements and democratisation in Latin America" in *Third World Quarterly*, vol.14, no.3, 1993, pp.573-87

Williamson, John, *Latin American Adjustment: How Much Has Happened?*, Institute for International Economics, 1990

Williamson, John, "Democracy and the 'Washington Consensus'" in *World Development*, vol.21, no.8, 1993, pp.1329-1336

World Bank, *The World Bank Development Report*, Oxford University Press, 1993

World Bank, *The World Bank Atlas 1996*, The World Bank, 1995

World Bank, *The World Bank Atlas 1994*, The World Bank, 1993

World Bank, *Learning from the Past, Embracing the Future*, World Bank, 1994

World Bank, *The East Asian Miracle: Economic Growth and Public Policy*, Oxford University Press, 1993

World Commission on Environment and Development: *Our Common Future*, Oxford, 1987

Part II

Anderson, Benedict, *Imagined Communities*, Verso, 1992

Barrett, Sean: "Measuring poverty in Ireland: an assessment of recent studies", in *The Economic and Social Review*, vol.20, no.4, 1989, pp.353-60

Barry, Frank, "Industrialisation strategies for developing countries: lessons from the Irish experience" in *Development Policy Review*, vol.9, 1991, pp.85-98

Barry, Frank, "Review symposium" in *The Economic and Social Review*, vol.21, no.2, 1990, pp.235-244

Barry, Frank and John Bradley, *On the Causes of Ireland's Unemployment*, Centre for Economic Research, UCD, Working Paper WP 91/1, 1991

Barry, Frank and Aoife Hannan, "Multinationals and indigenous employment: an 'Irish Disease'?" in *The Economic and Social Review*, vol.27, no.1, 1995, pp. 21-32

Bielenberg, Andy, *Cork's Industrial Revolution 1780-1880: Development or Decline?* Cork University Press, 1991

Boyce, D. George, *Nationalism in Ireland*, Croom Helm, 1982

Bradley, John, José-Antonio Herce and Leonor Modesto, "The macroeconomic effects of the CSF 1994-99 in the EU periphery" in *Economic Modelling*, vol.12, no. 3, 1995, pp.323-33

Brady, Ciaran, ed., *Interpreting Irish History: The Debate on Historical Revisionism*, Irish Academic Press, 1994

Breen, Richard and Christopher T. Whelan, *Social Mobility and Social Class in Ireland*, Gill & Macmillan, 1996

Breen, Richard and Christopher T. Whelan, "Social class, class origins and political partisanship in the Republic of Ireland" in *European Journal of Political Research*, vol.26, no.2, 1994, pp.117-133

Breen, Richard, et al., *Understanding Contemporary Ireland*, Gill & Macmillan, 1990

Breuilly, John, "Reflections on nationalism" in *Philosophy and Social Science,* vol. 15, 1985, pp.74-5

Brown, Terence, *Ireland: A Social and Cultural History 1922-1979,* Fontana, 1981

Byrne, Sean, *Wealth and Poverty in Ireland: A Review of the Available Evidence,* Combat Poverty Agency, 1989

Caherty, Térèse et al, eds, *Is Ireland a Third World Country?* Beyond the Pale Publications, 1992

Callan, Tim and Brian Nolan, *Income Inequality and Poverty in Ireland in the 1970s and 1980s,* ESRI Working Paper 43, 1993

Carter, Alan, "The nation-state and underdevelopment" in *Third World Quarterly,* vol.16, no.4, 1995, pp.595-618

Castañeda, Jorge G., *Utopia Unarmed: The Latin American Left after the Cold War,* Vintage Books, 1993

Chandhoke, Neera, *State and Civil Society: Explorations in Political Theory,* Sage, 1995

Cherry Orchard Faith and Justice Group, *One City, Two Tiers: A Theological Reflection on Life in a Divided Society,* Cherry Orchard Faith and Justice Group, 1996

Clancy, Patrick, et al., eds, *Irish Society: Sociological Perspectives,* IPA, 1995

Clancy, Patrick, et al., eds, *Ireland and Poland: Comparative Perspectives,* Department of Sociology, UCD, 1992

Clancy, Patrick, et al., eds, *Ireland: A Sociological Profile,* IPA, 1986

CMRS, *Towards Full Citizenship for All,* Justice Commission, CMRS, n.d.

Combat Poverty Agency, *Community Work in Ireland: Trends in the 80s, Options for the 90s,* Combat Poverty Agency, 1990

Combat Poverty Agency, *Pictures of Poverty: Twelve Accounts of Life on Low Income,* Combat Poverty Agency, 1989

Commins, Patrick, "Rural development in the Republic of Ireland" in Michael Murray and John Greer, eds, *Rural Development in Ireland,* Avebury, 1993, pp.41-53

Community Workers' Co-operative, *Partnership in Action,* CWC, 1996

Conniff, Michael L, ed., *Latin American Populism in Comparative Perspective,* University of New Mexico Press, 1982

Connolly, Bernard, *The Rotten Heart of Europe,* Faber and Faber, 1995

Council for Social Welfare, *Conference on Poverty 1981,* Council for Social Welfare, 1982

Craig, Sarah, *Progress through Partnership*, Combat Poverty Agency, 1994

Crotty, Raymond, *Ireland in Crisis: A Study of Capitalist Colonial Undevelopment,* Brandon, 1989

Curran, Catherine, *The* Irish Press *and Populism in Ireland,* unpublished PhD thesis, DCU, 1994

Curtin, Chris and Thomas M. Wilson, eds, *Ireland from Below: Social Change and Local Communities,* Galway University Press, 1990

Daly, Mary, *Irish Industrial Development and Cultural Identity,* Gill & Macmillan, 1992

Deane, Seamus, ed., *The Field Day Anthology of Irish Writing, 3 vols,* Field Day, Derry, 1991

De Long, J. Bradford, "Productivity growth, convergence, and welfare: comment" in *American Economic Review,* vol.78, no.5, 1988, pp.1138-1154

Department of Enterprise and Employment, *Growing and Sharing our Employment:*

Strategy Paper on the Labour Market, Department of Enterprise and Employment, 1996

Developing the West Together, *A Crusade for Survival*, Euradvice, 1994

Di Tella, Torcuato S., *Latin American Politics: A Theoretical Framework*, University of Texas Press, 1990

Dix, Robert H., "Populism: authoritarian and democratic" in *Latin American Research Review*, vol.20, no.2, 1985, pp.29-52

Driever, Klaus, "Closing the gap: Ireland's experience with integration in the EU/EC" in *Aussenpolitik*, vol.45, Part 4, 1994, pp.315-324

Douthwaite, Richard, *The Growth Illusion*, Lilliput Press, 1992

Dunphy, Richard, *The Making of Fianna Fáil Power in Ireland 1923-1948*, Clarendon Press, Oxford, 1995

Evans, Peter B. et al., eds, *Bringing the State Back In*, Cambridge University Press, 1985

Faughnan, Pauline and Patricia Kelleher, *The Voluntary Sector and the State*, IBI and CMRS, n.d.

Fernandes, Rubem César, *Private but Public: The Third Sector in Latin America*, Civicus and Network Cultures – Asia, 1994

Forfás, *Shaping Our Future: A Strategy for Enterprise in Ireland in the 21st Century*, Forfás, 1996

Foster, R. F., *Modern Ireland 1600-1972*, Allen Lane, 1988

Garvin, Tom, *Nationalist Revolutionaries in Ireland 1858-1928*, Clarendon Press, Oxford, 1987

Geary, Patrick T., "Ireland's economy in the 1980s: stagnation and recovery" in *The Economic and Social Review*, vol.23, no.3, 1992, pp.253-281

Gellner, Ernest, *Encounters with Nationalism*, Blackwell, 1994

Gellner, Ernest, *Nations and Nationalism*, Blackwell, 1983

Gereffi, Gary and Donald L. Wyman, eds., *Manufacturing Miracles: Paths of Industrialization in Latin America and East Asia*, Princeton University Press, 1990

Girvin, Brian, *Between Two Worlds: Politics and Economy in Independent Ireland*, Gill & Macmillan, 1989

Gibbons, Luke, *Transformations in Irish Culture*, Cork University Press, 1996

Goldthorpe, J.H. and C.T. Whelan, eds, *The Development of Industrial Society in Ireland*, Oxford University Press, 1992

Guiomard, Cathal, *The Irish Disease and How to Cure It*, Oak Tree Press, 1995

Hachey, Thomas E. and Lawrence J. McCaffrey, eds, *Perspectives on Irish Nationalism*, The University Press of Kentucky, 1989

Hechter, Michael, *Internal Colonialism: The Celtic Fringe in British National Development 1536-1966*, Routledge and Kegan Paul, 1975

Hederman, Miriam, ed., *The Clash of Ideas*, Gill & Macmillan, 1988

Hirschman, Albert O., "Exit, voice and the state" in *World Politics*, vol.31, no.1, 1978, pp.90-107

Hitchens, D. M. W. N. and J. E. Birnie, *The Competitiveness of Industry in Ireland*, Avebury, 1994

Hutchinson, John, "Irish nationalism" in D. George Boyce and Alan O'Day, eds, *The Making of Modern Irish History: Revisionism and the Revisionist Controversy*, Routledge, 1996, pp.100-119

Hutchinson, John, *The Dynamics of Cultural Nationalism: The Gaelic Revival and the Creation of the Irish Nation State*, Allen and Unwin, 1987

Hutchinson, John and Anthony D. Smith, eds, *Nationalism*, Oxford University Press, 1994

Inglis, Tom, *Moral Monopoly: The Catholic Church in Modern Irish Society*, Gill & Macmillan, 1987

Jacobsen, John Kurt, *Chasing Progress in the Republic of Ireland*, Cambridge, 1994

Jacobson, David, *New Forms of Work Organisation in Ireland: An Annotated Bibliography*, DCU Business School, 1996

Jacobson, David and David O'Sullivan, "Analyzing an industry in change: the Irish software manual printing industry" in *New Technology*, vol.9, no.2, 1994, pp. 103-114

Jacobson, David, "Theorizing Irish industrialization: the case of the motor industry" in *Science & Society*, vol.53, no.2, 1989, pp.165-191

Keane, Colm, *The Jobs Crisis*, RTÉ/Mercier, 1993

Keating, Paul and Derry Desmond, *Culture and Capitalism in Contemporary Ireland*, Avebury, 1993

Kelleher, Carmel and Ann O'Mahony, eds, *Marginalisation in Irish Agriculture*, Economics and Rural Welfare Research Centre, 1984

Kelleher, Patricia and Mary Whelan, *Dublin Communities in Action*, Community Action Network and Combat Poverty Agency, 1992

Kennedy, Kieran A., "European unemployment and lessons for Ireland" in *Regional Studies*, vol.29, part 5, 1995, pp.439-451

Kennedy, Kieran A., *Facing the Unemployment Crisis in Ireland*, Cork University Press, 1993

Kennedy, Kieran A., "Real convergence, the European Community and Ireland", paper given to the Statistical and Social Inquiry Society of Ireland, 1992

Kennedy, Kieran A. et al., *The Economic Development of Ireland in the Twentieth Century*, Routledge, 1989

Kennedy, Kieran A., ed., *Ireland in Transition*, RTÉ/Mercier, 1986

Kennedy, Liam, *The Modern Industrialisation of Ireland 1940-1988*, The Economic and Social History Society of Ireland, 1989

Keogh, Dermot, *Twentieth Century Ireland: Nation and State*, Gill & Macmillan, 1994

Kirby, Peadar, "Valuing social change in Ireland" in *Doctrine & Life*, vol.44, September 1994, pp.418-425

Kirby, Peadar, *Ireland and Latin America: Links and Lessons*, Trócaire and Gill & Macmillan, 1992

Kirby, Peadar, *Dialann ó Nicearagua*, An Clóchomhar, 1990

Kirby, Peadar, *Has Ireland a Future?*, Mercier, 1988

Leddin, Anthony J. and Brendan M. Walsh, *The Macro-Economy of Ireland*, Gill & Macmillan, second edition, 1992

Lee, Joseph, *Ireland Politics and Society, 1912-1985*, Cambridge University Press, 1989

Lee, Joseph, *The Modernisation of Irish Society 1848-1918*, Gill & Macmillan, 1973

Leftwich, Adrian, "Bringing politics back in: towards a model of the developmental state" in *The Journal of Development Studies*, vol.31, no.3, 1995, pp.400-427

Litton, Frank, *Unequal Achievement: The Irish Experience 1957-1982*, IPA, 1982

Mac Laughlin, Jim, *Ireland: The Emigrant Nursery and the World Economy*, Cork University Press, 1994

Mac Laughlin, Jim, "Emigration and the peripheralization of Ireland in the global economy" in *Review*, vol.17, no.2, 1994, pp.243-273

McAleese, Dermot and Fiona Hayes, "European integration, the balance of payments and inflation" in J. W. O'Hagan, ed., *The Economy of Ireland: Policy and Performance of a Small European Country*, Gill & Macmillan, 1995, pp.265-94

McAleese, Dermot, "Political independence, economic growth and the role of economic policy" in P. J. Drudy, ed., *Ireland: Land, Politics and People*, Cambridge University Press, 1982, pp.271-295

McCarthy, John F., ed., *Planning Ireland's Future: The Legacy of T.K. Whitaker*, Glendale, 1990

Matthews, Alan, *Managing the EU Structural Funds in Ireland*, Cork University Press, 1994

Mjøset, Lars, *The Irish Economy in a Comparative Institutional Perspective*, NESC, 1992

Mjøset, Lars, "Comparative typologies of development patterns: the Menzel/Senghaas framework" in Lars Mjøset, ed., *Contributions to the Comparative Study of Development*, vol.2, Institute for Social Research, Oslo, 1992

Mouzelis, Nicos, "The state in late development: historical and comparative perspectives", unpublished paper

Mouzelis, Nicos P., *Politics in the Semi-Periphery*, Macmillan, 1986

Mulhall, Terry, *The State and Agrarian Reform: The Case of Ireland 1800-1940*, unpublished PhD thesis, LSE, 1992

Munck, Ronnie, *The Irish Economy: Results and Prospects*, Pluto, 1993

Murphy, Antoin E., *The Irish Economy: Celtic Tiger or Tortoise?* Money Markets International, 1994

Murray, Michael and John Greer, "Rural development and paradigm change" in Michael Murray and John Greer, eds, *Rural Development in Ireland*, Avebury, 1993, pp.255-268

Nairn, Tom, *The Break-up of Britain*, New Left Books, 1987

NESC, *The Economic and Social Implications of Emigration*, NESC, 1991

NESF, *Long-term Unemployment Initiatives*, National Economic and Social Forum, Opinion no.3, 1996

Nolan, Brian and Tim Callan, eds, *Poverty and Policy in Ireland*, Gill & Macmillan, 1994

Nolan, Brian, *The Wealth of Irish Households*, Combat Poverty Agency, 1991

Norton, Desmond, et al., *Economics for an Open Economy: Ireland*, Oak Tree Press, 1994

Nowlan, Kevin B., "The Gaelic League and other national movements" in Seán Ó Tuama, ed., *The Gaelic League Idea*, Mercier, 2nd edition, 1993

Ó Cinnéide, Séamus and Jim Walsh, "Multiplication and divisions: trends in community development since the 1960s" in *Community Development Journal*, vol.25, no.4, 1990, pp.326-336

Ó Cinnéide, Séamus, "The extent of poverty in Ireland" in *Social Studies*, vol.1, no. 4, 1972, pp.381-400

O'Connell, Declan, "Sociological theory and Irish political research" in Mary Kelly et al., eds, *Power, Conflict and Inequality*, Turoe Press, 1982, pp.186-98

O'Donnell, Rory, *Ireland and Europe: Challenges for a New Century*, ESRI, 1993

O'Donnellan, Niall, "The presence of Porter's sectoral clustering in Irish manufacturing" in *Economic and Social Review*, vol.25, no.3, 1994, pp.221-32

Ó Gráda, Cormac, *Ireland: A New Economic History 1780-1939*, Clarendon Press, 1994

Ó Gráda, Cormac and O'Rourke, Kevin, "Economic growth: performance and explanations" in J. W. O'Hagan, ed., *The Economy of Ireland: Policy and Performance of a Small European Country*, Gill & Macmillan, 1995, pp.198-227

O'Hearn, Denis, "Global restructuring and the Irish political economy" in Patrick Clancy, et al., eds, *Irish Society: Sociological Perspectives*, IPA, 1995, pp.90-131

O'Hearn, Denis, *Putting Ireland in a Global Context*, Department of Sociology, UCC, n.d.

O'Hearn, Denis, "Innovation and the world-system hierarchy: British subjugation of the Irish cotton industry, 1780-1830" in *American Journal of Sociology*, vol. 100, no.3, 1994, pp.587-621

O'Hearn, Denis, "Global competition, Europe and Irish peripherality" in *The Economic and Social Review*, vol.24, no.2, 1993, pp.169-97

O'Hearn, Denis, "The road from import-substituting to export-led industrialization in Ireland" in *Politics and Society*, vol.18, no.1, 1990, pp.1-38

O'Hearn, Denis, "The Irish case of dependency: an exception to the exceptions?" in *American Sociological Review*, vol.54, 1989, pp.578-96

O'Malley, Eoin, *Industry and Economic Development: The Challenge for the Latecomer*, Gill & Macmillan, 1989

O'Rourke, Kevin, "Emigration and living standards in Ireland since the Famine" in *Journal of Population Economics*, vol. 8, part 4, 1995, pp.407-21

O'Sullivan, Mary, "Manufacturing and global competition" in J. W. O'Hagan ed., *The Economy of Ireland: Policy and Performance of a Small European Country*, Gill & Macmillan, 1995, pp.363-96

O'Toole, Fintan, *Meanwhile Back at the Ranch*, Vintage, 1995

OECD, *Ireland: Local Partnerships and Social Innovation*, OECD, 1996

OECD, *OECD Economic Surveys 1995, Ireland*, OECD, 1995

Office of the Tánaiste, *Interim Report of the Task Force on Long-term Unemployment*, Office of the Tánaiste, 1995

Orridge, Andrew W., "The Blueshirts and the 'Economic War': A study of Ireland in the context of dependency theory" in *Political Studies*, vol.31, 1993, pp. 351-69

Patterson, Henry, *The Politics of Illusion*, Hutchinson Radius, 1989

Peillon, Michel, "Placing Ireland in a comparative perspective" in *Economic and Social Review*, vol.25, no.2, 1994, pp.179-95

Peillon, Michel, *Contemporary Irish Society: An Introduction*, Gill & Macmillan, 1982

Periwal, Sukumar, ed., *Notions of Nationalism*, Central European University Press, 1995

Persell, Caroline Hodges, "Taking society seriously" in *Sociological Forum*, vol.9, no.4, 1994, pp.641-657

Report of the Industrial Policy Review Group, *A Time for Change: Industrial Policy for the 1990s*, The Stationery Office, 1992

Rowthorn, Bob, "Northern Ireland: an economy in crisis" in Paul Teague, ed., *Beyond the Rhetoric: Politics, the Economy and Social Policy in Northern Ireland*, Lawrence & Wishart, 1987, pp.111-135

Ruane, Frances and Francis O'Toole, "Taxation measures and policy" in J. W. O'Hagan, ed., *The Economy of Ireland: Policy and Performance of a Small Country*, Gill & Macmillan, 1995, pp.127-58

Senghaas, Dieter, *The European Experience*, Berg, 1985

Seers, Dudley et al., eds, *Underdeveloped Europe: Studies in Core-Periphery Relations*, Harvester Press, 1979

Shafer, D. Michael, *Winners and Losers: How Sectors Shape the Developmental Prospects of States*, Cornell University Press, 1994

Shirlow, Peter, ed., *Development Ireland: Contemporary Issues*, Pluto, 1995

Shirlow, Peter, "Transnational corporations in the Republic of Ireland and the illusion of economic well-being" in *Regional Studies,* vol.29, part 7, 1995, pp.687-705

Smith, Anthony, "Ties that bind" in *LSE Magazine,* Spring 1993, pp.8-11

Smith, Anthony D., *National Identity,* Penguin, 1991

Snyder, David and Edward L. Kick, "Structural position in the world system and economic growth, 1955-1970" in *American Journal of Sociology,* vol.84, no. 5, 1979, pp.1096-1126

Storey, Andy, "Industrial development, industrial policy and social exclusion in rural areas", an unpublished report for NESF, 1996

Tovey, Hilary, "Environmentalism in Ireland: two versions of development and modernity" in *International Sociology,* vol.8, no.4, 1993, pp.413-30

Vilas, Carlos M., "Neoliberal social policy" in *Nacla,* vol.29, no.6, 1996, pp.16-25

Whelan, Christopher T., *Values and Social Change in Ireland,* Gill & Macmillan, 1994

Whelan, Christopher T., "Social class, unemployment, and psychological distress" in *European Sociological Review,* vol.10, no.1, 1994, pp.49-61

Whelan, Christopher T., *In Search of the Underclass: Marginalization, Poverty and Fatalism in the Republic of Ireland,* ESRI Working Paper 51, 1994

White, Gordon, "Towards a democratic developmental state" in *IDS Bulletin,* vol.26, no.2, 1995, pp.27-36

White, Gordon and Robert Wade, "Developmental states and markets in East Asia: an introduction" in Gordon White, ed., *Developmental States in East Asia,* Macmillan, 1988, pp.1-29

Whyte, John, *Interpreting Northern Ireland,* Clarendon Press Oxford, 1990

Wickham, James, "Dependence and state structure: foreign firms and industrial policy in the Republic of Ireland" in Otmar Höll, ed., *Small States in Europe and Dependence,* Austrian Institute for International Affairs, 1983, pp.164-85

Wickham, James, "'Industrialisation by invitation' crashes" in *The Irish Times,* 26 February 1993

Index

Other Titles in the Trócaire World Topics Series

A series on aspects of Third World affairs for the general reader – factual, accurate and up to date.

1. **BREAD AND FREEDOM: BASIC HUMAN NEEDS AND HUMAN RIGHTS** *John Grindle*

Basic needs – food, shelter, water, health, education, a living income and security – are the minimum human entitlement. *Bread and Freedom* outlines an approach to development which could provide these basic needs for all.

Political freedom and basic needs are inseparable. While great advances have been made in the Third World more progress is possible at little cost. All that is lacking is political will.

John Grindle has worked as an economic consultant in several developing countries and for the Irish Government.

"Some valuable ideas" *Sunday Tribune*
Trócaire and Gill and Macmillan, 1992, £4.99, 0 7171 1967 X

2. **IRELAND AND LATIN AMERICA: LINKS AND LESSONS** *Peadar Kirby*

Our links with Latin America have always been strong through Irish missionaries, traders and soldiers. Part One of this book is a concise history of the region from pre-Columbus days to independence, military rule and democracy.

Part Two tells the story of leading Irish migrants to Latin America and Church and solidarity links. The author suggests Ireland and Latin America have much in common: both need to overcome a colonial legacy and find the right development model. Each can learn much from the other.

Peadar Kirby, a journalist and author, has written widely on Third World development.

"a valuable insight ... a fine read" *Sunday Tribune*

"a compact account" *Sunday Independent*

"highly recommended for both seasoned and first-time readers on Latin America" *Fortnight*

Trócaire and Gill and Macmillan, 1992, £4.99, 0 7171 1969 6

3. THE POOR RELATION: IRISH FOREIGN POLICY AND THE THIRD WORLD *Michael Holmes, Nicholas Rees, Bernadette Whelan*

Does Ireland have an overall foreign policy towards the Third World and, if so, who decides it? How great is EC influence on that policy? Do Irish decision-makers really care about the Third World? These are some of the questions this book tackles.

The authors argue for wider consultation on policymaking. They also urge Ireland to adopt a more planned approach rather than reacting to events as they happen.

Michael Holmes lectures in the Department of History, UCC; Nicholas Rees lectures in European Studies and International Relations at the University of Limerick. Bernadette Whelan lectures in Modern History at the University of Limerick.

"a mine of information on the foreign policymaking process" *The Furrow*

"a comprehensive analytical framework and accessible style add up to a strong candidate for an introductory text on Irish foreign policy" *Irish Political Studies*

Trócaire and Gill and Macmillan, 1992, £4.99, 0 7171 1970 X

4. THIRD WORLD DEBT: TOWARDS AN EQUITABLE SOLUTION *Mary R. McCarthy and Thomas G. McCarthy*

Third World debt repayments reduce health and education spending, causing malnutrition and child poverty.

This book examines the scale of Third World debt and its effects on the poor. The authors argue that responsibility for the problem lies with the rich, industrial countries as much as the debtor countries. They analyse responses to the debt crisis from various groups and suggest that most focus on protecting lenders' interests rather than on the welfare of poor debtors.

The authors propose drawing up a fairer, more just solution to the problem of Third World debt. They also offer concrete policy proposals for putting these ideas into practice.

Mary R. McCarthy works for the Commission of the European Communities, Brussels. Thomas G. McCarthy lectures in Economic at St. Patrick's College, Maynooth.

Trócaire and Gill and Macmillan, 1994, £4.99, 0 7171 1968 8